Raised by the Stars

Raised by the Stars

Interviews with 29 Children
of Hollywood Actors

NICK THOMAS

McFarland & Company, Inc., Publishers
Jefferson, North Carolina, and London

LIBRARY OF CONGRESS CATALOGUING-IN-PUBLICATION DATA

Raised by the stars : interviews with 29 children of Hollywood
actors / Nick Thomas.
    p.   cm.
Includes bibliographical references and index.

ISBN 978-0-7864-6403-6
softcover : 50# alkaline paper ∞

    1. Children of motion picture actors and actresses — United
States — Biography.   2. Children of motion picture actors and
actresses — United States — Interviews.   3. Motion picture
actors and actresses — Family relationships — United States.
I. Thomas, Nick, 1956–
PN1998.2.R35   2011
791.4302'80922—dc23
[B]   2011034485

BRITISH LIBRARY CATALOGUING DATA ARE AVAILABLE

Front cover image: Rosalind Russell and her three-and-a-half-
year-old son, Lance Brisson, 1947; cover design by David K.
Landis (Shake It Loose Graphics)

Manufactured in the United States of America

McFarland & Company, Inc., Publishers
  Box 611, Jefferson, North Carolina 28640
  www.mcfarlandpub.com

Acknowledgments

This work would not have been possible without the generous and gracious assistance given to me by all the children of the actors discussed in this book. Some of these children were in their seventies or eighties but still very active and busy. So I do appreciate the many hours they spent sharing stories of their families and for providing photographs.

I am also grateful to Bob King, editor of *Films of the Golden Age* magazine and *Classic Images*, for permission to reprint several of my interviews that appeared in those publications. For lovers of old movies, these are two of the last remaining publications that feature the classic film period. Likewise, my thanks to editor Lee Pfeiffer, for his permission to reprint a couple of my interviews that appeared in *Cinema Retro*, a fabulous magazine that celebrates movies from the '60s and '70s. These past interviews from *FGA*, *CI* and *CR* were updated and expanded for this book. A portion of the interview with Harry Crosby appeared in the *San Francisco Chronicle* on December 26, 2010.

And although it had no direct involvement in this project, I must say "thank goodness for Turner Classic Movies" for continuing to help keep classic Hollywood alive. Finally, I am also thankful for Debby Thomas, and that my lousy typing was no match for her keen proofreading skills!

Table of Contents

Preface

My interest in classic movies goes back to a time and place far removed from the glamour of Hollywood, and America. I must have been five or six when my mother first told me about the "famous movie star" who had been born and raised in our little town. She didn't reveal much at first, just waved a hand out the car window as we drove past a nondescript road in the early 1960s: "A famous movie star used to live down there," she told me, pointing to some place that barely interested me at the time. Years later, after I had been assailed with this piece of local history on numerous subsequent passings, more details eventually emerged: the road was Duke Street; the town was Hobart, Tasmania; and the star was Errol Flynn.

Of all the memories I have of those early days growing up in Tasmania, that one stuck with me, even though Flynn had been dead for years when I first heard his name and his family had long since abandoned Australia's beautiful southern island state. Nevertheless, armed with this tenuous connection to Tasmania's most famous son, I eventually developed an interest in Errol Flynn, his movies, and old films in general. Like Flynn, my own career would also take me to America, but into the very different world of science, research, and teaching. Yet I remained an amateur enthusiast of what are now called the "classic movies" from the '30s, '40s and '50s.

Curiously, too, my early interest in science had an indirect Hollywood influence. I was around ten and we had moved to Melbourne, when I was enchanted one afternoon by a movie featuring Mickey Rooney; it was called *Young Tom Edison*. For years after, I just couldn't escape the mental image of young Tom and his exciting science experiments. One that especially caught my imagination was the mixing together of hydrochloric acid and ammonia solutions, resulting in a cloud of "smoke" that emptied Tom's school room and brought the local fire crew running. What mischievous school kid wouldn't want to reproduce that scene in his classroom!

Though uncharacteristically accurate for a Hollywood biopic, artistic

1

license wasn't totally abandoned in that wonderfully charming film. I eventually got my hands on the two aforementioned chemicals, only to be utterly disappointed when I failed to recreate the same menacing cloud of choking white vapors young Tom had so easily produced on film. Nevertheless, as I later learned, there remained an element of truth in the on-screen experiment, for the mixing of vapors from the two substances does indeed produce a very modest amount of white vapor, consisting of a substance called ammonium chloride. (I'll end the chemistry lesson there!) But the story serves to illustrate that movies can have influences — large and small, good and bad — on our lives, because I would indeed go on to spend much of my life in chemistry labs and lecture halls. Thanks, Mickey!

In 2004, when I began to write features for newspapers and magazines, I was naturally drawn to write about topics of interest: science and nature, people with unusual hobbies or businesses, and old movies and their stars. When the opportunity arose to interview Mickey Rooney for the *Ottawa Sun* in 2009, I was naturally quite enthusiastic. It was a brief interview — he was beginning a 15-city tour of Ontario at the tender age of 89 — but I did get the chance to tell him how his *Young Tom Edison* role had stirred my interest in science. The same year I was asked to write a piece for the *Washington Post* to celebrate the centenary of Errol Flynn's birth — another writing task I readily embraced. That story included interviews with actors who had shared the big screen with the great Aussie actor, as well as his third wife, his two grandsons — and daughter! Flynn had been gone for 50 years, but how fascinating it was to talk with the daughter of the legendary actor who has been raised so close to my childhood home.

My interest aroused, other similar interviews with actors' children followed — with Glenn Ford's son and Gene Lockhart's daughter — and these appeared in *Films of the Golden Age* magazine and *Classic Images*, respectively. Wouldn't it be fun, I thought, to gather together and publish a collection of interviews with the children of popular actors from Hollywood's Golden Age? Fortunately, McFarland shared that belief, and the result is this book — interviews with children (or, in one case, a grandchild) of film and television stars from Hollywood's Golden Age.

To assemble the collection, I began with a list of my 100 favorite actors and actresses and included major stars, like Flynn, as well as popular supporting and character actors. I felt that such a diverse collection would be of most interest to fans of classic movies. Then, for various reasons, the list was trimmed. For instance, some of the actors on the list never married, never had children, or, if they had, their children had passed away. In other cases, I simply could not locate the offspring, or they were of advanced age, in poor health, or they simply did not want to be interviewed. Others had plans to "one day" write their own book about their famous parent, and clearly did not relish any sort of competition, even from so humble a book as mine. Perhaps the most interesting response to an interview request was from the child of a very famous actor (mentioned several times in this book) who asked for payment of a mere $100,000 to grant an interview! I politely declined.

And so, the list was eventually whittled down to this collection of 26 — a stellar cast of delightful actors who appeared in some of the most popular films and television shows of all time, and whose children kindly granted me interviews. While some had talked previously about the challenges of being raised by a Hollywood parent, and a few had even penned their memoirs, others had rarely given interviews over the years. While each had a unique experience to relate and, for the most part, a positive one, in some cases the relationship with their famous mother or father was not always easy. Sure, the wealth and fame that accompanied their celebrity parent's status had an obvious appeal, but the lack of privacy due to constant media and fan attention, the busy shooting schedules, travel requirements, and hectic lifestyles of actors could be tough on family life and sometimes left children feeling neglected or abandoned. Nevertheless, all expressed an affection and love for their parent and, presumably, they have provided an honest account of being raised in the celebrity bubble.

As we all know, actors can also carry a lot of baggage — and I don't mean Samsonite. However, rather than ugly gossip or rumor, I have tended to focus on everyday stories about the actors, their families and their lives, as well as behind-the-scenes accounts of the filmmaking process, and facts that could be classified as movie trivia because I think these are the areas that die-hard classic movie fans enjoy reading about. Honestly, I would find it much more interesting to learn what color Errol Flynn's toothbrush was rather than who he may have shared it with! Therefore, while the interviews in this collection are personal, they are not explicitly intimate; nor are they intended to represent full biographies. There are countless books and websites devoted to many of the actors discussed in this book. I have only included books written or mentioned by the children, which may be about themselves or their parents, or official websites which may be authorized by the children or other family members.

I think this diverse collection featuring big stars, as well as supporting and character actors, will interest all who have a fondness for the classic movie era. What follows, then, is a collection of interviews with the children of some of my favorite actors; I hope they are some of your favorites, too.

1

Carey Harrison on Rex Harrison

Was there ever an actor who projected the English language more eloquently than Rex Harrison (1908–1990)? No wonder he owned the role of George Bernard Shaw's professor of phonetics, Henry Higgins. As the surly and impatient Higgins, Harrison won the Best Actor Oscar for My Fair Lady *(1964), a role he had played on Broadway for two seasons in the 1950s and also revived a quarter-century later at the age of 73. Harrison is also remembered for portraying the amusing, critter-loving veterinarian in* Doctor Dolittle *(1967) and for more dramatic roles, such as Julius Caesar in* Cleopatra *(1963). Harrison loved the stage and appeared in 15 Broadway productions, winning Best Actor Tony awards for roles in* My Fair Lady *and* Anne of a Thousand Days. *Labeled by some as a "difficult" actor, Rex Harrison, says his son Carey, was really a perfectionist at his craft. Carey's mother, German-born actress Lilli Palmer, was the second of Harrison's six wives and the couple worked together in several films during the '40s and '50s. Despite coming from a family of actors and being surrounded by entertainment celebrities growing up, Carey was more interested in writing than performing, and has published many novels, plays, and screenplays. Like his father's most famous character, Carey Harrison is also a professor—professor of English at the City University of New York.*

What do you know about your grandparents?

My maternal grandfather was chief surgeon at the Jewish Hospital in Berlin. I think he was as much Prussian as Jewish because he was not an observant Jew and I received no religion through my mother's side of the family. He also passed on his Prussian character and discipline to my mother who could be quite a stern woman. But I never knew him because he had a heart attack at the age of 56 and died before I was born. He left behind his own father, who later died in a concentration camp during World War II. My mother, her sisters, and my grandmother were able to get out of Germany in

Carey and Rex Harrison n Paris, on the set of *A Flea in Her Ear* (1968), a Feydeau farce transferred to the screen and starring the elder Harrison, Rachel Roberts, and Rosemary Harris. Carey had come from college to visit his father. He says: "Note my badly fitting cheap suit and his perfectly fitting one." (Photograph courtesy of Carey Harrison.)

the 1930s, but the rest of my mother's family died in the camps. Their escape from the Nazis was "anticipatory," in the sense that my grandfather saw what was coming in Germany, so it wasn't a hair's breadth escape as such. My grandfather put his family on the train to Paris and stayed behind — perhaps he thought there was a chance things wouldn't get too bad, or perhaps it was his sense of duty as a doctor which prevented him from fleeing when he had patients to look after. I got to know my maternal grandmother well. She had been quite a prominent actress when she was very young and played the leading part in Gerhart Hauptmann's *Hannele*. That acting tradition was carried down to my mother and her sisters, all of whom acted. But my grandfather had encouraged my grandmother to give up the stage because he didn't think acting was a respectable profession for a wife, at the turn of the century. My father's side of my family included two of his sisters of whom I was greatly fond, as I am of their children and children's children. My parents moved from London to Hollywood when I was barely one year old, and I didn't know my father's parents at all because they died while I was growing up in America. Strangely, I never heard my father speak about his childhood once in his entire life. He never talked about his mother or father, or growing up — ever!

So you never pressed your father for information about his parents?

I have never liked putting people on the spot about personal matters, even my parents. I love to listen, and will listen all night, prompting people to go on. But I hate trying to puncture someone's privacy. My father was a person who put the past behind him, and transformed himself with each new phase of his life. He was married six times and with each new marriage, he left the past behind him entirely. I did learn from my mother — my chief source of information about my father's upbringing and ancestry — that he was supposed to be descended from Edmund Kean, the eminent actor. So on both sides of my family there was theater in the blood. Many of Rex's descendants have appeared on stage: two of his sons — myself and my brother Noel — plus a number of Noel's children and mine. I added it up once, counting both sides of my family, and came up with over 30 relatives who had appeared on stage or screen.

Your dad was in the Royal Air Force during World War II. Did he talk about those days?

Not to me, but he did tell my mother about his experiences. She told me how much he loved being in uniform and enjoyed his days in the RAF. He wanted to be a pilot, but was too tall. He had a bad eye, the result of contracting measles as a boy, out of which he could only see light and dark, which definitively prevented him from being a pilot. The Royal Air Force needed plenty of ground crew and ground staff, and Rex was involved in an interesting project called "bending the beam," which I actually did ask him about once. When the German planes were returning home from a bombing sortie over Britain, they homed in on a radar source — a beam — to guide them home. The British developed a way to bend that beam which would take the bombers off course and cause them to land in the sea or run out of fuel. I'm not sure how successful it was, but my father was a part of that work, not in a scientific but an administrative capacity. He moved the little model planes, representing German bombers, across the huge map that kept track of their movements.

You were born during an air raid over London, correct?

Yes I was, in the London Clinic, during the later part of the Blitz, in 1944. A nurse came around to ask my mother for my name because they wanted it for their records in case we were all killed by a bomb. My parents were caught napping by that, partly because they were convinced I was going to be a girl, whom they planned to call Leslie — I'm quite glad not to be Leslie, which they could have used as a boy's name. My mother wanted Erika, which I'm also glad to have avoided. They hadn't even thought of a boy's name. So they gave me my father's names, Reginald Carey, and added my mother's father's name, Alfred, on the end.

Your father did a lot of Broadway in the '50s. Did you get to see him on the stage?

I saw pretty much everything he did there when I was a small child. *Anne of a Thousand Days*, in which he played Henry VIII, was the first play I saw him in, followed by *The Love of Four Colonels*, and I saw Rex as Julius Caesar in Shaw's *Caesar and Cleopatra*, which also featured my mother as Cleopatra. They acted together in *The Fourposter*, a two-handed play which later became a unique two-person screen comedy, again with Rex and Lilli. Then they did the even more successful *Bell, Book and Candle* which went from Broadway to London's West End. (Fatally, Kim Novak attempted Lilli's part in the movie.) Finally came *My Fair Lady* with Julie Andrews as Eliza Doolittle, when I was 11. I was allowed to stand offstage and watch, which was wonderful. I'll never forget the sight of Rex and Julie, after a particularly angry scene between them: the curtain would come down leaving half-light on the stage so that the actors could see to walk off, and Rex and Julie would stroll off arm in arm, having just been shouting at each other. This was striking, to an 11-year-old — that camaraderie of the theater was very moving to me, even at that age.

How would you compare his performance as Henry Higgins in the film and on Broadway?

He was a consummate film actor, but as good as his performance was in the movie, it could never be as great as his best stage performances as Henry Higgins. The relationship with a live audience always brings out unrepeatable effects from night to night. While there are no film recordings of him in that role on the stage, there are some interesting excerpts he did on TV shows such as *Ed Sullivan*, which give a glimpse of his stage Higgins. I never saw the '81 revival, but as a child, I was endlessly fascinated watching him perform and I continue to remain captivated by his art.

In general, how would you describe him as a performing artist?

He was widely regarded as a "light comedian," a term he detested. He was a "high comedian," which is something entirely different. High comedy begins with Shakespeare — whom Rex fled, fearing his little education excluded him. It didn't, of course, and to prove it there's a remarkable audio recording of him as Benedick in *Much Ado About Nothing*, opposite his fourth wife, Rachel Roberts, as Beatrice. High comedy continues into Congreve and the High Restoration dramatists, then eventually into Wilde, Shaw, Coward,

Orton, and others. Chekhov, for instance, excelled in comedy — high, light and low. David Niven, for example, was a light comedian. You'd hardly cast him as Caesar or as a pope — two roles in which Rex excelled. In light comedy nothing too grave is at stake. In high comedy there is always tragedy lurking. Comedy of menace was Rex's specialty, and his singular magnetism consisted in bringing many qualities not always comic — rage, heartbreak — close to the surface of his comic performance. He was not the greatest comedian of his generation — he was not Keaton or Chaplin — but he was the greatest high comedian, and recognized as such by those who appreciate varieties of comedy. His greatest performances were in Shaw, Chekhov and Pirandello, where everything is at stake, and souls are won and lost.

It's been said that your dad was a perfectionist when it came to acting, but he was also known as being difficult to work with. Do the two go hand-in-hand?

It is a fine line. He was definitely a perfectionist and was intolerant of colleagues whom he thought were not up to the mark. Very few of his fellow actors met his high standards, nor did a lot of directors. I'm on his side as far as that's concerned because actors have to work with a lot of pretentious, incompetent or otherwise ill-qualified directors, and he just wouldn't stand for that. It did give him the reputation as being a difficult person to work with. Perhaps with that reputation he was able to get his way more easily!

Perfectionists can also be hard workers. Did he put a lot of effort into his roles?

He always worked immensely hard and would put the same amount of effort into good films as he would into those that turned out to be dreadful. I worked with him on his memorizing process, and from the age of six would hear his lines. By doing that, I actually found that I became a whiz at sight reading, out of fear of letting him down. Believe it or not, I still remember to this day some of the lines he had to say in *Cleopatra*, the movie. I was 18 at the time and visiting him in Rome, and still helping him to learn his lines. He had terrible difficulty with them because Joe Mankiewicz had written so much pedantic Roman history into the film in an attempt to prove that Hollywood could be serious about historical drama. But it meant poor Rex had to remember names he had never come across with his limited education — he left school at 16 — and it was torture for him. He had to say, "When Sulla marched on Rome and Crassus lost the armies in Parthia." Well, he just couldn't remember which word went where. I was on the set when he had to do it, and he still got it wrong over and over. It was torment for me watching him. Elizabeth Taylor was just as bad. In the film, she has a sidekick called

Sosigenes, but she kept calling him Sisogenes. Then Sosigenes again. In editing the movie they tried to come up with a complete set of takes in which she only said one or the other. But they couldn't.

Actors can be private, shy people in real life who open up on stage or in front of a camera. Was your father at all like that?

In some ways he was. Among the personality types you find in actors, there are those who even off-stage or off-screen can't stop being the life of the party, telling stories, and mimicking everybody. Hayley Mills was like that already as a child. By the age of 12 or 13 everyone knew she was going to be an actress. Then there are other people who are shy and waiting for that moment under the lights when they can become someone they can't be offstage. My father was like that in several respects. Mimicry was not his art and he was surrounded, as I was as a child, by virtuosos. Sometimes we had Noel Coward, Gielgud, Olivier and Ustinov at our dinner table — four of the greatest storytellers and, in Ustinov's case, mimics, of their generation. Ustinov had once been in love with my mother — a tender fact I cherish.

How was the personality of Rex Harrison, the actor, different from Rex Harrison, the dad?

I never saw such vulnerability from my father in real life as I saw him exhibit on the stage. I don't think I felt envious of his stage persona, because I always recognized that this was what acting was all about for him. He simply wasn't able to easily show in life those emotions that he could on stage. His own father was a shy man — a nice, dear man from all accounts — but tremendously inhibited, as I understand from my aunts and from my mother. And this shyness was passed on to Rex, who couldn't openly show emotion with ease. I always loved my father and didn't really suffer from the fact that he didn't show me the same emotions that he showed on stage, although I rarely felt completely at ease with him — it was his own unease that communicated to me. This was nothing personal, as I was well aware. His father had been equally ill at ease around his children. As I say, I loved him nonetheless, and my love for him was rooted in earliest childhood, when he was more at ease with the infant that I was, as one can see from photographs. I had a governess, now in her '90s, who recently confirmed that I always adored my father, and never liked my mother, whose strictness grated on me.

Your parents owned a home in Italy. What are your memories of your time there?

Rex and Lilli started building a home in 1950 or so, when I was six, on the Italian Riviera, above the small fishing village of Portofino. It became our

Another shot of Carey and Rex Harrison in Paris, on the set of *A Flea in Her Ear* (1968). Harrison and co-star Rachel Roberts were married at the time of production. (Photograph courtesy of Carey Harrison.)

holiday home where we would spend summers every year. We really never needed to go anywhere else for vacations because of the extraordinary beauty of the villa and its surroundings, overlooking the bay of Rapallo. You could just sit and take in the view all day. My father imported a speedboat from America although, as he probably didn't realize, Riva, the Italian company who build some of the best speedboats in the world, had their manufacturing base directly across the bay from us in Chiavari. Every fine summer day we would head off in the boat and improvise picnics at various places around the bay. And each summer, a parade of famous people came to visit us. Once I wound up sitting on Greta Garbo's knee — which was quite uncomfortable because she was very bony and she hated children — because my mother requested it and was very keen that I should remember having sat on the knee of the most beautiful woman in the world. At that stage, Garbo was a middle-aged woman with a wispy moustache and sharp, withered features, and it really made no sense to me whatsoever to refer to her as the most beautiful woman in the world! Our visitors included the Duke of Windsor, who arrived with the Duchess to sing German folk songs with my mother. Gradually, our villa became almost a legendary place during the '50s, as Portofino became a world-famous haunt of movie stars and millionaires. My parents' "gang" was less the film stars than the theater actors like Gielgud, Olivier, and Coward, who formed a remarkable part of my childhood. Later, I was employed by Olivier at Britain's National Theatre, who took an option on my plays and my first job after college was as assistant to Gielgud on his West End production of Chekhov's *Ivano*. One of my early plays was compared to Noel Coward's plays — he had described me when I was a child as himself "reincarnated" — and my mother promptly dragged me to the Savoy to present Noel with a published edition of the play. And, finally, to crown my childhood connections, when Gielgud was 90, I wrote a play for him about the great 18th century architect Sir Christopher Wren at the age of 90, which Sir John performed on the BBC.

Did you have contact with many other "Hollywood kids" growing up? Do you keep in contact with any?

I really don't see many of the Hollywood kids that I knew. My own work has taken me into different areas, mostly with British actors who don't share that bratpack past. I haven't seen Hayley Mills for ages and Geraldine Chaplin I haven't seen for God knows how long. I did work with Raymond Massey's son, Daniel, who was a fine actor and recorded a play of mine. My mother worked with Gary Cooper in *Cloak and Dagger* [1946] and absolutely loved him, as I did at first sight. I saw Coop's daughter, Maria, in the summer of 2008 at the Museum of Modern Art when they were showing a season of films to honor my father's centenary, and I spoke about him. Maria was so sweet to come along and see me. She had been part of a previous event devoted to her father's films. When I meet up with people who share a background of celebrity parent actors, we tend to greet each other like explorers in the Gobi desert — hailing each other like people who have emerged, to the best of our ability, from an unusual upbringing not everyone survives.

Like your dad, you have a very distinctive British voice. You must have spent some time in Great Britain?

It was no great fun for a nine-year-old, sitting at a table with world-famous actors and listening to them tell stories that were completely over your head. I couldn't wait to be allowed to leave the table, and school was another kind of paradise for me. I was sent off to boarding school in England when I was nine. I loved it there because I longed for the company of kids my age. I had my half-brother, Noel, whom I adored, but we couldn't share childhood together because we were ten years apart. When I was little, I loved my preparatory school which is where you go until you're 12 or 13. This was Sunningdale School, most of whose boys went on to Eton. But because my grandfather had briefly gone to Harrow, a rival school, I was sent to Harrow, which I liked much less than I did Sunningdale. I was growing up and there were no girls around!

Your parents divorced when you were 13 and you had a succession of stepmothers. Did you get along with them?

After the divorce, I more or less lived with my mother and her sisters, though the idea was to spend alternate vacations with each parent. I got along very well with my father's other wives. I adored Kay Kendall, which was hard on my mother because my father had left her for Kay, and with heartless 13-year-old candor I didn't disguise how much I loved Kay. I also adored Rachel Roberts, my father's fourth wife. So I was fortunate to be very happy around my father and his glamorous new wives after the divorce, as well as with my mother and her sisters.

Your father wore a fancy ring on the little finger of his left hand which can be seen in some of his later movies. What happened to that?

I have the ring. His grandfather had a coat of arms made for the family which was green with the head of a lion and a scimitar. So the ring is a dark green stone with the family coat of arms on it. Kay had that made for him.

What's your favorite Rex Harrison film?

I think I like him best in *Unfaithfully Yours* [1948]. But I liked him in everything he did, even in some of the terrible films like *Cleopatra* and *The Agony and the Ecstasy* [1965] which were absolute clunkers apart from Rex. My mother was a most accomplished actor, too, but with a certain stagy artificiality — you can see the same in Audrey Hepburn.

Your dad played the Henry Higgins role in *My Fair Lady*, twice on Broadway, and for other productions. Did he object to being always identified with the character?

He loved the role. Actors know how lucky they are when they land a definitive role-of-a-lifetime — it didn't seem like it to Rex when rehearsals began! — and many will go through their entire career and never have that experience. He naturally got fed up with people asking him to sing "I've Grown Accustomed to Her Face," and made up an obscene version, referring to a part of the body far removed from the face, that he would sing if he really became annoyed! There was also a lot of himself in Higgins. Both were impatient, brilliant, vain and self-absorbed. Rex, who as I've mentioned was no mimic, invariably played himself.

Did he ever meet George Bernard Shaw [the author of *Pygmalion*, upon which *My Fair Lady* was based]?

He knew Shaw well and visited him at his home in Ayot St Lawrence. Shaw liked Rex's acting very much. When my father appeared in the film version of Shaw's play, *Major Barbara*, Shaw was on the set from time to time. I'm sure he would have been delighted if he had lived to see my father as Higgins. One time my father was going to visit Shaw, who was pushing 90 at the time, but instead went to see my brother, Noel, at school. He apologized to Shaw who said to him: "You'll be sorry — you can always see your son, but won't always be able to see me!" And as it turned out he didn't, since Shaw died shortly after.

Both your parents wrote autobiographies. Did you learn anything new from them?

Not really. My father had ghostwriters do his, but my mother wrote hers by herself. She was an instinctively gifted storyteller, and became a bestselling novelist, as well as a painter exhibited on both sides of the Atlantic. A triple threat! I gained an immense amount from observing her and learning from her, and absorbing her dedication to her several crafts, which matched my father's own dedication.

With two show business parents, was there a push for you to go into acting?

They were eager to discourage me, as many theatrical parents are, knowing how unstable the life can be. Fortunately, I had my own agenda. I was born a writer, as I think many writers are, and never had any doubt in my mind about what I would do, even from a very young age. I started writing novels when I was eight, and have never stopped writing. By contrast, language is rarely what draws actors to the stage. What draws them is being the focus of attention. Secondarily, they are drawn to playing a character, to the drama and the language. While some of them are deeply literate and love plays, it's just not the same instinct that draws someone to become a writer.

Did you ever incorporate anything from your parents' lives into your novels or plays?

None of my writing has been about my parents or their lives. I always kept away from that. But I did portray my stepfather, Carlos Thompson, who was my mother's second husband, in a novel — under another name, of course. He was a remarkable human being and a decisive influence on my life.

Do you think your career as both a writer and a college teacher has combined aspects of both your parents' talents?

It's true. Acting and writing are both involved. My mother and stepfather both wrote novels, and I've found the calling to be a wonderful one. I've written close to 200 plays and novels, the best received being a long novel, *Richard's Feet.* I've been fortunate to win numerous literary prizes for my novels and radio dramas. Writing is like climbing a mountain — solitary work, progressing inch by inch, always afraid of "falling off" and finding that the project has crumbled in your hands. But while you're climbing, you have your fate in your own hands. No one else can ruin the venture, only you. For me this has made for a very fulfilling life. I also founded a theater company in Woodstock, where I live, so that I can still keep my fate in my hands — and stage my own plays. I started teaching in 1971 and enjoy the resemblance to theater. Perhaps it's my way of carrying on the family's acting tradition, since in a classroom you have an audience whose interest you have to capture. Every class is a fresh improv.

Presumably, most of your students are young and don't know who your parents were?

Rex Harrison or Lilli Palmer are names that mean nothing to my students, unless they're avid film fans. Someone on campus actually did start a rumor that I was the son of Doctor Dolittle. After that, a number of students came up to me asking: "Is it true you're the son of Eddie Murphy?" I always say, "Yes!"

Carey Harrison on Rex Harrison. Telephone interview on 11/23/10. Carey Harrison's website is http://www.midgetinacatsuit.com.

2

Charlie Matthau
on Walter Matthau

Best remembered for playing grumpy, miserly men, Walter Matthau (1920–2000) just kept getting grumpier with age, at least as an actor. In real life, nothing was further from the truth, according to his son, Charlie. Walter Matthau appeared in 17 Broadway productions; in his final Broadway play he was Oscar Madison in The Odd Couple. *Matthau seemed born to play the role, and brought it to the big screen in 1968. He also appeared in over 100 movie and TV roles and, perhaps fittingly, won a best Supporting Actor Oscar (for* The Fortune Cookie). *Most memorable was his on-screen partnership with Jack Lemmon, which included comedies such as* The Fortune Cookie *(1966),* The Odd Couple *(1968),* Grumpy Old Men *(1993),* Out to Sea *(1997), and* The Grass Harp *(1995), which was directed by Matthau's son. Born to poor Jewish immigrants, young Walter rose from a life of extreme hardship to become one of the most beloved grumpy old comedic actors of the 20th century.*

Did you know your father's parents?

I never knew my grandfather because he died before I was born. As a matter of fact, my father only met his father two or three times. He kicked around from job to job and died in his thirties from tuberculosis, I think. So any influence my grandfather had on my father was only through his absence. He was rarely at home because he couldn't stand to be around my grandmother, and found her to be quite an impossible woman. However, I was pretty close with my grandmother. Her name was Rose, and she was from Kiev. She really was a very harsh woman and came over to New York alone. She had a very tough life working in sweat shops for very low wages on the lower East Side of New York. They had very little money and it must have been quite difficult.

How did your dad get interested in acting?

He said he became an actor because he was always trying to amuse his mother. He would try and make her laugh as a little boy, for instance, imitating the landlady who would come around asking for the rent. One of his jobs as a boy was selling sodas in a Yiddish theater in New York. So he really always wanted to be an actor, but I don't think he thought he could ever make a living at it. He lived with his mother until he volunteered for World War II. He did that so his brother wouldn't have to go, because his brother had a job and was providing an income for the family. I think he enjoyed going off to war because it was easier than living with his mother! It was a tough life they had in the early days, just Rose and the two boys, and they were constantly being evicted. When the war was over, he was able to take some acting lessons on the G.I. Bill and he just started doing jobs on Broadway and never really stopped working after that.

What was his first Broadway role?

His first significant acting job that I know of was in *Anne of a Thousand Days* on Broadway in the late '40s. He was understudy for Harry Irvine, the actor who played Bishop Fisher. I think that was his first real paying acting job. He actually auditioned for the role of bishop, but didn't get it because all the producer saw was this young Jewish boy from the lower East Side. The producer said he looked like he should be playing a cop, rather than an old English bishop in the court of Henry VIII. Rex Harrison was the star, and played Henry. But my father ended up filling in the role for a while and did very well. The next summer he auditioned for the same producer and this time it was for the role of a New York City firefighter. But the producer said, "Matthau's only good at English stuff!" My father went on to do many Broadway shows, and won two Tony Awards that I have in my office. He also received an award for Best Newcomer for an early play that he did. Unfortunately, I never got to see him on Broadway because I was too young. The only play I ever saw him in was *Juno and the Paycock*, in Los Angeles, in the late '70s with Jack Lemmon and Maureen Stapleton.

It's hard not to smile when you think of Walter Matthau and his great comedic talent. However, he began with serious roles, didn't he?

He had done some other comedy work on stage such as *A Shot in the Dark*, which was the predecessor to Inspector Clouseau. But in his early movies he quite often played the villain such as in *Charade* [1963], with Audrey Hepburn and Cary Grant, and in westerns with Burt Lancaster and Kirk Douglas. He had a very intense role in *Fail-Safe* [1964] with Henry Fonda.

Walter Matthau analyzes a scene for his son, Charlie, making his film debut in *Charley Varrick* (1973).

He loved Fonda and thought he was one of the best actors. I guess somebody eventually figured out Dad could be funny in movies.

His final Broadway show was *The Odd Couple,* from 1965 to 1967, with Art Carney as Felix. Did he want the role back when the movie was made?

He wanted to do the movie, but the studio wanted Frank Sinatra. So my father went to see Howard Koch, who was the head of Paramount at the time. He asked Koch if he wanted to be known as the guy who ruined *The Old Couple*! Well, Howard and Frank eventually got into some kind of an argument and Howard came to his senses and hired my dad to play Oscar Madison.

What was the first film you saw him in?

He took me to many of his movies when I was little, but I'm not sure which one was the first. It may have been *A Guide for the Married Man* [1967], when I was three or four. But I do remember saying to him, "The guy on the screen looks just like you!"

By the time you were eight years old, he was 50 and had experienced some serious health problems. How concerned were you about his heath?

When I was three, he had a massive heart attack and nearly died. The doctors thought that he would never work again. Every day there was a fear that he would have another heart attack, or that he would become sick. He continued to have heart problems for the next 30 years and he did have a couple more heart attacks, a bypass operation, several angioplasties, and a pacemaker installed. So I was always afraid of losing him. He was my best friend and I was very close to him. So I had that fear growing up. He was an incredible father and we did everything together, so I can't imagine having a better father. I think he wanted to be the dad for me that he never had.

Did learning lines come easy for him?

I remember him rehearsing at home and sometimes I'd read lines with him. He didn't enjoy memorizing material and said it was manual labor, but he must have had a facility for it. He did summer stock where you do a new play every week. So for a film, memorizing two or three pages of dialogue at a time was something he called "retirement acting" and was easier for him. That's one of the reasons I never became an actor: I just hate memorizing lines for some reason.

So was he a grumpy old man in real life?

No, in fact, he was quite the opposite of that. He really was the nicest person. Sure, he could be grumpy sometimes, but he just had the biggest heart of any person you could ever meet. So in a lot of ways he was the opposite of those roles he is well known for. Unlike Oscar in *The Odd Couple*, he was very neat and clean, but he was very funny. And very generous, too. He wasn't miserly at all, probably because his mother was so thrifty, let us say, in order for her family to survive, and he remembered that. In fact, he showed no respect for money with his gambling. He lost millions of dollars, which again was probably a way of rebelling against those early days of poverty. It was a problem until he started to make a lot of money, then it wasn't so much. He was always loaning money to other actors who would never pay him back. Or he'd give to any worthy cause and was always writing out checks or donating his time for a cause. Bums on the street would come up to him and he would give them $20, and he was always generously tipping people. So he was just an extraordinarily generous man and always thinking about other people.

How close were he and Jack Lemmon off-screen?

They were very good friends on-screen and off, and were always kidding around and joking off-screen. They would go round to each other's homes and their wives were friends, too. And I'm friends with his son, Chris, and daughter, Courtney. We'd all have Christmas together, and hang out all the time. The families would often travel together because the guys were working together so much. I remember one time I was traveling with them on the road to Palm Springs, in the desert. There was nobody around and we hadn't passed any cars for miles. We were running out of gas and called in to a service station. Dad got out of the car and started to pump gas. He and Jack were talking and this Native American guy who ran the service station came out of the office and said, "You guys can't fool me, you're the Odd Couple!" So I thought that was kind of cute — even in the middle of nowhere, they were recognized.

What was the on-screen magic between Walter and Jack?

It's hard to describe that kind of chemistry. You've got the streetwise Jewish New Yorker and the WASPy, uptight guy from Harvard — complete opposites that were just great together.

Ever wonder what *Some Like it Hot* might have been like if your dad had played Tony Curtis's part?

I've never thought of that. It would have been an interesting idea. I do know that Billy Wilder wanted to hire my dad for *The Seven Year Itch* [1955], and he actually did a screen test for that. Billy told him afterwards that he was 90 percent sure that he was going to get the part. But I guess he couldn't talk the studio into it, and they gave the role to Tom Ewell who had done the part on Broadway. Then later, when my dad was doing *The Odd Couple* on Broadway, Billy went to see him backstage and gave him a script for what became *The Fortune Cookie*, for which he won the Oscar. Dad asked him what happened to his role in *The Seven Year Itch* and Billy replied, "Haven't you ever bet on a horse that was 1 to 9 and lost?"

Did he have any stories about working with Elvis in *King Creole* (1958)?

He said Elvis came up to him on the first day and said, "Mr. Matthau, if you could help me with this acting, I'd appreciate it." Dad replied, "Elvis, I've seen you act, and you don't need any help." Actually, I think Dad spent most of his time playing craps with Colonel Parker, Elvis's manager.

Do you have a favorite line from a Walter Matthau movie?

The Sunshine Boys [1975] is my favorite performance with my dad. He played Willy Clark, an aging vaudeville actor who's going senile. And his nephew, played by Richard Benjamin, is trying to pitch him a TV idea. Willy keeps saying over and over, "What's the theme of the show?" although with his broad accent it comes out, "What's da teem of da show?" So my dad and I used to say, "What's da teem of da show?" to each other when we would meet, meaning "What's going on?"

You worked with your dad on several films as a fellow actor and you even directed him. Did you see him differently as a co-worker?

I was 11 when we made *Charley Varrick* [1973], but we were not on-screen together. However, he ended up actually directing me in the scene. Don Siegel, the director, left for a phone call so my dad took over. After we did the first take, he yelled, "Cut! No,

Charlie and Walter Matthau on the set of *The Grass Harp* (1995). (Photograph courtesy of Charlie Matthau.)

no, no, too much acting. Terrible!" After a while I asked, "When is the real director coming back?" Later, when I directed my father in *The Grass Harp*, I got to see him from a director's perspective and it was great. I always knew what he was thinking just by looking in his eyes, and he knew the same about me. It was really easy because we had fun together. Our relationship on the film reminded me of the very successful racehorse Zenyatta, and the jockey who says the horse will do anything he asks it to do. That's what directing my dad was like.

Why did it take 30 years to make *The Odd Couple* sequel?

I think back in the '60s when *The Odd Couple* was made, it wasn't cool to do a sequel. Now, of course, even if a film is a minor success, they make 15 sequels! And also, nobody else could write the sequel except Neil Simon, and he didn't write it until 30 years later. My father had a good time shooting it, but this was during the time that he was diagnosed with cancer, and I think he thought it was going to be his last film. He said, "I came in with *The Odd Couple*; I'm going out with *The Odd Couple*." I managed my father for the last ten years of his life, so I was usually involved in his work. But on *The Odd Couple II* [1998], my role was basically sneaking into his trailer and taking out all the fatty foods and replacing them with low-fat products which he always referred to as "taste-free foods." For instance, if he had ice-cream bars in the freezer, I'd replace them with yogurt bars.

Did he like doing the *Grumpy Old Men* films?

No, they were very hard for him because of his age, health and the cold weather. I think during the first one he had a heart attack and during the second he got sick, too. The producer was a friend of mine and asked me to read the script. I thought it was okay, but with Dad and Jack in it, I believed they could make it great, and they did. When I showed the first one to my father he said it was the worst piece of crap he'd ever read and wasn't going to do it. But I talked him into doing it. Jack, on the other hand, loved it and wanted to do it. Dad liked the second one better.

How did he handle growing old?

He was very graceful about growing old, even when he got cancer. I would call the doctor to get the results of tests and my father wouldn't even ask me about them; he'd just wait for me to tell him. I was calling the doctor every five minutes, but Dad was very calm about all that stuff.

Was there a character he played that was most like him in real life?

I don't think there was one character, but there were parts of him in all his films. For instance, in *The Bad News Bears* [1976] he was kind of laid back, gruff, and with a heart of gold. In *The Odd Couple*, he was laid back and a sports nut, which he was in real life. And *The Grass Harp* revealed his romantic side, which he never got to show in most movies. My mother, Carol, also helped him to see himself in a more romantic way and that he could be a leading man as well as a character actor.

So off-screen he enjoyed gambling and sports. What were his other interests?

He loved classical music and got to show a little of that in *Hopscotch* [1980]. Pretty much all he would listen to was Mozart. He'd blast the Mozart out on the stereo while he would go for a swim. Other times he would turn on the game, turn off the sportscaster, and put on the Mozart — unless it was

Vin Scully or someone he liked listening to. The music helped to calm him down, especially when he had a large bet going. He liked all of Mozart's music; maybe the 40th Symphony and *Don Giovanni* were among his favorites. He used to sing along, but if you watch *Hello, Dolly!* [1969], you'll see that singing wasn't his best skill.

What traits of his have you inherited?

I think his sense of humor, laughing your way through life and not taking anything too seriously, especially about myself. I am also a gambler, but since I have far less money, there are a lot less zeros on the ends of my bets!

After all those early years of struggling, his mother lived to see him successful. Presumably he took care of her once he started to make it?

He bought her a beautiful condo in Miami, and anything she wanted. I think he was always trying to get his mother's approval. But despite all his success, she was always reminding him that it could fall apart at any time. I think when he was working on *Hello, Dolly!* he told her, "Mom, they're paying me a million dollars to do this film." And she would tell him it wasn't too late to get into a line of work that was more stable, like being a pharmacist or something!

Was he pleased that you followed him into the film business?

Actually, he wanted me to be a doctor! But I didn't want that; it would have been too much pressure. I did some acting, but now am a director and run The Matthau Company, although occasionally I'll do a part if someone asks me. So in this business, unlike medicine, the worst thing I can do is make a bad movie — I'm not going to kill someone! But he was pleased with my success. Growing up, I was always with my father and watched him work with other directors, so I can relate pretty well to actors. *The Grass Harp* has been the best film we've produced, and it was my father's favorite film. I'm very proud of that one and that I got to work with my father and not embarrass him in the process!

Charlie Matthau on Walter Matthau. Telephone interview on 10/27/10. The Matthau Company, Charlie Matthau's production company site with a section on his father, is www.matthau.com.

3

Lance Brisson on Rosalind Russell

Some movies just seem to become more appreciated and treasured with age; the same can be said for some actors. This is clearly true for Rosalind Russell (1907–1976) and two of the all-time classic comedies she starred in, 18 years apart. Call her zany Auntie Mame or sassy reporter Hildy Johnson, Russell created two characters most actors can only dream about. Raised in Connecticut and on the stages of East Coast theaters (to which she would return triumphantly later in life), Russell found a home, career and husband in Los Angeles. Fresh off the boat from England, Danish-born actor's agent Frederick Brisson (1912–1984) twisted a friend's arm to secure an introduction to Miss Russell, whom he would marry in 1941. Brisson later became a successful Broadway and film producer. The couple's son, Lance, explains why his mother was a great lady off-screen, as well as on.

With two parents in the entertainment world, were you interested in a show business career?

My view is that offspring of well-known and highly successful people have to make a choice whether or not to pursue a career in the same field as their parent, or to strike out on their own. From the time I was mature enough to be thinking about it, I decided I didn't want to compete with the success that my parents had in show business and chose an entirely different path. Hollywood is a community in which nepotism is not only accepted, but is encouraged. I'm not being critical when I say that, it just is! I have great respect for sons and daughters of stars who have succeeded in their own right. But, ultimately, whether they have sustained success depends on their ability. My parents could have opened doors for me if I had wanted to act or produce, but I didn't have the talent to act or the motivation to produce. So with the exception of elementary school, I wasn't even in school plays and had no interest in acting. In high school, I became interested in journalism and was editor of the school newspaper, and had summer jobs as a copy boy for the *Los*

24

Rosalind Russell, shown here in her favorite role of mother, giving a bath to her three-and-a-half-year-old son, Lance Brisson, at their Beverly Hills home in 1947.

Angeles Times. By the age of 20, I was a general assignment reporter at the *Times* in 1963. I was there the day Kennedy was shot. Being the most junior reporter, I was assigned to take statements of sympathy and grief being phoned in by the local political officials, while more senior reporters covered the actual events. However, to be in the city room of a major newspaper on that day was one of the most memorable experiences of my life. Since 1987, I have worked at Winner & Associates in L.A., where I am the chief operating officer. It's a strategic communications company which helps clients — mostly large companies — manage difficult issues, including high-stakes crisis situations.

How did your parents meet?

My father was born in Copenhagen, in 1912, and moved to England when he was ten with his parents and aunt. The war in Europe started in 1939, but because he was a Dane, the British wouldn't let my father become an officer in the Army. So he left England some time after September 1939, and sailed to the U.S. where he eventually enlisted in the U.S. Army Air Force. The trip took about 12 days because the boat had to zigzag to avoid the U-boats. On my father's ship, the passengers had just one or two movies to watch, and one of them was *The Women* [1939], in which my mother was appearing. My father saw it several times during the voyage and was fascinated by my mother, who played a rather wacky character. When he arrived in New York, he sent a telegram to Cary Grant, who was a friend from the time both of them lived in London. Cary sent him back a telegram — which I still have — inviting my father out to Hollywood to stay with him, so he took the train to California. While there, he told Cary about this actress he had seen on the ship, Rosalind Russell, and asked if Cary could help him meet her. Cary told him he was in luck, because he was at that very time making a movie with her! The film was *His Girl Friday* [1940]. Well, Cary arranged to have dinner with my father at Chasen's, a well-known hangout for celebrities at the time, where my parents would eventually meet. My mother told the story this way: she was thrilled to be making a movie with Cary Grant, who invited her to Chasen's for dinner one evening. She got all "dolled up" and was sitting there with Cary when "this Danish guy, Freddie Brisson, comes over and plops down at the table." She thought she was on a date with Cary Grant, but this Freddie guy kept trying to get her attention. She eventually shooed him away, but not before he got her phone number and address. He started sending her flowers and she said she put him off for weeks before finally agreeing to go out on a date with him. And the rest is history.

Did you ever meet Cary Grant?

Cary was actually best man at my parents' wedding in 1941, and he delivered one of the eulogies and was a pallbearer at my mother's funeral in 1976. I met him a number of times and spoke with him on the phone a few times. He was a very nice guy.

By the time you were born, in 1943, your mother was a well-established actress. What do you remember about her career as you were growing up?

I grew up in Beverly Hills where I went to a Catholic elementary school from the first through fourth grade. In the early 1950s, my mother's movie career was in a bit of a trough, so she decided to go back to her roots in the theater and agreed to go on the road in a play called *Bell, Book, and Candle*. This was around 1952. I was young at the time, but looking back, it was quite a remarkable thing for her to do — she wasn't even going back to Broadway; it was a touring company! She had been a big movie star in the '30s and '40s, and for her to take that step, to leave Hollywood and big film roles to appear in a play in places other than Broadway, was taking a big career risk. But the reviews and attention she got as a theatrical actress led to her being cast in the Leonard Bernstein Broadway musical *Wonderful Town* in 1953. This was a remarkable piece of casting because she could not sing well. Yet she won the Tony for best actress in a musical! It turned out to be one of the highlights of her career, especially from a courage point of view. She went on to create the role as Auntie Mame in the Broadway production in 1956, and then the movie.

What happened to you when your parents moved back to New York?

We lived in a hotel while my mother was in the theater on Broadway. From the fifth through the eighth grade, I was a student at a private school in New York. From there I went to a prep school in Connecticut, which was where my older cousin, Sean, had attended. It was a boarding school called Hotchkiss, and many of the students were from elite East Coast families that were connected to investment banking or corporate law. My family was from show business and came from the West Coast, so it was almost like I represented diversity at the school! I remember one year, my parents dropped me off in a chauffeur-driven limousine, and I felt extremely uncomfortable because all the other kids were in station wagons. I didn't want to be known as the "movie star's kid!"

Did you appreciate how famous your mother was when you were young?

Growing up in Beverly Hills, it was an environment in which my early childhood friends and acquaintances were the offspring of actors, actresses, producers, and people like that. But I had no recognition of that when I was four or five years old. The realization that I had a famous mother and a very successful father was gradual — there was no epiphany. Over time, I would see people coming up to the table at restaurants asking for my mother's autograph and at some point it all sank in.

Was it difficult having such a busy, famous mother?

There were positive and negative aspects to it. From my perspective at the time, one downside to having a celebrity parent was that in public situations people were often paying attention to my mother — asking her questions and seeking autographs and so on. This could be frustrating sometimes when you are young and you want your mother to pay attention to you. When I complained to my mother about it, I remember she said, "This is part of how Mommy makes a living and helps pay the bills." Because of the demands of my mother and father's careers, we had a lot of separations, and we sure didn't have a typical 1950s family life. I did spend quite a lot of my growing up time with people other than my parents — I had a governess during some of the time I was in elementary school, spent some summers with relatives, and was away at boarding school as I got older. When I was 12, we were living in New York City. My parents told me they had to move back to California for about a year — I think it was between the time my mother was appearing in *Wonderful Town* and *Auntie Mame*. They asked me if I wanted to go with them or stay on the East Coast. I didn't want to change schools for just one year and then go back to New York, so I ended up staying, and lived with a governess for that school year. But not having the traditional family life with a mom who was in the kitchen cooking when I came home from school wasn't all bad. I had to learn to become independent at an early age. I had to travel on my own — initially by train, then later on planes. That's not a big deal so much today, but back in the '50s it was. When I was 13, I flew by myself from L.A. to Denmark which was a 23-hour flight. So the independence led to a certain amount of self-reliance. I was also an only child and spent a lot of time around adults. In those days misbehavior was not tolerated, so I have to wonder whether I lost a little bit of my childhood in that type of environment. I was expected to be a young gentleman whenever other people were around. But there were a lot of positives about being the son of successful parents. I consider myself to have been really lucky to have been born into this family. I came to understand that both their careers were important to them, and I was very proud of them. And for all our separations, I never doubted that both my parents loved me a lot, and I always felt connected to them.

Mothers can be very possessive about an only child. Was yours?

I thought so at the time, but now that I'm a parent of three children, I think it was remarkable that I had as much independence as I did. I don't think that she was possessive in the sense of clinging to me, but she did worry about me. She didn't have me on a tight leash as I grew older, but when I was a teenager and had a car and was going out on dates, she would worry. But I don't think that's being possessive; that's just parental concern. I always had an independent streak and was anxious to grow up and work for myself. Some of the girls I went out with were daughters of my parents' friends, but because I went to school in the East, many of my friends had nothing to do with Hollywood or the entertainment industry.

Was the family able to get away for many vacations?

Oh, sure. The first one I remember was spending the Christmas of 1950 skiing at Sun Valley, Idaho. I learned to ski there and became a lifelong skier. My parents skied, too, but not very well. Golf was my father's sport. We had beach holidays in California, and several trips to Europe. I remember going to Copenhagen around the summer of 1955 to visit my grandfather, Carl Brisson, who was dying of cancer. The following year we returned for a memorial service and there was a special dinner with the prime minister of Denmark. I was asked to get up and give a speech, which I did, but have no idea now

Rosalind Russell and infant son Lance Brisson meet Sister Elizabeth Kenny, whom Russell portrayed in the 1946 film *Sister Kenny*.

what I said. I just remember my parents being very proud of me. Carl Brisson was very famous in Scandinavia and well known to European audiences for his work on the stage in Great Britain and in silent films. He had been a successful boxer in his teens, then became a very successful singer and entertainer in England. His second movie, *The Ring* in 1927, was about boxing and was directed by Alfred Hitchcock. Being a small country, Denmark didn't have a lot of celebrity connections, so whenever my parents visited, there was tremendous news coverage.

Was it odd to see your mother up on the big screen?

I'm often asked that, and the answer is no. I always viewed it as what my mother did, and it was no big deal. The person on the screen was just my mother wearing a costume. What was great about our relationship was that we shared a lot of interests outside the entertainment profession. We were both interested in politics and social issues and discussed them all the time. She was also a huge baseball fan, read the sports pages every day, and we went to a lot of games together. Her team was the Dodgers, and we went to Ebbets

Field often. When the Dodgers moved to Los Angeles, she was friends with the owner, Walter O'Malley, and she obtained season's tickets right next to the owner's box at Dodger Stadium. Those tickets are still in the family.

You mentioned her interest in politics. What were her views?

Both my parents were Eisenhower Republicans, so I would consider her views to be moderate/conservative. My father had served on Eisenhower's staff during World War II, and they were good friends with Mamie and Ike before, during, and after his presidency. I was, and still am, a Democrat, so that made for some interesting family conversations!

At one point, your parents formed a production company. Did they work well together?

They formed Independent Artists, in 1946, and made four or five movies over a six-year period. As a producer, my father was a combination of very astute businessman and a person with artistic sensibilities. He was very involved in guiding and collaborating on my mother's career. They worked very closely in terms of making decisions, and she would consult him. In some ways, he was more her agent than her real agent was. One of their films, *Mourning Becomes Electra* [1947] featured a young Kirk Douglas, although it was not a commercial success. The Douglases actually lived behind our house, across an alley, and had a tennis court; we didn't. They told me I could go over and play tennis any time I wanted!

Did you ever see your mother perform on Broadway?

I saw her performing on Broadway many times. When she was on Broadway in *Wonderful Town*, I was living with my parents in a hotel in New York and going to school there. On Friday nights I often went with my mother to the theater. The show was a great success and she was a huge star at the time. I wasn't awed by the experience. I hung around with the crew and learned a lot about what goes on backstage. Sometimes, the lighting guys would let me guide the spotlights on my mother. When she first found out about it, she nearly had a heart attack! I also saw her perform a number of times in *Auntie Mame*, but I was away at prep school much of that time.

Do you see any of the real Rosalind Russell in the Auntie Mame character?

The craziness of the Auntie Mame character was not at all like my mother. Auntie Mame did a few things that were fun on the stage or screen but might have been a bit reckless in real life. My mother was not irresponsible at all; she had both her feet on the ground. However, they both cared about people and didn't like snobs or stuck-up people. They both liked to have fun and could be a bit zany at times. A good example of my mother's fun side was the Christmas Eve parties our family held. We invited a lot of friends from the entertainment business, but not because they were in show business; they were just nice people and my parents enjoyed being with them. Each year, some would join our family for a Scandinavian meal and we would play games after dinner. Gary Cooper and his family were often guests. For one of the games, my mother would collect a stack of paper bags from the Safeway store and I would help her fill them with ribbons, cheap costume jewelry, other decorative items, and a package of straight pins. The lights would be turned off, with maybe a few candles for light, and everyone had ten minutes to make a hat from the bag and items. It was quite funny to see someone like Gary Cooper — who was a wonderful guy, but a very shy person — walking around in these crazy hats! We might have Gregory Peck, Jimmy Stewart, or Van Johnson and their families with us. This went on from the time I was a small child until my late teens during those years when we were home for Christmas. The way I look at it, there was some of my mother in Auntie Mame, and more than a little of Auntie Mame in my mother.

Did your mother view her Auntie Mame character, as well as Hildy Johnson in *His Girl Friday,* as breakthrough roles for women?

They were pioneering roles in terms of showing a professional woman taking charge and sassing back to a man at a time when women were not portrayed that way. Although she never told me that she was really proud of those roles for that reason, I think they did reflect her view of herself because she really was a strong, smart woman. She was also a great writer. She wrote, uncredited, some of the script for the *Auntie Mame* play and movie — I saw her do it. She also wrote a couple of screenplays and books under a pseudonym. So she was comfortable playing those roles, but it wasn't her nature to say she was proud of them. *His Girl Friday* will be studied by film students as long as there are movies, and numerous papers have been written about it and [Howard Hawks's] directorial style.

She did a lot of charity work throughout her life. How did she start that?

One of the things that interested her in the '40s was the treatment of polio. When I was five, she took me to a hospital in Los Angeles where people were being treated for polio. In those days, there was no polio vaccine and parents were terrified that their kids might contract it. She met Sister Kenny, an Australian woman who was convinced that most doctors of the day were not treating polio patients properly. So my mother became an advocate for Sister Kenny, and used her star power to get a movie, *Sister Kenny*, made about her in 1946, even though she knew it was unlikely to be a commercial success.

Your mother had her own health problems throughout her life. How difficult was it for the family?

She had two mastectomies, the first in 1961 at a time when breast cancer was poorly understood. The second was some years later and she died from metastasized breast cancer. The final years of her life were particularly difficult for her because she was also very ill with rheumatoid arthritis, which was all through her body. At one time she was resuscitated, although I'm not sure if her heart actually stopped, but they had to "bring her back." As an Irish-Catholic, born in the early part of the 20th century, she believed, as far as it was possible, to suffer silently. So she was very brave and a fighter, and not one to give up. We never talked about her dying, and it would have been very difficult for me to initiate that conversation. I think we all maintained the façade that she would continue to live for a long time. In her final years, she even tried to protect me and my father from having our lives dominated by her pain, which tells you something about her amazing character. She also had a health problem after I was born, which I think was due in part to post-partum depression, because she had been working fairly intensely right up to near my birth. I don't know the full story about it, but there were other factors involved. My father was serving in the U.S. Army Air Force from 1942 to around 1945, so he was away much of the time. She also had three brothers away at war, two of them in heavy combat. So it was a very stressful time for her.

She also did a lot of work raising awareness for arthritis?

Yes. She became stricken with arthritis in 1969, and if you look at photos of her from the mid–'70s, her face is bloated from the high doses of steroids she was prescribed. Back in the early days, it was a disease that people didn't talk about much, and was not well understood. It was generally thought that people just got these aches and pains as they aged. Nor was there any significant government support for research. So President Ford named her to a commission to study it, although she was suffering terribly at the time. Nevertheless, she still traveled around the country, drawing attention to the disease, which resulted in an increase in public awareness and, ultimately, more federal spending for research. After she died, in 1976, Congress had a competition among universities to set up a research center and the University of California San Francisco won. It's now a major center for arthritis research in the country and is named the Rosalind Russell Medical Research Center for Arthritis.

Your mother was obviously a class act both on and off the screen!

She never forgot her roots; never forgot about people. She was a big believer in giving back, not just money, but her time, even though she had great difficulties herself. That was a theme throughout her life.

Lance Brisson on Rosalind Russell. Telephone interview on 1/3/11. The Rosalind Russell Medical Research Center for Arthritis website is www.rosalindrussellcenter.ucsf.edu.

4

Kelly Stewart on Jimmy Stewart

If you don't think Jimmy Stewart (1908–1997) put the "classic" in classic movies, check out these titles: Harvey, It's a Wonderful Life, The Philadelphia Story, Mr. Smith Goes to Washington, You Can't Take It with You, Anatomy of a Murder, Rear Window, The Stratton Story, *and the list goes on, including four classic Hitchcock films. No wonder Stewart appears near the top of just about every list of all-time most popular actors. With such a resumé, it's hard to imagine that the man didn't develop an ego the size of a giant rabbit. Yet according to his daughter Kelly, the respectable, unpretentious, all-American guy he often portrayed on film was also the real Jimmy Stewart. He was married to his beloved Gloria for 45 years; together they had two sons and twin daughters.*

How long did you live at home with your parents?

I was living at home until 1969, when I graduated from high school. Then I went to Stanford for four years, but would come home for Christmas and during the summer each year. Two weeks after I graduated I went to Rwanda and eventually got my Ph.D. in England. So I really lived outside of America from 1973 to 1989. My parents lived in the same house, on North Roxbury in Beverly Hills, for most of their lives, so I always enjoyed coming home to the house I grew up in. They lived in my mother's house for a brief period, then bought the other, larger house when they realized they were going to have twins. After Dad died, we sold it, and the new owner tore it down and built a monstrosity.

You have a brother and sister — what do they do?

Judy, my sister, lives in Santa Barbara, raised two kids, and has become a masterful gardener. Mike first went into law, then became a high school teacher for many years, and now manages investments. He lives in Phoenix. My other brother, Ron, was killed in Vietnam in 1969.

The first Stewart family safari in Kenya in 1965 — and the first time in Africa for twins Kelly and Judy. Stewart has a beard because he was making *Flight of the Phoenix*. In fact, he took a break from shooting to fly to Kenya to be with the family for a few days. From left to right are Stewart; son Ron, who was killed in Vietnam in 1969; wife Gloria; son Mike; and daughters Judy and Kelly. (Photograph courtesy of Kelly Stewart.)

Did any of the children have an interest in an acting career?

None of us did. We didn't have the slightest desire to make entertainment our careers. As for why none of us wanted to go into show business: for one thing, we weren't surrounded by it growing up because Dad didn't bring his work home with him. We didn't really know it any better than any other profession. As for the negatives — and I'm speaking only for myself here — even though I'm sort of a ham, the life of an actor didn't really look like that much fun to me. We went to Dad's set a couple of times — once I remember when he was making *How the West was Won* [1962]; another time during the filming of *The Man Who Shot Liberty Valance* [1962]. It looked very tedious to me — short takes, just a few minutes long, after which people come rushing up to you, touching up make-up and hair. One was constantly surrounded by people, hovering and fussing and looking. I remember thinking, "I could never do this." From what I could see, the life of an actor meant you were stuck indoors all the time under glaring lights. I wanted to be out in nature with wild animals. Today, acting seems to me a mysterious, unfathomable ability and I am in awe of anyone who can do it.

**Well, you got your career wish because you work with wild animals —
gorillas! How did that come about?**

I wanted to be a naturalist from an early age. My mother got me interested in anthropology when I was young, too. She gave me Robert Ardrey's
Territorial Imperative and Konrad Lorenz's *On Aggression*, two books for the
interested public that came out in the '60s. When I was 14, my parents took
us to Africa for a photographic safari. We were the only ones there, sleeping
in beautiful tented camps, and surrounded by animals. I remember Dad had
grown a beard because he was making *Flight of the Phoenix* [1965]. In fact, he
took a break from shooting to fly all the way to Kenya to be with us in camp
for a few days. Later, in college, I dug up fossils in Kenya with palaeoanthro-
pologist, Richard Leakey. In my junior year, I met gorillas while on a trip
with my mom and sister to the Congo, which in those days was called Zaire.
I've been captivated by and involved with the animals ever since. I'm a research
associate in the Department of Anthropology at the University of California
Davis and have worked with my husband, Sandy, who is also an anthropol-
ogist, and who retired in June 2010. I have lectured for various university
courses, but more commonly I give talks to general audiences such as school
children, zoo organizations and conservation groups, on the behavior, ecology
and conservation of wild gorillas.

**How did your dad feel about you living in the jungles of Africa with
gorillas?**

He loved the fact that I was over there; they both did. In fact they came
over to visit in 1981 and I took them to see the gorillas. My husband and I
were running the research center in Rwanda for two and a half years while its
founder, Dian Fossey, was away in the States. I had Dad and Mom crawling
on their stomachs through the bamboo forests in Rwanda looking for animals.
Dad got right up close to the gorillas, maybe five meters away, and took some
great photos. But I didn't get any pictures of him with the animals, which I
wish I had. Gorillas are not easy to photograph with their black fur and faces,
especially if they are in the shadows.

**You have taught at college over the years. Do your students know Jimmy
Stewart was your dad?**

Most of them don't, although quite a few grew up watching *It's a Wonderful Life* [1946] because their parents would watch it each Christmas, so
some college-age students know him through that movie. Every now and then
I might get an email from a student, or faculty member at Davis, who finds
out and wants to tell me he was one of their favorite actors. And that's quite
fun for me to hear. When I came to Davis in 1989, even a lot of people in

my department didn't know that I was Jimmy Stewart's daughter. Most found out when Dad died and there was local publicity. Some were just surprised to find out about my Hollywood connection, and others were excited because they were fans of his and loved his movies. But I tend not to run around talking about who my dad was. I've had a bit of horror of that sort of thing since I was a child. I think it all started when my sister and I had a governess who took us to see one of his films when we were nine. I don't remember which film it was, but there was a long line of people waiting to get in to see the movie. I remember the governess, whom we called mademoiselle because she was French-Canadian, pushed her way to the front of the line saying, "Excuse me, I have Jimmy Stewart's daughters." One guy yelled back, "I don't care who you've got, lady — get to the back of the line!" It was just so humiliating to me — a cringe-worthy moment. It stuck in my mind and I never wanted anything like that to happen again.

Your father has always been rated high on most popular actor lists, and he was a huge fan favorite. Do you think he really appreciated just how popular he was?

I think he might have, because he received so much fan mail and high praise from his peers. As to what he thought about his acting, I believe he was proud of his work, although he was extremely modest and judged himself by his own high standards. He didn't talk about his career or work a lot, and I think he would have been surprised at the accolades after he died — we certainly were. I didn't realize how big an icon he was until then and was totally amazed at the outpouring after his death. He was very close to his fans and he always said he had a partnership with them. He answered his fan mail faithfully. That was very important to him because he believed his public was his "bread and butter." I've had people come up to me and tell me they wrote him a letter when they were in high school and got a personal response back. He had a secretary helping him, of course, but he signed all the letters. I never saw him say "no" to an autograph seeker, even when there where crowds of people. I remember I was with him in New York during a tribute to him from the American Museum of the Moving Image in 1988. After the ceremony, we were leaving out the back door of the theater at midnight and it was pouring rain, and a crowd of fans was waiting by the door. Dad stopped and signed everything for them all. I remember thinking that was pretty amazing.

Did you watch his movies as a teenager?

I watched a few at the movie theater, like *Two Rode Together* in 1961. But most I watched in the family basement where we had a screening room. Dad would get copies of the films on those big reels and I can picture him standing

Jimmy Stewart takes high school-age daughters Judy (left) and Kelly on a trip to British Columbia to look at colleges, 1966. (Photograph courtesy of Kelly Stewart.)

there threading the film into the projector. We watched all his Hitchcock films there.

He did four Hitchcock films — were they friends?

He didn't hang out with Dad, but we would see him at Chasen's Restaurant. Mom and Dad always got the same booth when they ate there, and the Hitchcocks had the booth next to ours, so I can remember sitting right next to him. He would come over to parties my parents would have in their home.

How did your father prepare for his roles?

Every evening before dinner, we would gather in the library. Mom and

Dad would have the news on and be sipping their cocktails, while the kids would be talking about what happened at school. Dad sat in a big comfy armchair that had a matching footrest, and no one else ever sat in that chair when Dad was home! When he was working on a movie, he would sit with the script in his hands and his lips moving, saying his lines to himself. He never said anything out loud. I have that image of him burned into my mind. We never read any of the lines with him. Except for that, he rarely brought his work home with him. I do recall an exception, however, when he was making *The Flight of the Phoenix*, which was about a plane crash in the middle of the Sahara. One day he came home with his makeup on, cracked lips, peeling skin and all. It was quite alarming.

That famous Jimmy Stewart slow drawl delivery — was that how he talked around the house?

That's how he really talked! Whenever we told stories that were about him, we would imitate his voice — it's hard not to talk like him when you're talking about him. He loved to tell stories about his own experiences and he had great timing. He just took a long time to come out with the punch line!

He always seemed like a mild-mannered man in interviews. Did he have a temper?

Dad would let things simmer and you could tell when he was getting irritated about something. He would remain very quiet and then had his way of letting you know he'd had enough. It was kind of a steely sternness that suddenly came out, but he didn't yell or scream. So he did get mad, but not often. My sister and I were quite the hell raisers in school and one year we got a bad behavior report, and that upset him. Typically, he'd say: "How could you do this to your mother!" And then Mom, when she got mad, would say: "You're killing your father — how could you do this to him!" One time they took us to Pacific Ocean Park, an old amusement park in Santa Monica. Judy and I were 12, and we started teasing a girl because she had a funny hairstyle. My parents were shocked at us being so mean. As for punishment, forget about taking away any privileges — all they had to say was that they were very disappointed in us, and we were crushed.

How did your friends cope when first going to your home and meeting Jimmy Stewart?

I'm sure some of my boyfriends were intimidated. I was a teenager of the '60s, when bare feet were the fashion. If I brought someone home who wasn't wearing shoes, I could tell Dad disapproved. He also frowned on any guy with a limp handshake who didn't look him in the eye. When I went to college, my parents took me to help set up my room. My roommate had just arrived for the first day. She was unpacking and had lingerie in her hands, and when she turned around and saw Jimmy Stewart there, she was pretty shocked.

Was it chaotic for the family to go out in public?

We did go out as a family, but in Beverly Hills where we grew up, people were used to seeing him around town. At less-frequented places like the LA Zoo, or a baseball game, he drew more attention, and there would always be people who came up and asked for his autograph. When I was nine, we went on a family holiday to Europe. When we landed, there was a huge crush of photographers clamoring for photos. Then there were all the interviews in hotel rooms. So it was much more obvious to me that he was a movie star when we traveled. It was actually a kick to get that glimpse of Dad's fame.

How did your mother handle being married to such a famous celebrity?

Both my parents were incredibly unpretentious, so she handled it fine. They were married for 45 years — pretty rare in Hollywood. They kept each other laughing and had incredible respect for each other. I think that was their secret. Mom was very funny and all their friends loved her because she was so unassuming, but charming. She made people feel at ease, and was such good fun.

Some sources have said he didn't like to be called Jimmy. True?

He went by Jimmy and his really good friends called him Jim.

Was your father religious?

Yes, but quietly religious. He didn't try to convert anybody. We went to church every Sunday when I was growing up. Every night, he would kneel by his bed and say his prayers. Even when the rest of the family stopped going to church, he still went every week. I think he was sorry that faith didn't become important to any of us, like it was for him, and that it was a failure on his part that we didn't become religious. He always felt his belief really helped him in life.

As a scientist, you probably don't have a problem with evolution. Did he accept it?

Yes, he wasn't ridiculously religious! We had some discussions about it over the years, and he believed in evolution.

There's a story that's been floating around for years that your dad smug-

gled the hand of a Yeti out of Nepal many years ago. Of course, there's no conclusive evidence for the existence of Yeti, but what do you know about that tale?

As the story goes, an artifact known as the Pangboche hand was stolen from a Buddhist monastery in 1959. If anything, it was probably from a human hand. According to the story, Dad was asked to smuggle it into London so a famous anatomist could examine it. Dad had a little mischief in him, and if he got the chance to harmlessly fool someone in authority, he would. So the idea of smuggling something out of a country would probably have appealed to him. But I never heard Mom or Dad ever talk about this incident. Dad was a great raconteur — very funny and engaging. If this story was true, I can't imagine him not spinning a wonderful anecdote out of it, to captivate his family and friends. So I do find it hard to believe.

There are many museums scattered around the U.S. honoring various entertainers, but some have had financial problems. For instance, The Roy Rogers Museum had to close in 2010 due to declining numbers of visitors. How's the Jimmy Stewart Museum in Pennsylvania doing?

It's in trouble as are many non-profit institutions when the economy goes into a decline. However, my family and I have hopes for it because it would be a terrible shame if it had to close. The Jimmy Stewart Museum is modest, but wonderfully done — a real little gem of a place in Dad's small home town of Indiana, Pennsylvania. It's a fantastic resource for people to learn about the life and times of Jimmy Stewart, and of course, for my brother and sister and me, it is a gift to have a place like this carrying on our father's legacy. We sent them some items from the house we grew up in, including the front door! And there are some personal items like the old sweaty hat with holes in it that he wore in the westerns, his boots, and they even have Dad and Mom's booth from Chasen's. The building is on the corner of a street and there are pedestrian lights that have the electronic countdown in seconds to tell you when you can cross. Well, it's hooked up to the lights and they got Rich Little to do Dad's voice which announces: "Hi, this is Jimmy Stewart and you've got five seconds to cross." It's hilarious.

It's fairly well known that your dad fell into great despair after your mother died in 1994. How did you handle it?

He really retreated and I think he had just had enough of the world. We went home as often as we could and spent a lot of time with him. We tried to get him to go out and see his wonderful friends, but he just didn't feel up to it. Dad was the most stubborn person I've ever met. You couldn't make him do anything he didn't want to do. Well-meaning people would tell us we should get him a personal trainer or to take him out for a drive to see the sunset. But they didn't understand. Dad was going to do what he wanted. At the end, I believe he appreciated his wonderful life, and knew he was loved. But he just wanted to hunker down inside his beloved home, with his two dogs. He did have an amazing housekeeper who took devoted care of him. She moved to Ireland and we still visit her.

So how would you describe Jimmy Stewart as a father?

He taught us to do the right thing, without ever sitting us down and telling us to do the right thing. He wasn't a hands-on dad — he didn't help us with our homework and I doubt he ever changed a diaper. But he taught by example and just had a very quiet way about him. I remember growing up and doing things based on whether I thought Dad would approve or not approve.

What was your dad's favorite food — exotic and fancy, or simple and plain?

He was a very conservative eater and always liked the same thing. But his favorite was ice cream. Always, for dessert, he would have one scoop of vanilla ice cream. Not very flashy or extravagant, but just perfect for Jimmy Stewart!

Kelly Stewart on Jimmy Stewart. Telephone interview on 1/18/11. The Jimmy Stewart Museum website is www.jimmy.org.

5

Bill & Minnie Marx on Harpo Marx

The Marx Brothers — Groucho, Chico, Harpo — officially appeared together in their last feature film, Love Happy, *in 1949. Although fans have little "love" for it and the brothers were not "happy" making it, the film did provide some enjoyable moments showcasing Harpo's silent talents. Along with brothers Zeppo and Gummo, the five Marx Brothers grew up in New York City. Gummo dropped out of the act and the four brothers traveled the country as stage performers before taking Hollywood by storm, starting with* Cocoanuts *in 1929. Straight man Zeppo eventually bailed, too, and the three remaining brothers went on to become arguably the greatest comedy team ever. Between them, the five brothers raised a dozen children and a few went into the entertainment business. Bill Marx and Minnie Marx Eagle are two of Harpo's four children. While Minnie had no interest in a show business career, Bill is enjoying a successful career as a musician, composer, comic, speaker, and writer. They talk about life with Harpo (1888–1964) and his brothers, with Bill concluding the interview by paraphrasing his Uncle Groucho's biting sarcasm!*

Bill, you published a book, *Son of Harpo Speaks!*, in 2007. What was it about?

It's not really a book about the Marx Brothers. It chronicles my relationship with my dad and our working together for 12 years. My stories have never been told before and I guess I'm one of the last people left who actually worked with the Marx Brothers firsthand. I also have an audio book of *Son of Harpo Speaks!* which contains material that nobody's heard before.

Were you interested in a show business career?

MINNIE: I never did anything in entertainment; I was never even in a

Left to right, top: Minnie, Harpo and Bill; left to right, bottom: Jimmy, Harpo's wife Susan and Alex, circa 1961. Alex died in 2006. (Photograph courtesy of Minnie Marx Eagle).

school play. My dad never encouraged nor discouraged us from show business. My mother, however, encouraged us to go in a different direction. I have been married since 1964 and was a stay-at-home mom. My children and grandchildren are all grown now so it's the time of my life to just enjoy and travel.

BILL: I'm what you'd call a sit-down/stand-up/sit-down/stand-up comic! I sit down, play the piano, then stand up and tell stories, then sit down again and so on. Then I do Q&A sessions. I've been a composer and jazz pianist most of my life — doing film scores, symphonic writing, and arranging. I've played with many of the great jazz artists of the 20th century.

Did Harpo influence your musical career?

BILL: Absolutely. When I was two years old, he recognized my musical ability, but he never forced anything on me. I was not a disciplined young musician — I hated scales and lessons. I wanted to play baseball! When I was 16, I wound up as his personal arranger and conductor. We did two albums together for Mercury Records. When he appeared on TV programs like *The Lucy Show*, he often played the harp and I did all the musical arrangements for him. I was only in my late teens then, so he helped validate me as a composer and musician.

Do you play the harp?

BILL: No. Dad used to say, "One harpist in the family is enough!" I have written a couple of concertos for the harp and did all the pop arrangements for my dad later in his career.

Did Harpo play the harp at home for the family much?

BILL: Not really; he'd play to practice. He loved to practice; he'd do it for two to three hours a day, whether he was working or not. He just loved the harp — its feeling, its sensuality, the vibrations, and the harmony and sounds of the chords. The harps you see in the films were his personal instruments.

What happened to his harps? They would be priceless Hollywood memorabilia today.

BILL: When he passed away, my mother and I went to Israel and donated them to the Rubin Academy of Music, now the Jerusalem Academy of Music and Dance. Students are still playing them, which is wonderful.

What about his other old movie props — have they been saved?

BILL: I have a lot of stuff— his prop chest, his coat, his hat, and wigs. I'm looking for a place to have it all displayed. I turned down the Smithsonian because I don't want it stored in a vault. These are pieces of American film history and they need to be on permanent display somewhere.

What happed to his famous walking stick with the honker?

BILL: My sister has that. But it doesn't work anymore because the bulb has worn out over the years.

How would you describe Harpo's personality and nature?

MINNIE: He was a wonderful dad. I think because he had kids later in life he was much more tolerant. He never raised his voice to us, ever. We were each treated with respect and love. My dad always tried to listen to what each of us had to say. In the early days when he had to travel a lot for his work, the time with the kids became very special times. He always made sure to spend quality time with each of us when he was home, because there wasn't a lot of quantity. After we moved to the desert of course, that was different as he was home all the time then. Harpo was a very simple man. He never drove a fancy car, didn't wear expensive clothes from France or Italy, or live an extravagant lifestyle. Simple things made him happy.

Do you have a favorite Marx Brothers film?

BILL: It's *Go West* [1940], only because I thought Dad was phenomenal in it. It was written by a great friend, Irving Brecher, who passed away in 2008. He was one of the funniest guys ever. I recommend reading his book, *The Wicked Wit of the West*, which is full of delightful stories. I also love *Monkey Business* [1931] and *A Night in Casablanca* [1946]. *The Big Store* [1941] was the first Marx Brothers movie I saw, when I was four or five. I love the scene where Dad is playing the instruments in front of the mirrors. It's very charming. I think *A Night at the Opera* [1935] is probably their best film. But everyone has a different take on their movies and what appeals to them.

MINNIE: I don't really have a favorite Marx Brothers film. I enjoyed all of them. It was fun as a child to see their movies and think, "Hey, I know those brothers." I always enjoyed the scenes with Harpo playing the harp because it was so much like my dad, not the character.

Did you have a favorite uncle?

BILL: Not really. Gummo was the easiest for me to get along with. He was very laid back. He could construct a sentence with three words and take four minutes to say it! I got to know Groucho the best as I spent a lot of time with him in his later years. Groucho had to work all the time and was miserable if he didn't. He had to have an audience and perform; that was his greatest joy in life.

MINNIE: I enjoyed all my uncles for different reasons, but if I had to choose I would have to say that my favorite uncle was Gummo. He was a very soft-spoken and gentle man. To me, he was just a nice person to be around.

It's often claimed that Zeppo was actually the funniest in real life. True?

BILL: He was in many ways. He was a great raconteur. He could tell stories that would make Groucho fall apart — the only man who could make him tear up with laughter. Each brother had a different sense of humor. Chico could tell you the latest jokes, and Dad was kind of a prankster around people. Gummo was very subtle, the least overtly humorous of the bunch, but still a good sense of humor.

Off-screen, did the brothers always call each other by their stage names?

BILL: Yes, although for the most part without the "o" — Grouch, Chic, Harp, Zep. But Gummo was always Gummo.

Did you get to visit any of the Marx Brothers film sets?

BILL: I was only on two, *A Night in Casablanca* and *Love Happy*. I was 12 during *Love Happy*, and it was a difficult film for Dad to do. Originally, it was going to be his movie. But in order to get financing, the producer had to write Chico and Groucho into the story. So the final film was nothing like

Dad originally had in mind. Dad was lied to by the producer and it was an awful experience for him, but he had to do it as he was under contract.

MINNIE: Because Bill is seven years older than I, he visited more of the sets than I did. I do, however, remember being on the set of *Love Happy*, mostly because I got a Beany and Cecil hat! It was all pretty routine for us to visit a set. We actually sometimes were more interested in what other things were happening because we were used to what my dad did.

Do you think your parents spoiled you?

MINNIE: My brothers and I may have had a nice life with a lot of perks, but we were not spoiled. My mother saw to it that we were raised with good values and education, and didn't allow us to be doted on. We all went to public school and were never treated "different" because of what my father did for a living. We all had chores, didn't get an allowance, and when we got old enough to want for things we were expected to get a job. Even though we lived in Beverly Hills, my parents made sure we lived an ordinary life. Our mom was a Cub Scout leader and a Girl Scout leader, both at the same time.

How did your dad influence your life?

MINNIE: My dad taught me that you always have to look for the good in people. Never look for the bad in people and dwell on that. I never heard my dad say he didn't like a particular person. He never had a negative thing to say about a person, at least that I ever heard. He also taught me to think before you speak, especially when you are mad. If you are mad at someone and say bad things in anger, you can never take it back.

Do you and your cousins still get royalties from the Marx Brothers films?

BILL: We get a few bucks now and then from *A Night at the Opera* and *A Day at the Races* [1937]. But nothing from the other films.

Is it true that Harpo smuggled out secret documents during a trip to Russia in 1934?

BILL: Yes. His friend, Alexander Woollcott, arranged a concert tour of Russia. But he really went there to avoid getting married! While he was there, the U.S. ambassador asked him to secretly take some papers back to America. But he never knew what was in the documents. When he returned, he realized how much he had missed her. He had been a confirmed bachelor for 47 years. Our mother was Susan Fleming, an actress. But she really couldn't stand show business. She stopped acting the moment they were married.

All the Marx Brothers gave their daughters names beginning with "M,"

Christmas with Harpo Marx, circa 1950. Bill is sitting next to his father; Minnie is in the middle; Alex is on the bottom left; and Jimmy is on the bottom right. (Photograph courtesy of Bill Marx.)

in honor of their mother Minnie. Did the Marx children carry on the tradition with their kids?

BILL: For the most part. Although Groucho's daughter, Melinda, has a daughter called Jade, who is an actress.

There are some audio and video clips of Harpo actually speaking that have appeared on the Internet. Have you heard them?

BILL: Yes. Those clips don't sound exactly like him when I knew him, but they're similar. We were all actually very disturbed when those things came out. It was contradictory to his philosophy of the character he created and the public embraced. That's why he once turned down oodles of money from a TV network to say just one word. He felt that would violate the public's trust in the mime they knew as Harpo, thus diluting its curious mystique. By revealing these tapes, it served no real positive purpose, and I am more than sure it would have saddened him greatly.

Are there other recordings of his voice that you know of?

BILL: I've got some audio recordings of his, but they will never be heard publicly. There's not a whole lot, mostly family recordings. I've got him singing and doing a German dialect.

Did he speak much in public?

BILL: He would rarely speak for any sort of public relations event or on TV to pitch something. Very rarely did he ever speak on stage. The night he retired from the entertainment world he was doing a show with Allan Sherman. He actually spoke to the audience and they were astonished. It was a special night. He passed away not too long after, in September 1964.

He suffered two heart attacks — how did that affect him?

BILL: After his first one, he became very morose. The Marx Brothers were all very athletic and did all their own stunts until they reached their mid-fifties. For example, in *The Big Store* you can see it wasn't them in some of the scenes. So it was very depressing for Dad not being able to do many of the things he once easily could. But after his second heart attack, he actually snapped out of the depression.

For the last decade of his life he lived in Rancho Mirage, California. What was the place like?

BILL: Dad built a home there in 1956 and called it El Rancho Harpo. He loved the serenity of the place. He had lived the city life and traveled the world, so he was ready to enjoy watching his kids grow up there. It was a great final chapter in his life. It was very spartan when he built it, but has been renovated over the years by a number of owners. It's quite an astonishing place now and has been designated an historic site by the city. It's privately owned and not open to the public, although the owners use it for fundraisers and other projects.

MINNIE: We moved to El Rancho Harpo when I was 12 years old. I was just entering junior high school and the move from Beverly Hills to unknown surroundings was not easy. My mom and dad did their best to make the transition a positive experience. I was given a horse and could keep it as long as I took care of it, and eventually I became a horse trainer and guide. After a few months of getting settled in the new house and meeting new friends, things were great. El Rancho Harpo was a wonderful place to be. Lots of family around, lots to do, and most important, lots of love. Every Sunday was set aside for family day. We played games, cards, and just talked about what we had all been doing for the week. There were a lot of parties at El Rancho Harpo also. My mom and dad would let my brothers and I have school parties quite often. At school reunions a lot of the alumni from high school still talk about what great parties we had. That was, of course, way before the days of drugs and alcohol. We never needed them to have a good time. By the time we were at El Rancho Harpo my dad was pretty much retired. I have such wonderful memories of him painting and playing the harp.

Did the brothers get together often as a family?

MINNIE: I remember the brothers getting together quite often, especially at the holidays. They used to play piano, clarinet, harmonica, and sing together a lot. You really knew these brothers loved each other. Even as a child I could see that. We had a big round dining table in our house that sat everybody. There was a lot of joke telling, and a lot of laughing. I never remember my dad or any of the brothers telling an off-color joke. Everything was about family. After my dad died, family and friends all came to Gummo's house. Groucho, Zeppo, Jack Benny, George Burns and others all told wonderful stories about Harpo. It was truly a celebration of his life. There was no funeral because my mom didn't want people to remember my dad as being gone — just keep telling the wonderful stories as if he were still here. My father died just two months before I was to be married. It was a difficult time, but all my uncles were there for me.

Well, thank you, Minnie and Bill, for sharing some great memories of your family for this collection of interviews.

BILL: You're welcome. I'm sure it will be a great book. But quite frankly, Nick, I wouldn't read any book that had you as one of its authors!!

Bill & Minnie Marx on Harpo Marx. Telephone interview with Bill on 7/15/09; email interview with Minnie on 12/11/10. *Son of Harpo Speaks,* is the title of Bill Marx's website (www.sonofharpospeaks.com) and also his 2007 biography, published by BearManor Media. Bill's other site, www.harposplace.com, is a tribute site to his father and family.

6

Peter Ford on Glenn Ford

Glenn Ford (1916–2006) appeared in close to 100 films from 1937 to 1991, and was a hugely popular draw at the box office, notching up performances in numerous westerns like The Fastest Gun Alive *(1956). There was also a host of other classics, such as* Gilda *(1946),* Teahouse of the August Moon *(1956),* Blackboard Jungle *(1955),* Pocketful of Miracles *(1961), and* The Courtship of Eddie's Father *(1963). While he never achieved that superstar status of a John Wayne or Cary Grant, he was a gifted actor. Married four times, Ford was first married to Eleanor Powell, a union which lasted 16 years and produced one child. Though she only appeared in a dozen movies, "Ellie" was regarded by many as the best female tap dancer to ever appear on-screen. Oddly enough, the first biography on Glenn Ford didn't appear until 2011. It was authored by his son, Peter, and contained some surprises about his famous father.*

When did you begin preparing the book about your father, *Glenn Ford: A Life*?

I started working on it around 2004, abandoned it for a while, and then my dad became ill and needed my wife's and my constant care. After he passed away I had a lot of estate problems to deal with, so it wasn't really until about a year later that I started working on it in earnest. It's a complete biography of his life. He lived 90 years, and performed for seven decades in the movies and had many associations with famous people. There has never been a biography written about Glenn Ford or his career, so people with a fascination for movies and life during the Golden Age of Hollywood will find it interesting. My father did write a book in the '70s called *Glenn Ford: RFD*, referring to Rural Free Delivery, which was about raising me on our rural area of Beverly Hills and raising chickens and growing vegetables. It was a folksy book, sort of a hillbilly Glenn Ford, and not at all related to the film industry or his career.

What resources did you use for the book?

My father kept a diary every day of his life since 1933 and I have every one of them, so there was an enormous amount of material there. If you picked any day since then, I could tell you what he had for breakfast, where he went, what he did, what he thought, who he talked to, etcetera. He also talks about directors he worked with, actors he liked, and actors he didn't like. My dad didn't have many bad things to say about his peers but his first director, Ricardo Cortez, was a "lemon" as far as Dad was concerned. He loved working with Anne Baxter and Geraldine Page and aside from Rita Hayworth, who could do nothing unappealing in my father's eyes, probably Barbara Stanwyck was the most accomplished, professional actress that he recalled. I interviewed many people for the book, such as Sidney Poitier, Shirley Jones, Debbie Reynolds, and Anne Francis. I also had about 50 pages of quotes from my farther that I have accumulated over the years on topics such as acting, acting styles, women, etiquette, and others, and I thought it was important to include some of these so people could hear him in his own words.

Your dad had quite a few women companions through his life. Did he talk about them?

Yes, he had quite a crew. He's perceived by the public as a Jimmy Stewart — a wholesome, all-American guy. He was that, but he also had a lot of Errol Flynn in him. In reviewing all my sources, I counted 146 women he had dalliances with, including Marilyn Monroe, although they are not all mentioned in the book. My intent was not to write a sensationalistic book, but to portray a man of enormous talent with all honesty. But he did have a lot of affairs.

Did that surprise you?

Oh, no — I knew about many of his relationships. I was his only child, and we talked a lot. He was a very complex person. He was an incredibly gifted actor who, in my opinion, never gave a bad performance. But there was a bit of a dark side to him that will surprise people.

How did your parents meet?

This is a long and interesting story. The short answer is that Mom and actor Pat O'Brien met on a U.S. Bond tour together. Pat had worked with my dad and thought they would make a nice couple and had a party after the tour specifically to introduce them.

Your mother was only in about a dozen films, then stopped acting shortly

Peter and Glenn Ford on the set of *Heaven with a Gun* (1969) at Old Tucson where Peter was the dialogue coach. (Photograph courtesy of Peter Ford.)

before you were born, in 1945. Despite her brief career, she is well known to fans of classic movies for her dancing. What made her so memorable and what were her best dance sequences on film?

My mother was the greatest dancer in film. This assessment is not only held by me and many other students of the field of dance, but Fred Astaire as well. Fred told me this in person. She had no regrets when she left dancing. She had a new role as wife and mother and threw herself into these new duties with the same zeal with which she approached her dancing. I was blessed with having the best mom a young man could possibly have; she was kind, honest, sweet, caring of all humanity — the best. She had a major comeback after her divorce from my father in 1959 that took her to Las Vegas and venues throughout the United States and Europe. As far as her best dance sequence, I think all her work was sensational. But look at the Adagio Dance with her and Fred in "Begin the Beguine" from *Broadway Melody of 1940*, and the "Drum Dance" from *Rosalie* [1939].

In addition to his many romances, your dad was married four times. Was there a great love of his life that slipped by him?

That was Rita Hayworth. She was in his life very early, and he was a pallbearer at her funeral (in 1987). Rita was also our next-door neighbor and was at my wedding. She was a dear, sweet friend, fragile and vulnerable and nothing like her screen image.

After your dad died, what did you do with all his belongings?

I inherited his house on Oxford Way, in Beverly Hills, that was built in 1961. It's 9,000 square foot, and huge for just me and my wife to live in. It's just mammoth — my daughter learned how to ride a tricycle in the master bedroom! So we want to move. We had to auction off much of Dad's stuff, but there is so much more we still have. The auction house took two 26-foot-long trucks out of here loaded with stuff.

So he was a bit of a pack rat?

He saved everything. I have every letter he ever received and copies of letters he wrote. I have his baby teeth, the lock of hair from his first haircut, the dish he used as a baby, and every report card from school. Most of that stuff, his mother kept — he was her only child, so she doted on him. There's also thousands of photographs, and thousands of books — he loved to read. Wherever he went, he would take scraps of paper and write his thoughts. Often, he would stick these randomly in books, along with letters, Christmas cards and even money. We've given away hundreds of his books to the library, but have to check each one because we never know what he may have hidden in it. For instance, I found many letters from Sophie Tucker! My father had an opinion on everything, and just loved to jot down his thoughts about life. I have a three-page diatribe he wrote when he visited New York Central Park one winter, and he was incensed at the horses being used to pull the hansom cabs in the park and made to work in the cold. So between all the letters, notes, diaries, his film and television work, and all the people he knew, there was just an enormous amount of information to wade through for the book.

What were some of the items that you sold at the auction?

There was a dime slot machine that Frank Sinatra gave him. And a couple of pianos, including one that Judy Garland gave him. I guess the plaid couch that he bedded Marilyn Monroe on after he brought her back to the house after a party was a high-ticket item in the auction! But there was still a ton of his stuff that didn't go to the auction — wardrobes full of clothes. I mean, what do you do with 200 Glenn Ford shirts? They all have his name in them, and he did wear them, so we gave a lot away to charities that auctioned them off. We were happy to see them do some good for a worthy cause.

Did your father have any quirky habits?
He didn't like to fly. In the early days, to get to Europe, he'd take a train to New York, then take a ship across the Atlantic. He also loved any kind of exotic food. He'd eat Rocky Mountain oysters, fish eyeballs, cow brains, anything. He loved to travel, and he traveled the world. He would always eat the local cuisine, whether it was eels, ants, or crickets. And he became involved with ESP through Cary Grant, who was our neighbor at one point and was into Transcendental Meditation and mind-enhancing experimentation. He also liked to secretly record conversations — which I guess was illegal! In our old house, he had a phone tap installed in the '50s. I have a stack of old reel-to-reel recordings that I've never actually listened to. Then he had a system set up in the new house and he recorded conversations with people on cassette tapes — I must have 100 to 200 of them. I've listened to some of them. He has some of President Richard Nixon. Isn't that ironic? The most infamous taper himself getting taped! But he and Nixon were good friends. When Bill Holden died (in 1981), who was his very closest friend, he was quite depressed and sat by the pool and opined onto the tapes about the early days at Columbia and working with Bill and Rita Hayworth. So those types of tapes are quite interesting to listen to. Some of them are, shall we say, a little spicy, so I'm not sure if I should give them to the Academy or a local college. But they're full of interesting information about my dad's life.

You must have met some interesting people over the years.
I was raised in the heart of the Golden Age, so sure, they all came through our house. Charlie Chaplin was our neighbor and he actually ran over my dog and killed it. Across the street was David O. Selznick; down the street was James Mason; up the street was Fred Astaire; and Billy Wilder was a neighbor, too. I sat on Mary Pickford's knee when I was little and I can clearly remember taking my first real drink when I was nine. It was a martini that was mixed by Fritz Lang, who was making *The Big Heat* [1953] with Dad, and would stop by the house. I mean, if you've got to start drinking, why not have Fritz Lang mix your first martini for you! When Dad married Kathryn Hays, Edward G. Robinson, Chuck Connors, Joseph Cotton, Elke Sommer,

Van Heflin and Rod Taylor were guests at the wedding. I was Dad's best man. After the ceremony, Andy Williams sang "The Hawaiian Wedding Song" back at the house and Oscar Levant played the piano that was a gift to my dad from his girlfriend, Judy Garland.

Kathryn Hays had a long career in *As the World Turns*, and is known to all *Star Trek* fans as the mute alien Gem, in the episode "The Empath." How did the two meet?

They met in late 1964, at a party that my father's agent threw. Actor Don Murray and his wife, Bettie, were at the party and were friends of Kathy's and they introduced my father to her. When my father and Kathy married, Bettie was her matron of honor. Actually, Don had previously married Hope Lange, who my father had a crush on, and it was a great sadness of his life when she wouldn't marry him. Anyway, to further explain their time line together, Kathy was at our house helping to decorate the Christmas tree later that year. Then in November 1965, Dad had a party at our home on Oxford Way, and announced their engagement. Some time before that, Dad had given Kathy a $15,000 five-and-a-half carat diamond "friendship ring," as he called it, which I guess was really an engagement ring. They took out a marriage license early March 1966, and were married at Westwood Unity Methodist Church. Robert Goulet sang the Lord's Prayer.

How did you get along with your stepmother?

I remember Kathy fondly and was very happy for the two of them when they got married. I was 21 and the best man at their wedding, and Kathy's six-year-old daughter was the flower girl. But the marriage only lasted three years.

So was your father's not wanting Kathy to work a main issue leading to the divorce?

I think so. I have notes which indicate that on December 21, 1967 Dad, Kathy, me, my wife, Lynda, and Sherrie, Kathy's daughter from a previous marriage, went to the premiere of *Doctor Dolittle*. Then we had a big party at the house on New Year's Eve, and everything seemed pretty good. But they had separated by March 8, 1968. By June, they were in court. She told the court that my father would give her the "silent treatment" if he did not wish to discuss questions such as her acting career, which I think is the essence of why they got divorced. From the notes I have, which I think came from a newspaper, Kathy is quoted as saying: "Before we were married, my husband advised me to sign a film contract, but after we were married he did not want

Peter and Glenn Ford in Philadelphia in 1971 for the first TV movie Glenn Ford did, entitled *America*, which aired on September 10, 1971. It was a tour of the United States set to music performed by popular artists.(Photograph courtesy of Peter Ford.)

me to continue with my acting career." It went on to say that he often failed to talk to her and was often given to long periods of silence. Dad didn't talk about it much to me, but I think he wanted a wife who would stay at home and take care of him. I suspect he probably didn't tell her that before they were married. I know from experience that was how he dealt with problems — he would just tune out and brood about them, and that doesn't make a happy family. So he should have come clean with her at the beginning. I was actually living with my mother and looking after her around this time, and I was acting and singing and trying to make my way in show business. I was really just an occasional visitor at my dad's home to see him and Kathy, and didn't know the inner workings of the details of their relationship. But Kathy was serious about her career. She was a fine actress, and obviously went on to be very successful in the business.

Some sources say your dad was a direct descendant from a president. Is that true?

No, he was not. The studio would fabricate this sort of stuff and Dad would just go along with it. I thought we were related to the eighth president, Martin Van Buren, but after tracing our family tree, I don't see it. It has also been said that he was related to the first prime minister of Canada, but that is absolutely not the case.

Why do you think he never gained that "John Wayne" acting status?

John Wayne played John Wayne in all of his films. He was a bigger-than-life character. He wasn't necessarily a great actor, but he was an imposing personality who could act. My dad was just your average guy, which is why a lot of people could identify with him. He didn't have that Wayne swagger, and he wasn't flamboyant. Also, Wayne had the chance to work with great directors of the era, like John Ford and Howard Hawks. Dad never did.

Nevertheless, he gave some greats performances, but he never got an Oscar?

Not even nominated. He was the top box-office draw in 1958 and had huge success and popularity in the '50s. He had tremendous fan appeal and made a lot of money for the studios. All the critics raved about his performances and predicted he'd win or be nominated for an Oscar. But he was never bitter about it, although it's very rare that an actor who was so popular and busy like him didn't even get nominated.

Is it true that Glenn Ford could draw a gun faster than anyone in Hollywood?

Oh sure, he could draw and shoot in three-tenths of a second. So it was quite appropriate that he starred in *The Fastest Gun Alive*— and he used me to pretend to be co-star Broderick Crawford when I was a kid! He would put a holster on me and we'd practice drawing down on each other in the bedroom. He was also a gun collector, and I still have most of his guns. He used the same gun in most of his movies. We had a four-acre estate with huge eucalyptus trees behind the property. As a youngster, he'd set some targets up on those trees on the fourth of July and we'd go out onto the balcony of his bedroom, and my job was to shoot every gun in his collection. Even though we lived in a rural area of Beverly Hills in those days, we did have neighbors, so I suppose it was a bit dangerous. And as a little kid, some of those rifles had quite a kick.

How was your father in his final years?

After I left acting, I was a home builder and built custom residential homes until about 1999 when I retired and moved in with my dad to take care of him. He was very lonely and wanted to get married again at 78. He still loved women and I think he felt that, without a woman by his side, he was unfulfilled. He also loathed to be alone and always wanted people around him. He was dating these 30-year-old girls and that caused some problems between us, because he attracted his fair share of floozies who were not planning to be there for him, but for themselves. And he didn't want to hear that.

He would give himself over completely to these people, to the exclusion of his family and friends, so we had our ups and downs during that time. So my family and I eventually moved in to look after him. I remember putting a picture of Rita Hayworth on one end table next to his bed and another of Judy Garland on other — two of his past girlfriends — and I said, "You look at them and forget about those young girls!" Towards the end of his life he started drinking a bit and was very morose and depressed. All of his friends — John Wayne, Henry Fonda, Bill Holden, Rita Hayworth — had died.

Many great actors came from extremely poor families; did your father as well?

He came from a sturdy working man's family of paper makers in Canada. They were not wealthy in the sense of opulence, but they were self-sufficient and wanted for nothing. The family emigrated from Canada to California in 1922. The family could only afford to have meat once a week, and at Christmas, Dad would get a piece of fruit for a present — and be grateful! When he first worked for Columbia, the publicity folks said his father, Newton Ford, had been a railroad executive. But he had really been a railroad engineer for the CPR — the guy who waved the lantern at the back of the train — on the run between Montreal and Quebec. So when they came to the U.S., they didn't have any money at all. Dad was always worried about not having enough money. He elected to become a contract player, not for the big dollars, but to guarantee a steady check for his family. That meant he was sometimes stuck with films that he didn't want to do, like *The Loves of Carmen* [1948] with Rita. Columbia dressed him in a strange costume for his character, Don Jose; he just hated that film. So he had to do the bidding of people like Harry Cohn. He may not have received the kudos that others did, but he always had work!

And about *Cade's County*, the TV series you starred in with your dad in the early '70s. Did you see him in a different light working more closely as a regular on the show?

No, by age 26 when we did *Cade's*, there wasn't much left for me to discover that I didn't already know about my father on every level. He was a fine actor who left a great legacy to his craft.

Peter Ford on Glenn Ford. Telephone interview on 8/28/08. A shorter version of the interview appeared in *Films of the Golden Age*, Winter 2009. *Glenn Ford: A Life* is Peter Ford's biography of his father, published in 2011 by the University of Wisconsin Press. Peter has two websites: www.peterford.com and www.glennfordbio.com.

7

Samantha Hale
on Alan Hale, Jr.

When Samantha Hale sits down to watch an old film on Turner Classic Movies, or a '60s sitcom on a retro TV channel, it's sometimes like watching old family home movies. Sam's great grandfather, Alan Hale, was a prolific supporting actor who appeared in some 250 films during the first half of the 20th century. His last role was in 1950, the same year he died. But the Hale acting genes didn't just fade away. That same year, Hale's son, Alan Hale, Jr., appeared in his first television role, having already co-starred in about 30 films throughout the '40s. Alan Junior gladly accepted the acting baton and quickly took to the trade "like father, like son." The junior Hale went on to appear in over 200 film and TV roles, prior to his death in 1990. Despite this large body of work, Alan Hale, Jr., will forever be recognized by TV fans the world over for his role as the long-suffering but affable Skipper in the '60s comedy Gilligan's Island *(1964–1967). After his father died, the younger Hale dropped the generational suffix; however, it will be used here to avoid confusing the two. Although Alan Hale, Jr.'s son never took to acting, his granddaughter, Samantha, followed her grandfather and great-grandfather with a career in entertainment. Oddly enough, when I caught up with Sam, she was busy house sitting for none other than Dawn Wells, a.k.a. Mary Ann from* Gilligan's Island!

You were quite young when your grandfather passed away. What do you remember about him?

I was his first grandchild and was seven years old when he died. My most vivid memory is going over to his home in West Hollywood from my house in Woodland Hills, about 25 minutes away. He lived in a cute little house which had a warm, welcoming feeling. There was green Astroturf—fake grass—in the backyard, and I would sit on his lap the whole time on the patio outside. He was a big guy, and it was really just like sitting in a large, comfortable chair. So we would all sit around, tell stories, and have a big lunch. He had two little French poodles and loved those dogs so much. I actually have a home movie of him putting one of the dogs, Dolly, on his lap and pretending to sneeze. Then the dog would start sneezing, too. It was really cute. He also had a television room filled with *Gilligan's Island* memorabilia, and we would sit there and talk with the family. Unfortunately, we don't have any of that stuff anymore. My step-grandmother, Naomi Hale, gave it away to charity without telling us. So I wasn't too happy about that — it would have been nice to keep some of those memories. Naomi was my grandfather's second wife. His first wife was Bettina Hale, and she was so gorgeous. She was kind of quiet and

Alan Hale, Jr., and baby Samantha, 1985. (Photograph courtesy of Samantha Hale.)

very smart, read a lot, and took a lot of walks to admire nature. Unfortunately, she suffered from dementia in her final years and passed away in 2006. I also remember my grandfather coming over to our house for birthday parties, and he would hang out in the back and watch all the kids play. He was just a happy and sweet person all the time. I recall him giving me a beautiful porcelain doll of Amy, from *Little Women*, for my fifth or sixth birthday, I think. I still have it somewhere in a cupboard. I used to play with it all the time and my dad would often remind me that it was a gift from my grandfather.

Your father didn't follow the Hale family acting tradition. What happened?

No, my dad, Brian Alan Hale, was not an actor. When he was younger, he thought about pursuing it and he told me he did some work as an extra a couple of times to see what it was like. But he just didn't have the burning desire to act. I think he was also afraid that he wouldn't be as good as his dad. He worked in sales, and his last job involved selling ATM machines. He passed away in 2005.

Was your grandfather disappointed that your father didn't go into acting?

My father never told me that his father was disappointed about that. And actually, I don't think he would have been. A lot of actors tell their kids not to go into acting because they know how hard it is. I'm sure he was proud of the fact that my dad went out and did his own thing.

Alan Hale, your great-grandfather, and Alan Hale, Jr., your grandfather, looked and sounded so much alike. Did your father also resemble them?

It's amazing how my great-grandfather and grandfather looked so much alike. Yes, my dad looked and sounded like them too. This was especially true as he got older and started to get a bit heavier and as his hair turned whiter. They all had the same build and were just bear-huggable, lovable guys. When I was in fourth or fifth grade and my dad would take me to school, people would ask, "Is that the Skipper dropping you off?"

Do you remember meeting any stars during your childhood?

I met a lot of people, but was really too young to know who they were. I do remember a pool party at the house when I was three or four, and running around the pool right into Bea Arthur! She was so tall and had such a deep voice that I started screaming. I was so afraid of her, and ran away.

It must be awesome to turn on the TV sometimes and see your grandfather or great-grandfather staring back at you!

I just feel incredibly lucky that I can see them. Some kids don't get to meet or see their grandparents, or even have memories of them, let alone their great-grandparents. But I can YouTube my grandfather, and see clips of him from films and TV shows — how many kids can do that? I can also see interviews he did. He and the cast of *Gilligan's Island* were on a celebrity episode of *Family Feud* in the 1980s, and that's on YouTube, too. I used to watch the reruns of *Gilligan's Island* on FOX after school, and I'm pretty sure I've seen every episode. However, now it's sometimes sad for me to watch *Gilligan's Island* because my grandfather sounds just like my dad and that makes me miss my father. I mean, it's sad but also beautiful at the same time. I remember one night when I came home from an acting class and was not feeling so great about having a career in the entertainment business. I mean, it's very different from the "old days" and I actually feel more connected to old Hollywood due to my family connections. So I wasn't sure if I wanted to continue to work in the business. Anyway, I turned on the television and *The Andy Griffith Show* came on, and it was the episode called "The Farmer Takes a Wife." My grandfather was playing the role of a farmer from the Midwest who came to town

Naomi and Alan Hale, Jr., with son Brian Alan Hale, circa 1985. (Photograph courtesy of Samantha Hale.)

to find a wife. He was just so cute on it and that made me feel so much better. But that sort of thing happens all the time. I might be watching other shows, like reruns of *Rosanne* or *Married with Children*, and there's tons of *Gilligan's Island* references with Gilligan and Skipper jokes, which I think is really cool.

As you grew up, did you realize what a popular actor your grandfather was?

I think I realized he was an actor when I was in elementary school and was aware of the fact that he was so well known then. Now, I really appreciate it. I mean, how many people can say that they have a DVD box set of their grandfather running around on a deserted island in a grass skirt?

There were quite a few dangerous-looking stunts on *Gilligan's Island*. Did your grandfather ever get injured?

One day on the set, he fell out of a tree and broke his arm. But he carried on as if everything was fine and didn't tell anyone until they were done filming. He didn't want to bother people. He had to go the hospital after they finished filming. That's the sort of person he was. People ask me what's the dirt or scandal on my granddad and I tell them there is none!

Aside from Dawn Wells, how many of the seven "castaways" did you know?

Actually, Dawn is the only one from *Gilligan's Island* that I have met. I never even met Bob Denver. He lived out in West Virginia, so our paths never crossed. But I did become friends with his wife on Facebook.

How did you first meet Dawn and end up house sitting for her?

I met her through Allen Funt's son, Bill, who really enjoys bringing people together. He connected me with Dawn, as well as Bob Denver's wife, Russell Johnson's daughter, and Tina Louise's daughter. So I left Dawn a phone message and we played phone tag for a while because she travels so much. But we got to know each other and got along really well, and we still get together for Christmas, or Easter parties, or barbeques. So when she asked me to house sit for her, I said, "Sure!"

What do you know about your great-grandfather?

My great-grandpa's name was Rufus MacKahan, before he changed it to Hale. In fact, I didn't even know that my last name was a stage name until I did a family tree report in eighth grade. My great-grandfather met his wife, Getchen Hartman, on a set of a film around 1914, and he was playing the villain. I got most of the information about him from my dad. He would tell me stories about people who came over to their house when he was growing up. One story involved Béla Lugosi who visited for a party. He arrived before everyone else, and sat down in one of the chairs. My grandma then walked in, not knowing that he was there. Just to mess with her and have some fun, he said to her suddenly, "Good evening!" in his best Dracula voice. That just freaked her out! Now, when I watch the old movies my great-grandfather was in, I think it's just not fair — all those great people he got to work with! People like Bette Davis, Barbara Stanwyck, Errol Flynn; he worked with everybody, including many times with Flynn.

You must meet people who want to know more when they find out your family background?

I've noticed that when I mention "Alan Hale" to young people, they usually have no idea who he was. But if I say "The Skipper," then they know. People who are in their forties or fifties will usually recognize his name and often know all about his father, too. Some even know more about their work than I do. They can tell me what movies or TV shows they were in, and some I've never heard of.

Many '60s actors were typecast and came to hate the roles they were known for. Did your grandfather like that recognition?

He really did enjoy being known as the Skipper, and would wear one of the hats all the time. Later in life he opened a restaurant called the Lobster Barrel. I've met many people who visited his restaurant, and they tell me he would show up wearing his Skipper's hat. Unfortunately, I was too young and never got to go to the restaurant. But I've been told he would warmly greet visitors and talk to everyone who came to the restaurant. I remember my dad telling me it got to the point where he couldn't run the place because so many people would want to talk with him, and he would stop and sit down with them.

Actors rarely get royalties from videos and DVDs of TV shows they did in the '60s. Did your grandfather receive anything?

No. I believe the only one who did get residuals was Dawn Wells, because she was married to an agent who knew about those things and got them for her. But everyone else was out of luck. I think Ted Turner bought all the rights to *Gilligan's Island*, so I'm sure he made some money from it. I don't even know if Sherwood Schwartz, the show's producer and writer, made anything from the show's DVDs. He was very sweet, by the way. On his desk, Sherwood kept one of the hats my grandpa wore, which he had bronzed as a statue.

Your grandfather's sister, Karen Hale Wookey, also worked in the film business. What do you remember about your great aunt?

She lived in an old Spanish-style mansion behind Grauman's Chinese Theater until 1998, when she passed. It was originally my great-grandfather's house, and actually was the main family house where everyone came together and connected as a family. They held a lot of glamorous Hollywood parties there. Everyone would dress up and people like the Barrymores would come over. Karen worked as a script supervisor on many films such as *All the President's Men* [1976] and *Patriot Games* [1992]. Script supervisors work very closely with the director and their main concern is continuity, and making sure that all the shots are going to match. So if someone was drinking coffee in his left hand in the first shot and then it's in his right hand in the next shot, the script supervisor would point that out so the actor can switch hands and the editing can flow. She was very close with Warren Beatty for years and worked on most of his pictures. She took me to a set once where I met him, and I have bumped into him a few times since. He's super nice. Karen also took me to the set of *Fight Club* [1999] when I was 12, where I met Brad Pitt, who was very sweet. He was so personable and friendly, and shook my hand for something like 30 seconds.

So after your grandfather died, was Karen an influence on your career as you grew up?

When I decided I wanted to act, I mentioned it to Karen and she said that was wonderful, but told me I had to go to college first. "We'll talk after you get your degree!" she told me. But she did start taking me to film festivals and introduced me to people in the entertainment world. I do remember one funny incident involving her. I was staying with her one summer around 1996, and we walked down to the Chinese Theater because they were doing a Technicolor film festival. They were showing some old films that had been restored, and one of them was the original *Adventures of Robin Hood* [1938] with Errol Flynn and Alan Hale, who was Karen's dad, of course. It was a full crowd, and during the movie there was a group of people sitting right next to us who were cheering and yelling and hooting and hollering throughout, and having a great time. After the film was over, Karen went up to one of the ladies and said, "Excuse me, you guys were so into the film, did you have family who worked on it?" And the woman said, "Oh yeah, Errol Flynn was my dad!" And Karen said, "Really? Alan Hale was my dad!" It really was Flynn's daughter, but I'm not sure which one.

Did having the Hale name help your career?

Things are just so different today. My grandfather started acting when he was very young. Back then they had apprenticeships where a young person could come on the set and shadow someone to learn. I'm sure that's how he learned when my great-grandfather took him to work. But they don't do that anymore which is a shame, because it's a great idea to see how the business works. Regarding my career, a lot of people assumed that I had it easy because of who my grandfather was, but it hasn't made a difference at all. I've had friends of the family say they were going to help me, but never did. I think it has been different for me since I'm a generation separated from him. And, of course, a lot of people who worked with my grandfather have retired or passed away, and were just not around anymore. So that made me a bit disconnected from that earlier period. Again, it's just so different from my great-grandfather and grandfather's era when talent was so important. You don't necessarily need talent to be an actor now. You just need to know somebody, or look good, or just do a reality television show. None of that existed in my grandfather's time. Don't get me wrong—there are a lot of actors around these days who are incredibly talented. But there are a lot who aren't and they're "famous" for no good reason at all.

Did you go to your grandfather's funeral?

No, my dad didn't want to take me because I was too little. They held the service on a boat and scattered his ashes at sea, which is what I did for my dad. Dad was actually quite upset because there were helicopters from the tabloids flying overhead, taking pictures. Dawn was the only one from *Gilligan's Island* who was able to make it.

Do you feel the need to carry on the Hale acting legacy?

I always knew that I wanted to be an artist from an early age, even before I realized my grandfather was a TV star. But given my family background, I like to say I'm genetically diseased to be an actor — once you get bitten by the acting bug, it's hard to shake off. Artists, whether it be film, music or painting, just aren't meant to have a nine to five cubicle job and can't thrive in that environment. But other people do like that routine and stability. When I was a kid, I used to organize talent shows in my neighborhood. For example, I wrote a Christmas play and all the kids would come over. In fact, I remember my grandpa coming to that, although I don't recall what he thought about it. After college, things were going well, but that's when my dad passed away, so I got out of it for a while. My way of dealing with it was going to concerts. Then I decided to do a documentary about other people's experience with music and how they used it as therapy. I never thought I would become a filmmaker, and always intended to be on the other side of the camera. So I took some money I earned from a Visa commercial and made *Map the Music*, which I worked on for four years; it was released in 2010. I've also been doing some stand-up comedy here in L.A. So I don't think about the "Hale legacy," because that would be a lot to worry about. I like to live day to day, and enjoy all the different things I'm doing. As they say, it's not the destination but the journey that makes life enjoyable.

Samantha Hale on Alan Hale, Jr. Telephone interview on 9/23/10. Samantha Hale's website is www.mapthemusic.com.

8

Sara Ballantine on Carl Ballantine

> *He never won an Oscar, an Emmy, or a Tony, but Carl Ballantine (1917–2009) was surely one of the most naturally funny comedic actors on stage or screen. Often portraying the wisecracking used-car salesman-like huckster, Ballantine could have sold cheap cigars to Castro! In addition to his movie and television career, including four seasons as the gangly Lester Gruber in the '60s hit* McHale's Navy, *Ballantine traveled the country for much of his life performing his legendary comedy magic act billing himself as "The Amazing Ballantine." Sara Ballantine says her dad really was amazing, both on-screen and off.*

How did your dad begin doing a comedy magic act?

My father first became interested in magic when he was a little boy. A barber used to come to the house to cut his hair and, like all little boys, he was full of energy and very wiggly. So to keep him still in the chair, the barber started doing coin tricks. My dad loved it. It fascinated him, and he started doing the tricks and trying to amaze his barber. That was what hooked him. When his father died, he was only 12, so he became the breadwinner for the family — performing magic and making a living. In Chicago, he had to support his mother and sister, who also worked odd jobs. By the time he was old enough to work in clubs, his act had evolved into comedy when one night things didn't go right and the tricks didn't work. He improvised some comedy lines and the audience loved it. The owner of the nightclub suggested he should think about adding comedy to his act, so that's what it evolved into — a magic act where the tricks didn't work well. He wrote most of the material himself, although at times he had a few writers. Even though he was doing magic, he always thought of himself as an actor. He really believed you have to fully commit to whatever you're doing, whether it's drama or comedy, because it's the same energy that goes through you.

Sara and Carl Ballantine circa 1961 in Manhattan. (Photograph courtesy of Sara Ballantine.)

In 2007, comedian Steve Martin presented your dad with a Lifetime Achievement Award from the Magic Castle in Hollywood. Was your dad the first to combine comedy and magic?

He was the original comedy magic act! Many other comedy magicians owe their careers to my father paving the way- Mac King, Amazing Jonathan, The Great Thomsoni, to name just a few. Steve Martin also followed him and used comedy in his early magic acts. Steve was around 16 and working at Disneyland when he and my father became friends. Steve started doing magic and my dad thought he was great. I always wished they could have done a film together.

Your dad had mostly guest-starring roles in about 20 films, and didn't do his first movie until he was 47. Did he try to get into film when he was younger?

When he first came out to California from New York in the 1940s, he did try for the movies and even had a meeting with Louis B. Mayer. Mayer had seen his magic comedy act and, as was usually the case, the stage was a mess after the act with torn up newspapers and props tossed all over the floor.

At the end of the meeting, Mayer told my father that if he ever needed a guy to throw things all over a stage, he would call him. My father was so hurt by that. It was another 15 years until he got into television, which led to the movies. In those days, you could be a character actor and make a living if you had talent — you didn't have to have the looks of a model to get work.

Was he a hard worker?

At the height of his magic career, he could do three or four shows a day. In Vegas and Tahoe, he could work six nights a week. When he booked club dates, he could adjust the time of his act, so he could do a fast 10-, 20- or even a 40-minute set. He never felt his act should go on too much longer than that.

He appeared on a lot of variety shows throughout the '50s and '60s, including several times on *The Ed Sullivan Show*. Sullivan was renowned for his lack of humor; did he enjoy your father's routine?

Ed Sullivan only had my dad on the show because he knew the audiences loved him. Sullivan didn't get the act at all. My father was kind of baffled by that and wondered how Sullivan could host such a big show and be smart enough to know what the people wanted, but didn't have any sense of humor himself. But that was Sullivan's talent.

Did your dad enjoy working with Elvis in *Speedway* (1968)?

That was a great experience for him — how incredible that he got to work so closely with Elvis. Elvis was known for giving away cars and tried to give my dad a Cadillac, but my mother (who had a Mercedes at the time, said) "That's sweet of him, but honey, we don't need a Cadillac — you tell him to keep it; we like our Mercedes." I wish we had taken the car because it probably would have been mine! Dad had a great time on the film and always said Elvis was a doll. One night, Elvis took them all to the movies and bought out an entire movie theater for the cast and crew, and both my mom and dad went. In 2010, I went to the new *Cirque du Soleil* called "Viva Elvis" in Las Vegas. They used a clip from *Speedway* in the show and my dad was in it, so I looked up to heaven and said to myself, "Dad, you're back on the Strip!"

His big break came as one of Ernest Borgnine's eight crewmen in *McHale's Navy*, from 1962 to 1966. How important was that for his career?

It changed his life. As a stage actor, prior to *McHale's*, he went from job to job, so having a weekly series meant regular work. They made around 36 episodes each season, then had a break. So he was glad to know he had work waiting for him after the time off. He loved his part and the scripts were fun.

He become good friends with Ernest Borgnine, who took us to every good Italian restaurant in town. He was also great friends with Yoshio Yoda, who played the Japanese prisoner of war. He was a young heartthrob in Japan before he came over here and got the role. And he loved Joe Flynn, who I think was one of the funniest men who ever lived. There was one episode called "A Purple Heart for Gruber," the second episode of the show, that was all about my dad. He was just fantastic in that one and the producers tried unsuccessfully to get him an Emmy nomination for that episode. So it was a happy time for my whole family. I visited the set many times and, on one occasion, Dad invited my whole Girl Scout troop to visit and they got to meet everybody. While the show was in production, I remember we would have big parties at our house with hundreds of people. There were so many, we would make fruit salad in the bathtub!

Aside from acting, what were his other interests?

Horse racing was another passion, and both my sister and I grew up around race tracks. In fact, he named us both after race tracks. He named me Saratoga after the race course in New York. My dad's grandmother was named Sara, so that worked out and my mother liked the idea, too. My sister was called Molly Caliente, named after a course in Tijuana he visited often when we first came to California. It burned down in 1971, but was rebuilt.

You've also worked in the entertainment business. Were your parents supportive?

They were very encouraging. My dad told me to take acting classes and he paid for all my lessons- tap, ballet, jazz, acting, since I was nine — he supported me completely. By 18, I was working in TV commercials, and he was so proud of the fact that I could pay for my own college tuition when I went to LAMDA, the London Academy of Music and Dramatic Art, in England. The best way he showed support was by coming to all my performances, and offering notes and encouragement. I did a waiver play once at the Matrix Theatre in Hollywood, about Fatty Arbuckle and I played Mabel Normand. As an avant-garde theater piece, we ended Act One with the entire cast in an elaborate nude scene. My mom and dad were there opening night, and when the director asked my dad what he thought of the play, he replied, "I liked Act Two!" When I started doing a political sketch comedy act, "The White House Chicks," my parents schlepped out to Santa Monica for every performance; same when I sang with The Little Big Band. You can't ask for any more support than that!

Sara and Carl Ballantine on Sara's birthday in 2007 at the Magic Castle. In this shot, Carl Ballantine was 90 years old. (Photograph courtesy of Sara Ballantine.)

And you did some voice work for a famous cartoon series in the '90s?

I was the voice of Mary Jane in the Spider-Man cartoons, and even got my dad a role in one of the episodes. He did the voice of Lenny, the janitor. Usually it's the parent who gets the jobs for their children, but I got my dad a job! That show was so much fun, and Stan Lee would come in for the tapings. We had a tremendous cast with people like Ed Asner, Malcolm McDowell, Eddie Albert, Brian Keith, Martin Landau, and Mark Hamill.

You produced an interesting documentary in 2010 called *Troupers*, featuring some great veteran actors. How did that come about?

We wanted to show the world all the viable talent who were still plugging away at their craft, doing what they love, and still dreaming big into their eighties and nineties. My dad was the second artist we interviewed. He is tremendous in the film, but honestly, our inspiration came from many places: Largely from the feeling that Hollywood is such a youth-oriented town. I had a partner, Dea Lawrence, and we made it on a shoestring budget, directing and producing it. We interviewed 12 fabulous actors. For instance, Betty Garrett, Marvin Kaplan, Harold Gould, and Ivy Bethune were all in a local theater group I'm in, so I knew them. Others, such as Kaye Ballard, Jane Kean, and Pat Carroll had been good friends with my mother.

Your mother, Ceil Cabot, was also an actress. How did your parents juggle work and raising a family?

My mother was ten years younger than my dad, and was his second wife. They met in Cleveland after her nightclub act and he told her, "You're the first broad that made me laugh in five years!" So they started going out together. They moved to New York, where I grew up. My mother performed in nightclubs as a cabaret singer and comedienne, sort of a cross between Carol Burnett and Imogene Coca. She didn't get home until four A.M. and would sleep until noon, so my dad did all the cooking, took me to school and to ballet lessons. So he was a very good father. When I had birthday parties, he would do magic for all the kids. It wasn't the comedy magic because kids don't get the humor in magic tricks that don't work. I remember he was once on *The Bill Cosby Show* and did his act for the Cosby kids. Bill Cosby was laughing hysterically, but the kids were not impressed. They wanted to see magic that worked!

It seems like he had a naturally funny personality. Was he fun offscreen?

He would always find a fun way to do the most mundane things. For instance, he would make my breakfast with crazy hats on his head, and sing "Jada" at the top of his lungs. His stage personality wasn't that far apart from how he was in real life. He was funny, but he wasn't always "on." Towards the end of his life he would tell me, "I like being with you because I can just be myself." When he was in public he did turn it on for people because that's what they expected. He was very appreciative of people when they recognized him and didn't have a bad word to say about anybody. One night, my dad and I were leaving one of our favorite restaurants, Musso Franks, and we were approached by a stranger. I was always shielding my dad from fans, because you never really know if they are good people or not. Anyway, this man very respectfully introduced himself to us, and said what a great fan he had been of my dad's work. He insisted we take the portfolio under his arm, which turned out to be a musical he had written about Al Jolson. He became a great friend to my dad till his last days. Dad was a very outgoing person and would meet people on the street or in the supermarket and they would become friends. I remember a guy who turned up in our yard one time with a dog, which he said he couldn't afford to feed. So my dad gave him a bag of dog food. He was always very kind to people.

Did he work up until the end?

He continued to do the magic two years before he died. On the last day of his life, I had spent the day with him. I went to an audition at the beach and he came with me and I even got him to put his toe in the ocean. We had a really nice conversation and he said to me, "You know I love you, sweetheart." I told him that, of course, I did and he said, "So we're right with that?" and I said of course. That night my boyfriend and I had dinner with my father at his home on Beachwood Canyon, in the Hollywood Hills. At ten P.M., my boyfriend went home and I told Dad I was tired and was going to sleep in the back bedroom and would see him in the morning. So I went to bed, but in the middle of the night heard a noise. When I went to his room, he was up and he said, "I've got to get out of here." I asked him where he wanted to go and he said, "I've got to go home." I told him he was home. But he said he wanted his robe and shoes so he could leave. Well, he seemed okay after a while, and it was three o'clock, so I went back to bed. Next morning I went to his room but he wasn't there, so I searched around the house. At some point, he must have got out of bed, and walked to the other side of the house. I found him sitting by the desk, next to a window, with his robe and shoes on and a smile on his face. He had even brushed his hair. All I can say is that he went home.

Sara Ballantine on Carl Ballantine. Telephone interview on 12/10/10.

9

Rory Flynn on Errol Flynn

Best known for his exciting roles in films such as Captain Blood *(1935),* The Adventures of Robin Hood *(1938), and* The Sea Hawk *(1940), or as the dashing hero in war adventures and westerns, Errol Flynn (1909– 1959) appeared in some 50 movies— including nine with Olivia de Hav- illand— during his 26-year career in Hollywood. He was born in Tasmania, the southern island state of Australia. Much of 2009, Flynn's centenary, was set aside in the city of Hobart (Flynn's hometown) to celebrate Tasma- nia's most famous Hollywood son. Special guests at the celebrations were Flynn's daughter Rory and grandson Sean. Rory Flynn was just 12 when her father died; she inherited just a handful of items from him, as most of his estate went to his third wife. When she visited Tasmania, Rory gave much of her Flynn memorabilia to the Tasmanian museum for display, including love letters from her dad to her mom. Flynn married three times: first, to French actress Lili Damita (one son, Sean, a photo- journalist who went missing during the Vietnam war and was never found); second, to Nora Eddington (two daughters, Deirdre and Rory, who had one son, also named Sean); third, to actress Patrice Wymore (separated from Flynn but never divorced, she lived on Flynn's old plantation in Jamaica after his death; one daughter, Arnella, who died in 1998, had one son, Luke). Rory recalls her trip to Tasmania and memories of her larger-than- life dad.*

There was a lot of interest in Errol Flynn in 2009. How did you get involved in the Flynn centenary festivities in Tasmania?

There's a big fan club down there, the Errol Flynn Society of Tasmania. They started organizing the events a couple of years before the centenary and asked me to come down. I went to Warner Bros. and got film clips and stills for the celebration. It was great that Tasmania — and Australia — honored their native son in 2009, because Hollywood didn't. They're much more involved in their current stars, whereas Europe and other parts of the world are very considerate towards the stars of the Golden Era.

What did it mean to you to visit Tasmania?

Errol Flynn and daughter Rory in 1950. (Photograph courtesy of Rory Flynn.)

Well, I actually felt like I'd brought my dad home. That's where his roots are and they love him. I think the people there understand that my father was an extraordinary man. I have also learned more about my roots. My grandfather, Professor Theodore Thomson Flynn, was a zoologist and curator of the museum in Tasmania. My grandmother was a direct descendant of midshipman Edward Young of the HMS *Bounty*, so I feel like I came home, too.

What are some of your earliest memories of your father?

When I was around five, I used to lie on a bearskin rug in his den and I would fall asleep to the sound of his writing—the scratching of his pen. He was always writing. He was writing his autobiography from a very early age, and other books, documentaries and newspaper articles. I grew up with him until I was about seven. Then, after my parents separated, I would see him several times a year. Those visits became huge. He was really big about spending quality time with us when he could. He gave us parties and took us out, but didn't get to do it often, in between work and this and that. The way I look at it is that my dad was able to be a parent—a real family man—for about eight years of his life, then he went back to being who he was. But luckily, I was there for it, and so were my brothers and sisters.

In his twenties, Flynn sailed up the east coast of Australia to New Guinea,

where he had all sorts of real-life adventures, as recounted in his book, *Beam Ends.* Did that period of his life influence his acting? Did he ever tell you about his adventures?

Absolutely, this early period formed who he was. By the time he got to Hollywood, he was that "Tasmanian Devil," and he brought that to his films. But I was way too young for him to be talking to me about those adventures. Of course, he told my mother everything and she helped him type up the pages of his autobiography. So his stories were passed on to me, through my mother. But when you're a 12-year-old girl, you're more interested in the doll he sent from Spain, rather than those stories.

What do you think made your dad stand out as an actor?

My father invented the modern action hero that we see on the screen today. I think he bridged the gap between actors playing the tough American cowboy type who were simple and direct, and the European actors with sophisticated dialogue, like Leslie Howard. My dad bridged those two archetypes — he was able to be that action hero, and still hold an intelligent conversation on-screen. He came from the Outback to the center of Western culture and brought with him an independence that everyone has envied for years. No one had really done that before. I think he was also very unconventional, to the point that society at large embraced him.

Women loved him, but men thought he was pretty cool, too. Why?

I think one of the things that intrigued men was that he did what he damn well pleased! He was able to do that because he was a fully formed, independent, Aussie-spirited man before he started acting. He brought an independence and a life of adventures to Hollywood. Most actors come to Hollywood "naked" — they just don't have those experiences. Dad always did what he wanted, when he wanted. And when he didn't like something, he took off on his boat. There wasn't a man alive who didn't envy that! My father's real life was just as interesting, if not more, than his films.

His boat, the *Zaca*, had a long history, including being requisitioned by the U.S. Navy during World War II. After he died, your dad's lawyer got the *Zaca*, and it was later stripped down and left in a bad state sitting at a dock for years. What happened to it?

It is now restored and a tourist attraction in the South of France. My dad did a documentary called *The Cruise of the Zaca* [1952], and my grandfather and mother are in it.

Shortly before she died, your mother gave you the letters your father had

written to her — the ones you gave to the museum. What did you learn about your father from reading those letters for the first time?

I realized what a romantic man he was. He definitely romanced my mother through words in his letters, and kept her intrigued with his adventures. For me to see my parents in any situation where they were in love, I grasp at it, because I never really got to see them like that. For example, when I watch *The Cruise of the Zaca* documentary with my mother in it, and they're holding hands and looking into each other's eyes and he carries her over a waterfall, I can see they were in love and I start crying. So the love letters go with those images I see on the screen.

Did you know how sick he was towards the end of his life?

No, my mom didn't tell us about it. We know now that, shortly before he died, he told my mother that he was only given a year to live, but he only made it for three more months. His liver was shot, he had tuberculosis, malaria, terrible back problems — and there he was, still swashbuckling all over the place to the end.

It's been said that the Mulholland Drive house your dad lived in was later occupied by his ghost. What do you think?

Haunted? I don't think so; besides, it doesn't exist anymore. I lived for over 20 years just down the road from the Mulholland house. I would jog past my family home every few days and I watched in horror as they tore it down, for it should have been preserved. My father designed and built it and it was a part of Hollywood history.

So if your father had lived, where do you think his career might have taken him?

So many doors open at 50. After all the experience in life one has had by then, it becomes the backbone of any writer. My father was a writer, a good writer, and I could see him doing novels. I can see him continue his career just like Robert Mitchum did. He could have produced his own films and he could have done so many things. If only he could have turned that last corner.

Your dad had a sister, Rosemary. Were they close?

She and Errol were ten years apart in age. My grandparents separated for a few years as my grandmother did not like Tasmania — too small and isolated — and she took Rosemary to Paris. Therefore, they did not grow up together, and throughout my dad's life he only saw Rosemary occasionally. She passed away in 1999, with no children.

Your father's only other living child is Deidre Flynn. What does she do?

Deirdre, my sister, became a stunt woman. She worked for years with Michael Douglas on his TV show and early films. She is retired now.

Did you ever want to act?

Not really. I'm six feet tall and started out modeling in New York, London, and Paris until I was 27 years old. I took some acting classes with Peggy Furey. In my class was Sean Penn, who actually demonstrated every day what it took to be an actor, but I did not have the discipline it takes. I picked up the camera when I was modeling, so I went back to school to learn basics and hustled my way into becoming a reasonably good stills photographer on films. I like to be behind the camera.

Has there been a disadvantage being related to someone so famous?

There has never been a down side to being Errol Flynn's daughter. It is my inheritance. In the film world I am sort of old Hollywood royalty!

The grandsons, Sean and Luke, followed their famous grandfather into the entertainment world. What have been their interests?

My son, Sean, has been working in films from the age of seven. He starred in *Zoey 101*, a Nickelodeon series, for four seasons. At 17, he decided he wanted to be a singer/songwriter, but later gave up this idea. He felt there was way more talent out there than he could produce in music. So he went back to what he does best — acting — and is a chip off the old block! He really has the talent, and took time to go to school. Luke is a model in New York and Miami, and so is his girlfriend, Maggie. His father is a great fashion photographer so Luke also started working very young. He lives a charmed life and is writing scripts. The two boys are like brothers and spend as much time together as possible.

Your grandfather was an academic and college professor. Was he proud of his son's career in show business?

I don't know; I think he was, somewhat. I didn't get to see my grandparents often. I saw them when I was very young and we spent time together in Jamaica and on my father's boat. My grandfather was an intellectual and my father had something of that in him, as well as the adventurer. Errol did have a larger problem with his mother, but had a huge regard and respect for his father. He took care of them as best he could in his last years. But my dad still did what he wanted, and that was the "Flynn" in him.

During his career, did he really become tired of the swashbuckler films and want to tackle more serious roles?

Yes, he wanted to get out of type and was looking for some really meaty roles. I have letters from my father after he did *Captain Blood* where he says he really wanted to go back on stage because he thought of himself as a serious actor. I think he was basically "abused" as an actor by keeping him typecast as a swashbuckler. But on the other hand, he did do some amazing films such

as *Too Much, Too Soon* [1958], *Objective Burma!* [1945], and *That Forsyte Woman* [1949], in which he was outstanding. And he should have won an Academy Award for *The Sun Also Rises* [1957].

It was an excellent performance. Why do you think he didn't get the Oscar for that?

I don't think Hollywood took him seriously as an actor. He did not follow the rules, and was the black sheep of actors. He also was a writer and was interested in world politics. He went to Cuba to interview Castro, the freedom fighter, for the Hearst newspapers in 1957. He believed in freedom, and that human and animal rights were things to stand up for. His life was way more interesting than just making movies. He did what he wanted, with no fear of authority or bosses — Fearless Flynn!

Errol and Rory Flynn, mid–1950s. (Photograph courtesy of Rory Flynn.)

Perhaps Hollywood will see fit to officially honor Errol Flynn somehow, some day?

Well, they don't give posthumous Oscars, except for films made the year before the person died, like Heath Ledger in 2008. But I think they will honor him one day when they realize how great he really was.

Rory Flynn on Errol Flynn. Telephone interview on 6/3/09. A shorter version of the interview appeared on the Cinema Retro website, November 2009. Rory Flynn is author of *The Baron of Mulholland: A Daughter Remembers Errol Flynn*, which is available through her Errol Flynn website: www.inlikeflynn.com.

10

Bruce Morgan
on Yvonne De Carlo

Her very name conjures up the image of an exotic woman of mystery. No wonder Yvonne De Carlo (1922–2007) was the perfect choice for the sultry Anna Marie, in Salome Where She Danced, *her first lead role, in 1945. De Carlo continued to delight audiences throughout her 40-year career, no matter whether she shared the screen with Burt Lancaster, John Wayne, Charlton Heston, Clark Gable, Alec Guinness, Peter Ustinov, or Rock Hudson. Though she spent most of her career in motion pictures, such as De Mille's* The Ten Commandments, *like so many others who had success in a popular '60s TV sitcom she will forever be identified with one character—the pallid, yet alluring, Lily Munster on* The Munsters *(1964–1966). Yet even behind the layers of Munster makeup, Bruce Morgan says his mother's star status still shone through.*

What's your mother's family background?

She was born in Vancouver, British Columbia, as Margaret Yvonne Middleton. A biography about her claimed that her agent made up the name "De Carlo" while driving on Sunset Boulevard. Not true. The name comes from her grandfather, Michael De Carlo, who worked in the home of the British field marshal, Lord Kitchener. Michael was a livery servant and his wife, Margaret Purvis, was secretary to Kitchener. Their daughter, Marie De Carlo, and her husband, William Middleton, were Yvonne's parents. The bulk of Yvonne's childhood was spent between three or four places in Canada, one of which was a wild place called Whitehorse, where the flies take a bite out of you and sting. There were huge ice floes, giant barges moving down rivers, and large areas of timber harvested out of forests. It was a rough area to be raised around, but the region was populated with decent, reverent people. Unfortunately, her father was not one of them. He abandoned the family

While visiting Europe in 1963, Yvonne De Carlo and children Michael (left) and Bruce visit the set of *The Fall of the Roman Empire* in La Matas, Spain. (Photograph courtesy of Bruce Morgan.)

when Yvonne was three, and I remember Marie, my grandmother, referring to him in unflattering terms, calling him a bigamist. Yvonne only remembered crawling towards his feet and she never saw him again after he left. Many years later, she did receive a postcard from him that had scribbled on it, "Send me my daughter" after he found out she had money and fame. So he was a piece of work.

What factors contributed to her interest in acting?

I would claim that three things got her interested in acting. First, one cannot deny that there was something inside Yvonne, in a passive-aggressive way, wanting to draw attention to herself. Second, there was an idea planted by her mother, who was herself a frustrated performer and dancer, transferring that ambition to her daughter. Marie and Yvonne had a love-hate relationship that went on for years. Marie had sent her daughter out into the world to be her, or at least what she wanted to be, but Yvonne wanted to get away from that and claim that her success was her own. Finally, there was something Yvonne told me about herself as a girl, when she and her mother took several trips to California. One time, when she was ten years old in 1932, she walked around the main library in downtown Los Angeles, where she felt that she would one day be famous. Whether real or imagined, she was imbued with a sense of destiny.

What were the years like before she found that fame?

Before stardom, she worked in various theaters and nightclubs in Canada. Then she met impresario Nils Thor Granlund, known as NTG, who hired her to dance at the Florentine Gardens in Hollywood. My mother tells how Marie would go around to the audience inside the Florentine Gardens and encourage them to applaud louder for her daughter. If done intelligently, I can admire that, but if it's done indiscreetly it can be disastrous. I can't say Marie was right or wrong doing that, but she just did it. Taking the advice of one of the Dorsey brothers, Yvonne later went over to Paramount, where she worked as a film extra for a number of years. Basically, the studio didn't quite know what to do with her. During this time, she kept a diary and wrote about all that was going on. She wrote about dating servicemen who, in those war years, were bringing her food and extra supplies in order to win her hand. Most guys back then wanted to keep a woman barefoot and pregnant, but she seemed imbued with a sort of skittishness that kept her single, thank God. Much later, I remember asking her what had been her feelings when she married and she said, "My greatest worry was that it would end my independence." She was partially right because my father was a traditional guy and thought he had to control her. The diary also mentions going to Republic Studios for her first lead role. She was supposed to play Tremartini in *The Story of Dr. Wassell* [1944] for DeMille. But there was a trade at the last minute and she played Princess Wah-Tah, in the *The Deerslayer* [1943] instead, and her role in *Dr. Wassell* was taken by Carol Thurston. DeMille had his eye on Yvonne and discovered her long before *The Ten Commandments* [1956].

Did she keep a diary all her life?

No, and that's an interesting point. The diaries stop with the day after she starts her first fitting for *Deerslayer* at Republic Studios. It's as though she would no longer have any more time for writing. The diary was what I call a "cringing companion" as she writes about whether or not she will get roles or make it to stardom in general. This is around 1942 to 1943. In '44 to '45, she's in production for *Salome*. Her diary indicates she was very goal oriented but at the same time she had an interest in men.

When did you first see her in *Salome*?

I was probably in my early twenties. I saw the film projected in the screening room at someone's home. Even though it was my mother, I was extremely impressed with her talent at such an early age — she was only around 22 when she made the film. She had total command of herself and that surprised me. I think the very first time I saw her on-screen was at a drive-in. My brother and I had our pajamas on, so were very young. I was only vaguely aware that it was her up on the screen in the movie *La spada e la croce* (*The Sword and the Cross*) in 1958 which was made in Italy.

She worked with some of the greats. What stories did she tell?

For *Criss Cross* [1949], she told me Burt Lancaster wanted her out of the movie. But what kept her in was a contract written by the producer, Mark Hellinger, who died before he could make the film. But she had it in writing that she was to play the part, so Burt couldn't get rid of her. Tony Curtis was also in *Criss Cross*, and I remember meeting him and telling him that my mother had died. He looked down with sadness and said, "My first speaking role was with your mom in *Criss Cross*." He was genuinely sad when he heard she had died. They had even gone out together for a while. She enjoyed working with John Wayne in *McLintock!* [1963], but said he could be mean on the set. "Where's that big Irish bitch?" she said he asked, referring to Maureen O'Hara. And Yvonne said he treated the little Chinese cook terribly. She liked Wayne, but didn't like that abrasive aspect about him. It was the same with DeMille — she loved him, but didn't like the way he treated some people. For *The Ten Commandments*, she went to Egypt for filming. At one point they no longer needed her, but she stayed, I think, to cement her relationship with DeMille. He was so taken with her as an actress. In fact, he told her that when she had a baby, he wanted to be the godfather to her first born. So Cecil B. DeMille was my godfather! Actually, there was no material legacy to me as his godson, but it did enable me to meet his associate producer, Henry Wilcoxon, who told me how DeMille did things. To this day, that lesson serves well in that I work in the tradition of DeMille — a writer/producer/director. Yvonne worked with Rock Hudson on several films. She loved him like a brother, and they would play jokes on the director. One time they got in a station wagon and pretended to leave the set just before a take. She was such a powerful star, she could get away with that sort of thing. She also worked with Peter Ustinov and admired him for his brilliance. He was famously known as a socialist and claimed he actually understood communism. One time she was asked what was the most dangerous symbol in the world and she drew a sickle and hammer. According to Yvonne, Ustinov took it very seriously and their friendship soon grew cold.

In the early '50s, she was loaned out to do a few films in the UK, such

as *Hotel Sahara* and *The Captain's Paradise.* **Was that beneficial to her career?**

She grew as an actress in Britain. Suddenly, she had "thinking roles" and was treated as a real actress. Alec Guinness once turned to her and said, "I'm so glad you know what you're doing." Although she was a star in America, she grew into a full-fledged actress in the company of directors like Ken Annakin, and producer George Brown who turned out great little British films with a lot of wit, such as *The Lavender Hill Mob* [1951].

Your father, Bob Morgan, was a stunt man. Can you talk about the serious accident that ended his career?

He was a war pilot and an athlete of great ability. He became the person they would call when they thought someone could die doing a stunt. During the filming of *How the West Was Won* [1962], he was hurt badly during the train scene. In one segment, the logs roll off the train car, and after the take my dad fell under the train while it was still moving. They pulled his mangled body out and he had to have his left leg amputated. There are stories about what happened, such as my father being drunk on the set, but that was an accusation by some people who chose to strike at him under the cover of anonymity. I tend to side with the opinion that the assistant director really did mess up. He exercised his authority to reposition the logs on the flat cars without getting confirmation that it was safe to do so. When an accident occurs during a stunt, it could very well be the result of the stunt man's mistake. But when it happens after the stunt is done? My father was waiting on the logs after the stunt for the assistant director's directions. How do you blame a stunt man for an accident that occurs then? People who witnessed the incident said there was tension between my father and the assistant director before the accident. I think the guy was protected by someone higher up in the studio because he wasn't qualified to do what he was doing. Bob was not diplomatic to people and was hard to get along with, so it colors the circumstances about the incident, but I don't think there was anything intentional done; it was just incompetence. I remember when Bob won a Golden Boot Award in 1995. A guy came up to me and said, "I was one of the few people who got along with your father!" My mother took some time off from work to look after him and after a number of months she got a call from John Wayne telling her, "Yvonne, it's time to go back to work" and that's where *McLintock!* came from. Bob and Wayne had been drinking buddies — in New York of all places — and he was one of the few people who did get along with my father. Bob was very right wing. So much so, he made Wayne look like a liberal! My parents divorced in 1974. Yvonne hung in there for the sake of the kids, but the two were not suited on many levels. My father had some fairly base instincts in terms of spending other people's money and making excuses for his failures, whereas my mother had her act together and knew what she wanted. He would show up to meetings with producers and carry on like he was God's gift to the cinema. That sometimes cost my mother the role.

You had a brother, Michael. What happened to him?

He wanted to be a rock star, but it didn't work out and his life was not a happy one. He didn't have any personal guidance and fell under a bad influence. He did have some ability with poetry and piano playing. Other than that, he did odd jobs and lived with his mother. She doted over him, but that enabled more problems than it solved. She acted as a mother trying to save the situation, but it was a very stressful time for her. He passed away in 1997 and could have been murdered because he was leaving a halfway house with information about people who were trading drugs.

How important was the role of Lily Munster for her?

Long before *The Munsters* ever came along, my mother loved spooking people and enjoyed spooky movies. She had a library of books along the lines of sci-fi, horror and mystery, and she loved *Dracula*. So I had to laugh when she got the role of Lily Munster because something worked out that was meant to happen. Yvonne wasn't the first choice for the role; that was Joan Marshall. She was good, but looked too much like Carolyn Jones of *The Addams Family*. So my mother got the part and was told to play the role as if she was the mother in a normal sitcom. One thing she added was a lot of hand movements which she had remembered from seeing ZaSu Pitts, who used her hands a lot. She also understood what it meant to be in a hit television series, which could be meteoric in terms of your fame. She said, "It made me hot again!" I can remember going to the studio with her when it was still dark in the morning and driving passed Scotty, the guard, at the Universal studio gate. I would watch Abe Haberman make her up for the three to five hours needed, with all the base makeup and highlights that were designed for black-and-white filming. The makeup was green and blue and designed for the panchromatic film that was used. Black-and-white film sees color as shades of grey, so green was not the same as blue. There was a high level of technical quality on *The Munsters* considering it was a TV show. The set was done right, and the number of mechanical effects per show was surprising. It was not an easy series to do.

They had some great props on the show. Whatever happened to the bat necklace Lily wore?

My mother ended up with it. I'm not sure how, except that she was friends with the property manager. She was going to leave it to me, but ended up selling it to a collector. I also remember she ended up with a beautiful promotional painting from a film, *The Gal Who Took the West* [1949], which I gave away recently. I asked her one time, "Doesn't that belong to Universal?" She said that they often made doubles of everything and that the artist gave it to her. The painting was never seen in the film; it was purely for promotion and was featured in the December 1945 issue of *Life* magazine. I also had an original script from *The Ten Commandments*, which had Yvonne's notes on it. I sold it in 2008 for $5,000 to a person who appreciated her work. I kept a PDF of the script. I'm not planning on keeping a physical museum of her stuff because the essence of her memory is not the physical items, which really don't mean a thing to me.

Yvonne De Carlo and son Bruce Morgan attending the AFI Lifetime Achievement Awards in the early 1980s. (Photograph courtesy of Bruce Morgan.)

Did she keep in contact with Fred Gwynne?

A few years after the show ended, she got a letter from him. He invited her to go out to his country house and watch trees being chopped down! She didn't go, but he was a wonderful, if eccentric, guy. He actually had a secret place in a small town where he would go to write and paint, and nobody knew about it. He came from a very wealthy family and didn't have to do *The Munsters* for a living. He also went to Harvard and was in the Hasty Pudding Society, so he was a major brain. I remember on the set he once caught me talking about someone within earshot. He came over to me and laid his giant hand over my two hands and said, "You don't ever want to be saying anything like that within listening distance of other people." I could tell his chief concern was empathy for people, and he really had a good soul. But I wasn't going to argue with someone that big!

You're in the entertainment business now, but what did you do before that?

I have been a director of photography on small films, but am now producing Project Lodestar Sagas, a five-hour mini-series staring Academy Award-winning actress Margaret O'Brien. It won a Golden Halo Award from the Southern California Motion Picture council in 2010. I'm also working on a separate feature film of the same title, shot simultaneously with the series, which will probably be released overseas first. I'm working on a biography about my mother to be published in serial form in mixed media, tentatively entitled "Sapphire in the Sand." Long before I worked in films, I was a public servant for 30 years and rescued some 500 lives from the ocean as a lifeguard.

How would you sum up your mother?

Randal Malone, an actor I worked with on Lodestar, knew my mother and said he saw the quality of a little girl in Yvonne and I absolutely understood this immediately. Her acting coach, George Shadanoff, used to say, "She would put one shoulder forward as if protecting herself shyly." I saw that, too. She did have a quiet aspect about her, like a demure little girl. It was hard to pry loose her private thoughts, so in some ways I knew my grandmother, Marie, somewhat better than my mother. Yvonne was secretive, whereas Marie was far more talkative. She was very serious about her work and career. At the same time, she tried her best as a mother and we became friends very early. When I was six, she talked to me like I was an adult and I helped her read her lines. When I was seven, I even talked her out of suicide. I remember her dragging me to the hospital when I was nearly dead from asthma — obviously the act of a mother trying to save her son. But another time, she left me out in the car in the cold. When she realized what she had done she said, "What kind of mother am I?" She knew there were problems with her instinct as a mother, but I credit her for trying hard and love her for that. In my world, you don't have to be perfect.

Bruce Morgan on Yvonne De Carlo. Telephone interview on 11/20/10. Morgan controls the official Yvonne De Carlo site, www.officialyvonnedecarlo.com. His Project Lodestar website is www.myspace.com/project_lodestar_sagas.

11

Valentina Alonso
on Red Skelton

Most aspiring entertainers would consider their career a success if they achieved fame in one area of show business. But Red Skelton (1913–1997) wasn't like most. Skelton created a memorable cast of comic characters during his early radio years and brought them to his TV comedy series, The Red Skelton Hour, *that ran from the 1950s to the early 1970s. He also appeared in some 40 films—from a cameo in the original* Ocean's Eleven *(1960), to co-star of classic MGM musicals, such as* Three Little Words *(1950). He also composed thousands of pieces of music, wrote hundreds of short stories, and became one of the most successful celebrity artists of the twentieth century, with original paintings selling for up to $80,000 at the time of his death. Married three times, Skelton had two children, Valentina and Richard, with his second wife, Georgia. Val, who now lives on the Oregon coast, says her parents were devastated by the death of her brother in 1958, yet her father somehow managed to continue to make the world smile.*

Mystery seemed to always surround your father's birthdate and early years. What do you know about his childhood and family?

I believe he was born in 1913, on July 18, in Vincennes, Indiana, but he never really talked much about his childhood. He left home and school when he was in seventh grade, and I don't think he ever really strived to go on with his studies or to go to college. He had difficulty learning at school, probably because his family moved so many times when he was young. His father died two months before he was born and there is some question as to who his mother was. It seems his father had a girlfriend who got pregnant with my dad and she died giving birth to him — he was a big baby, weighing over 13 pounds. His father's wife remarried and took him in, so he was raised by her and a step father who also had three sons. But his half-brothers didn't like

Valentina, brother Richard, and Red Skelton at the beach, late 1940s. (Photograph courtesy of Valentina Alonso.)

him and gave him a hard time, which probably was part of the reason he left home so young. The family was very poor and he was raised in extreme poverty, so he was looking for a better life for himself. A lot of sources say that my dad's father was a circus clown, but I believe my dad fabricated that. His father worked in a grocery store and as a linesman. The family name was changed from Earhart to Skelton because the law was after one of my father's brothers, who was a troublemaker, and they had to move from town to town.

What got him interested in show business?

   The story is that when he was ten, and still living at home, he was selling newspapers outside of the Pantheon Theatre in Vincennes, where Ed Wynn was performing. Wynn walked up to my dad, who didn't know who Ed Wynn was, and bought all the newspapers and gave him a ticket to the show. So Dad went in to the show and was surprised when Wynn came out to perform. He really inspired my dad's interest in show business. Many years later, in the '50s, I remember meeting Ed Wynn when my dad and I went to a restaurant in Los Angeles. He was sitting in a booth, and my dad introduced me to him. I didn't really know much about him, other than seeing him in some Disney films. I thought he was a funny-looking little guy, but he was someone my dad really admired.

What do you know about your father's first marriage to Edna Stillwell?

The story I was told is that they met at a dance-a-thon when he was 18 and they married soon after. She turned out to be a big help in his early career because she was a very good businesswoman and very protective of him. Even after they were divorced and he had married my mother, they remained friends and she continued to work for him. He used to call her "Mommy," although I don't ever recall meeting her.

How did your parents meet?

From what I understand, they met through a friend who had invited my mother to Dad's house. My mother thought she was going to a party, but it turned out to be just my mom and dad. They were both redheads and my father called her "Little Red." She looked like Rita Hayworth and had that beauty about her. She was a model, a singer, and did a few bit parts in movies. For instance, she was one of the dancers in *The Harvey Girls* [1946] that starred Judy Garland.

Your father was best known for his TV show, but he did a few movies. Do you recall seeing him on the big screen for the first time?

Most of his movies were in the '40s and '50s, before I was born, or I was too young to remember them. He never really talked about his movies, but he did give some good performances, like in *Three Little Words*, where he came across as a free spirit and fun loving. And he also had a lot of empathy in some of his roles. I recall seeing him in a movie called *The Clown* [1953], in which he had a serious role about a washed-up clown and a young boy who befriends him. I was seven years old and he took me to see it while we were vacationing in Hawaii. At first, I didn't believe that it was him on the screen. When I finally realized it was him, I thought Wow!— because there I was, sitting next to this actor who was my dad! It was a real eye-opener for me because, until that moment, I don't think I really realized what he did for a living.

So you probably remember his TV shows more than his films?

That's right. I was born in 1947, so it's mostly his TV show from the '60s and '70s that I remember watching. Many of his famous characters like Clem Kadiddlehopper, Deadeye the Sheriff, Willie Lump Lump, and Freddie the Freeloader he brought to television from his days in radio. But I do remember when he created The Little Old Man, sometime in the '60s. He would try out new ideas on the family to see how we would react to skits he was planning for a TV show. Then we would watch it together on the night of the show. He would have several TV sets on in the house to watch other comedians on the other stations, like Jack Benny, Jackie Gleason and Ernie Kovacs. He liked to keep track of his competitors!

Your father always came across as a gentle and fun-loving person on TV. Was he more complicated than that in private?

He could be happy-go-lucky much of the time. If there was a sad situation, he would try and make a joke out of it to make people feel better, but sometimes his timing could be inappropriate. So he was always trying to see the lighter side of things, which I think probably stemmed from his childhood when he had to put up a shield against his hard, early life. But he could also be moody, and my mom was always trying to keep him from getting upset about things. However, I never saw him get really angry, so he was a fairly mild-mannered person. He had a drinking problem in his early years, but got over that. He didn't smoke, but often carried cigars, although he never lit them. They were expensive Cuban cigars, and were like props for him. My mother smoked Kool cigarettes and used a cigarette holder that gave her that elegant look that was common among actresses of the time. In many ways, my father was also rather flamboyant because he loved fine art, wearing diamonds, jewelry, fur, tailor-made suits, and eating at good restaurants. He also liked fine cars and had a Rolls-Royce which he loved. So he enjoyed the good things in life, which again, I think, had to do with the poverty he remembered from his childhood. Dad was also a Republican and loved Eisenhower and Reagan.

So were you spoiled as a child?

I suppose I was to a degree, but I didn't really like all the attention our family got and was much more of an outdoors person. I was into horses and trail riding, quite a free spirit!

He never used bad language in his acts. Did he ever use it around the house?

He wanted to keep all his material very clean, so the entire family could enjoy his shows. Maybe that came from his Midwest upbringing. His humor was more down-home — even corny, I suppose. He did not like comedians such as Lenny Bruce or Richard Pryor. He did have some "key words" he would use around the house — "friggin'" was one of them, but you don't hear that much any more. He tried not to swear around us, but if he really got upset with people he could let loose some real doosies!

His second wife, your mother, was Georgia Davis. Was she a housewife or a working mother?

She kept pretty much busy looking after my dad, so she wasn't your typ-

ical mother who prepared meals and went to the grocery store. She had a secretary, Dorothy, who was like a mother to me in my pre-teen years. She would
take us to the Farmer's Market and to Beverly Hills for chocolate eclairs, and
other fun trips. I would have preferred a more normal life, but it didn't happen
that way. We had nannies and governesses to look after us much of the time.
I remember one called Margaret, from Scotland, who had a strong accent. In
fact, my brother and I started speaking with a Scottish brogue, so they got
rid of her! Then there was Clair, a German nanny who was very strict, which
didn't work at all for me as I was getting more and more independent.

Your name, Valentina, is unusual. Who gave it to you?

My mother said that, when I was born, I had a heart-shaped face. She
had a book of baby names and chose Valentina — I guess she was thinking
about valentines! I used to cringe at school because it was so unusual and I
wanted to be a Jane or an Anne, but I learned to appreciate it as I got older.

Did you attend school with children of other entertainers?

I didn't know many kids from entertainment families at the schools I
went to: first, St. Martin of Tours, a private Catholic School, then a public
school for junior high, both in West Los Angeles. I do remember Burt Lancaster's son, John, was at the same junior high school, Emerson Junior High.
Marilyn Monroe and Jayne Mansfield also went there years before me, so were
not in any of my classes. I didn't hang out with kids of other actors. My best
friend's mother was a nurse and her father was a policeman, and my parents
tried to stop the friendship because they wanted me to be friendly with "well
to do" families. My dad actually got along better with "regular folks" than
my mom, who could be a little "high and mighty." When I was 16, my parents
actually wanted me to date J. Paul Getty's son, hoping I would marry him.
He was about three years older than me and was a perfect gentleman, but I
just wasn't interested in him. I was always going for the bad boys! So my parents were fighting with me during that period when I guess I was rebelling.
It can be difficult growing up in a family where a parent is always getting so
much attention and the child is always in the background.

Was your father protective?

My brother and I were fairly sheltered growing up, so we weren't exposed
to much of the Hollywood crowd, the parties, and all that went with it. There
were not a lot of celebrity visitors to the house, but I do remember Jonathan
Winters and James Arness visiting, men my father greatly admired. I also
remember Esther Williams and her husband, Fernando Lamas, visiting our
home. My parents were worried after the kidnapping of Frank Sinatra's son

and the Lindbergh baby incident was always in the back of their minds when we were young. But we lived in a community that was very private and secure.

Your brother's illness in the early '50s was obviously a terrible family tragedy. How did your father handle it?

My brother had leukemia for several years and died in 1958, when I was 11. Watching him get thinner and weaker was very difficult for both my parents. My father had always viewed Richard as the one to carry on the Skelton name in the world of entertainment. So when he died, it just shut the door on those plans and affected him terribly. He went on with his work, but there was a sadness building up inside that he didn't talk much about. In fact, my father and I rarely sat down together and had many good face-to-face talks throughout his life. People often turn to eating when they have problems, so he also gained a lot of weight, which you can see in his TV shows after 1955 and 1956, and he had a breakdown from work exhaustion in the early '50s, during the time my brother was ill.

The family took a trip to Europe in 1957 while your brother was ill, and even met Pope Pius XII at the Vatican. What do you remember about that trip?

My dad thought it would be better for the family to travel rather than just sit at home watching my brother get sicker, and that it would be better for Richard to be out and about. As sick as he was with all his treatments, I'm not sure that it was the right thing to do. But my brother did enjoy the trip — seeing all the shops and stores in Europe and riding the double-decker buses in London. We went to several countries such as England, France, Sweden, Denmark, and Italy. In Rome, we had a short, private meeting with Pope Pius XII who blessed my brother. It was very overwhelming for me going to the Vatican and St. Peter's Basilica with its tall ceilings, paintings, and old-world feeling. I felt very uncomfortable there because it was so overpowering for a small child and I don't think it really registered at the time how special the pope was. When we went to England, the newspapers were really rough on my dad with front-page news saying how my dad was traveling over Europe with his dying child just to get publicity. In spite of that and all the sadness, my dad thought it was the right thing to do — to get away from all the doctors and hospitals and blood tests. Travel was always a great escape for him and a way to forget about the problems of life. One place I remember visiting was a restaurant called Alfredo's, in Rome, where we had fettuccine for the first time and where the dish was invented. The flamboyant chef, Alfredo himself, came out and we watched him prepare the cheese and seasonings for the pasta.

Red Skeleton and daughter Valentina on Father's Day, 1995, at the Lawrence Welk Resort. (Photograph courtesy of Valentina Alonso.)

Your dad married a third time, to Lothian Toland, in 1973. Was she like your mother?

My mother had some personal problems, but was a very kind and generous person — very loving and giving. After they were divorced, my father was the type of man who needed a wife, so he remarried two years before my mother passed away. His third wife was very independent and, in that way, more similar to his first wife. Lothian was a realtor, had a pilot's license, and didn't have any emotional issues, which I think was quite refreshing for my dad. Her father was Gregg Toland, a highly respected cinematographer from the early Hollywood days who worked on *Citizen Kane* [1941]. Even though Lothian grew up in the Hollywood lifestyle, she wasn't caught up with the Hollywood glamour and was more down to earth and very matter-of-fact. She was much younger than my dad and still runs what's left of my dad's production company and estate.

Aside from his acting, your dad wrote a lot of stories and music. Could he read music?

No, he would hear the music in his head and transfer it to a recorder. Then a composer who worked with him would write the notes down on paper.

He was also famous as a celebrity artist, and especially known for his

clown paintings. Do you remember him painting much when you were growing up?

Dad began painting when he was very young, like 14, but it was very primitive stuff. When he met my mother, who was also a watercolor artist, he got into oils. So she was his biggest influence in the beginning. I know he began painting the clowns in the '40s, then from the '60s through the '90s, they became very popular. He also did limited edition reprints and plates that were more affordable. I think after Richard died, painting was a form of therapy for him. He didn't paint very much when we were living in Los Angeles, but when we moved to the desert, in Palm Springs, he converted a room in the house into his studio and painted more often. There was a bathroom off the studio room with a sliding-glass door that went to the backyard. He kept his easel and oil paints on one side of the room and there was a small bed there that I remember sitting on, talking to him as he painted. In his third marriage, he had a house in the mountains above Palm Desert and there was a spiral staircase leading to a loft which he made into his studio. He really produced a lot of paintings at that point after he quit TV in the '70s. They turned the house in Rancho Mirage into an office for his artwork. Once a week he would go in and sign his painting reproductions and they would be shipped off to different galleries.

Were you involved in his art business at all?

He wanted me to open an art gallery and sell his reproductions. I knew a little about sales from previous jobs, but knew nothing about running a business. I finally gave in and opened a small gallery, which was only about 200 square feet, in Pine Valley, about 50 miles east of San Diego. I sold a lot of his transfers on canvas in the beginning, but was not comfortable doing it six days a week. I was divorced and raising my 14-year-old daughter, Sabrina, and felt it was more than I could handle, so after about a year I gave the gallery up. However, art is now also my career, and I love to paint watercolors. It's very peaceful and relaxing.

Did you ever want to act?

Not really. My brother and I were in some of my dad's TV Christmas specials. In later years, when we were living in Palm Springs, I was asked to be Rodeo Queen and was on his show to promote that. His costume designer made me some outfits for the show and my dad interviewed me for about four or five minutes at the beginning of one of the shows in 1966. I was actually the first local girl to be Rodeo Queen; others included Marilyn Monroe and Jayne Mansfield. In my late teens I took acting classes at a school run by Agnes Moorehead, but it didn't click with me, although I remember Bobby

Vinton was in my class. The only other time I appeared on "film," was in family home movies! My father loved using his old 16mm movie camera. There's a lot of film from family vacations and Christmas. My stepmother has all those and had a lot transferred to DVD. Maybe some will be released to the public at some time, I'm not sure. I also studied interior design, to be a travel agent, and went to massage therapy school but was not successful at any of these businesses. So it's the art I stuck with, and I sell my work through local galleries. One of the most unusual jobs I had was driving public transport buses — the big 35-foot diesel Gillig buses. At first I was terrified, but I ended up doing it for six years. I never told people who my father was while I worked at the bus company. Today, I don't like to broadcast family connections. Sometimes, my father's name will come up and I'll mention our connection, but I try to live a fairly normal life now. It's far removed from the drama and craziness that I grew up with in Hollywood and show business families.

Valentina Alonso on Red Skelton. Telephone interview on 12/14/10. The official Red Skelton website is www.redskelton.com.

12

Maria Cooper Janis on Gary Cooper

There was nothing flashy about Gary Cooper on the big screen. Yet his performances were so honest and believable, he was nominated for five Best Actor Oscars, winning twice (for Sergeant York *and* High Noon*), besting the likes of Cary Grant, Orson Welles, Marlon Brando, and Kirk Douglas. Raised in Montana, the quiet yet intense Cooper was the box-office darling throughout the '30s and '40s. Though something of a playboy in his early Hollywood years, "Coop" settled down to marry Veronica "Rocky" Balfe in 1933. The couple briefly separated in the early '50s, but remained married for 28 years, until Cooper's death in 1961 at the age of 60. Their only child, Maria, is a talented artist who married one of the world's great concert pianists, Byron Janis. She shares memories of being raised by one of the world's greatest actors.*

Your father's parents settled in Helena, Montana, in the late 1800s. What was your grandfather like and how did he influence your father?

My grandfather was a lovely man but, from my perspective as a child, he seemed to be quite stern to me and wasn't the warm and fuzzy type. He became a Montana state supreme court judge. I understand that in many of my grandfather's legal rulings, he was very supportive of the powerless person against big corporations or companies, so he very much supported the "little guy." I think some of that rubbed off on my father's sense of what's right and what's wrong. Some of the characters my father played were like that, too. For his biography of my father, Jeffery Meyers did quite a bit of research into the Cooper family and his book is the best account of their days in Montana.

Is Gary Cooper still remembered in Helena?

Very much so. The first house the family lived in is preserved as a historical home, although it's privately owned and a family lives there. My husband and I visited around 2001 and the owners very kindly let us go through

Gary and Maria Cooper in California in the late '50s. (Photograph courtesy of Maria Cooper Janis.)

the home. We went upstairs and walked through all the rooms, and parts of the kitchen are still original. It's been kept up well, and the town appreciates that because there is a lot of affection for Gary Cooper in Helena. The house is not open to the public, but it's accessible to people who have a real interest in seeing it. Then there's also the family ranch that was on 600 acres, near Craig, which is about an hour and a half away. It's also privately owned. There were two houses on that property and the original has been enlarged, and people live in it today. Then there was another house a few hundred yards away with a big room with a huge stone fireplace and some of it still is exactly as it was when my father lived there. Nearby is the hill where my father and a friend had an accident when their car turned over. My father injured his hip in the accident and had problems with it for the rest of his life. Behind Helena in a newly built area; there are two intersecting streets that are named for Gary Cooper and western artist Charles Russell, whose work my father loved. Helena was also home to Myrna Loy, so she and my father are the two home-town kids who made it in the big world of Hollywood. She is also honored in Helena, and they have the Myrna Loy Theater there.

Your dad was born Frank James Cooper, and later changed his name to Gary. It must be strange for parents when they have a child who takes a stage name. What did his parents call him throughout his life?

I never really thought about that, but they always called him Gary. A lot of the family and old friends called him "Coop," so that stayed the same throughout his life. He changed his name to Gary for two reasons. Frank James was the name of another actor and there was also a notorious outlaw of that name, so it was thought a good idea not be identified with either of them. His agent was from Gary, Indiana, and she thought it was a nice name, so he took it.

Do you recall the first time you saw your dad in a movie?

I didn't realize my dad was in movies until I was about six or seven. My parents wouldn't let me watch his films before that because they felt it might confuse me and they wanted my upbringing to be as normal as possible and not colored by all of the Hollywood hype. The first movie I saw him in was *The Plainsman* [1936], when I was seven or eight. It was shown at our home for my birthday party on a 16mm projector that my father was running. It was the first time I ever saw him on the screen. There was a scene in the film where he had been captured by Indians and was being tortured. They had him hung by his wrists and were slowly lowering him into a fire and, during the scene, I became quite upset. But I remember, so clearly, turning around and looking at my father, who was standing behind the projector. He just looked at me and winked, and it was the most wonderful moment. It was like he was saying to me, "That's fantasy up there on the screen, not reality, and it's all okay." What solidified it for me was his attitude and humor, like he was laughing at it. So I understood at that moment that there was a difference between fantasy and reality, and that the two shouldn't be mixed. I suspect that came in handy for me as I was growing up.

Any thoughts about *Sergeant York* (1941) which was released when you were four years old?

I was too young to remember *Sergeant York* when it first came out. But I did have a wonderful opportunity to meet one of Alvin York's sons when I was invited to the National World War I Museum in Kansas City in 2009. They get a lot of tourists and school groups visiting the site and it's a wonderful place with state-of-the-art exhibitions. They asked if they could borrow the *Sergeant York* Oscar to put on display over the Armistice Day period in November. They invited one of Alvin York's sons, Andrew Jackson York, to come to the Armistice Day ceremony as well. He and I gave speeches, and the museum put the Oscar on display. Alvin York had eight children and named most of them after American historical figures. I found Andy York to be a charming man, and he was still living in the house that was built for his father by the community when he returned from the war. There's an Alvin York museum on the property now and I believe they have photographs of my father meeting Alvin York when he went down to Tennessee while he was preparing to work on the film. In fact, Alvin York said he would not allow the film of his life to be made unless Gary Cooper played him. I understand Alvin liked the way my father portrayed him.

Any stories about *High Noon* (1952) for which your dad won his second Oscar?

I was 15 and visited the set during filming, and got to really appreciate my father's acting ability. In the wedding scene, he had to pick up Grace Kelly, his bride, and lift her up onto on a high bureau — and she was not a petite woman. He had pulled his back and, in fact, had a bad back from childhood. He was in so much pain, but had to look like he was the happy groom sweeping his bride off her feet. His ability to hide the pain really gave me an added respect for how he handled his craft. *High Noon* was just supposed to be a simple little western, and no one expected it would amount to much, but it turned out to be a wonderful film. Fred Zinnemann, the director, was like a member of our family, and my father adored him. My father was also very good friends with Carl Foreman, who wrote the screenplay. He was one of the blacklisted people during that shameful period in Hollywood history when the McCarthy machine did its damage. When the producers tried to get Foreman off the picture, my father went to bat for him. He went into the their office and said, "If Carl Foreman goes, Gary Cooper goes," and walked out of the room. And of course, they caved in.

When your father was at home, did he rehearse much?

He really didn't bring his work home and left the moods and dramas of his roles at the studio. When he did come home with a script, he went into a room and shut the door. He didn't pace around the house saying his lines because that wasn't his style. I never read his lines with him. He was very private about his work. Work was work and home was home.

Several directors apparently felt that when they watched Gary Cooper doing his scenes, they were worried he wasn't doing them correctly. But when they saw him on the screen, they realized he had nailed it. How do you explain that?

I've read the same thing. He was a passionate person, but it wasn't in his nature to emote all over the place, and he was quite reserved. He really believed that it was very important for an actor to express his emotion in his face and eyes, rather than just using a lot of words. That showed the audience that the actor was a real, thinking person. He never went to acting class and he never studied technique. When he was a young actor, he learned his craft by watching and working with older, more seasoned colleagues like Ronald Colman and Charles Laughton, and he absorbed from people around him. Laughton and my father admired each other very much. My father was an artist and liked to draw, and was very observant of people, places, nature, and things around him. I think that power of observation probably gave him insight into personalities and behavior patterns which he then incorporated into his characters, and that came across on the screen.

You're an artist. Did your father encourage you to paint?

Well, both my parents encouraged me. I had two parents! That's the trouble, people forget about the other parent who isn't the celebrity and how important that other parent is, so certainly both of them encouraged me to paint. I went to the Chouinard Art Institute in Los Angeles, which was started by Walt Disney to train animators for the Disney studios. In fact, the year I graduated, Disney had just given 400 acres of land for what is now the California Institute of the Arts. I had a wonderful teacher at Chouinard and I'll never forget his advice on the first day of class when he said, "Put mileage on your pen!" Telling us to draw, draw, draw was the best advice for a young artist. My art is expressionistic and I've had quite a few shows in New York over the years. I've been on the road most of my life because of my husband traveling as a concert pianist, but I always take a suitcase along with me that contains rolled-up canvases and paints so that I can work wherever we are. In fact, much of my art had to do with musicians and scenes from backstage because that is a wonderful dramatic atmosphere that's so exciting to capture. My father did a lot of drawings and sketches throughout his life, and in his early career he wanted to be an artist. Growing up in Montana, Charles Russell, the famous western artist, was an influence, so my father drew lots of cowboys and Indians. During the war — World War I — his sketches reflected the period, and he would draw war scenes with warships and planes going down in flames. When he was older, he built a studio at his home which was actually an old dog kennel that he turned into his art studio, and he worked with watercolors and oils. But, with his acting, he didn't really have that much time to paint, and it frustrated him because he loved doing it. I still have a few pieces of his art, maybe about 20 pieces, although some of it has been lost or destroyed over the years. None of it has ever been on the market.

You mentioned your husband, Byron, who is a well-known pianist. He made quite an amazing discovery back in the '60s that was big news in the classical music world. What was it?

In 1967, we were in France and had been invited to have lunch at the Chateau of Thoiry, about 40 minutes outside of Paris. It's a remarkable property and the owners have had it in their family for over 500 years. To keep it in the family, however, they had to make it into a money-making operation, so they actually turned it into an African game reserve! It's become very popular with tourists. As we were being shown around by the owner, the Viscount Paul de la Panouse, he took us into an archive room that was filled with old manuscripts and letters. In the room, there was a trunk marked "old clothes" that was stuck in between a lot of old, beautiful dresses that were in storage. My husband looked inside the trunk and there was a folder in there with some papers. He picked them up and asked Paul what the papers were, and Paul said they were just scribblings of his grandmother's who used to write a little music and make notations. Byron said this was not Paul's grandmother's writing, but that it was the handwriting of Chopin! Well, it was quite an amazing moment — Byron had discovered the music of two Chopin waltzes. Later, they were authenticated and the Chopin manuscripts remain at Thoiry today. The story of the discovery was front-page news on the *New York Times*. But there's a second part to the story. Four years later, when Byron was at Yale discussing a master class, he visited their archive room which was filled with hundreds of boxes. For some reason, he pointed to one box way up on a top shelf, and asked, "What's that?" Well, they climbed up a ladder, pulled down the box, opened it, and there were two pieces of music in it. They were two Chopin waltzes — the same waltzes he discovered at Thoiry! These, however, were different versions of the same pieces, and Yale didn't know they had them. Byron recounts the story in his 2010 autobiography, *Chopin and Beyond: My Extraordinary Life in Music and the Paranormal.*

It was a fascinating book, and not just about music, am I right?

It was also about his medical struggle with severe arthritis and how he managed to play the piano. In spite of the toll arthritis took on his hands and wrists, as well as an accident to his little finger at the age of 11 which left it totally numb, he continues playing and adapting his repertoire to the conditions of the day. His experiences in the field of the paranormal seemed to be very natural to him as he has used "mind over matter" to help conquer the impediments of arthritis.

You also mentioned your mother; how did she get the nickname "Rocky"?

Her name was Veronica. When she was a little girl, she couldn't pronounce it and it came out "Rocky." So she began calling herself that, and it stuck. It turned out to be a wonderful nickname because she was a dynamic person, and very athletic. She was a great sharpshooter and made my father very proud because he loved to shoot.

How did she get interested in shooting?

I think a smart wife observes what her husband loves to do, so she can participate in it, too, and that develops another bond between the two of them. Knowing how much my father loved skeet shooting and hunting, she took up shooting, although she would never kill anything. My father was a super shot, and my mother actually became California's state woman's skeet champion. She wasn't better than my father, but she was better than a lot of his buddies which delighted him no end. Of course, some of them were chagrined by that!

Your mom acted under the name of Sandra Shaw in a few films in the early '30s, but stopped as soon as she was married. Did she enjoy her acting days?

She never liked the whole acting thing, and always said "Thank God Gary came along" and saved her from the terrible fate of trying to be an actress. She only had small roles in a few films, if you call being the girl who screamed out the window in *King Kong* being in a movie! I don't recall her telling any stories from that film, but my parents were friends with Fay Wray.

How did your parents meet?

They met through her uncle who was Cedric Gibbons, my grandmother's older brother. He was an art director at MGM for 27 years and, next to Walt Disney, he won more Academy Awards than anyone. Cedric was married to actress Dolores Del Rio. At the age of 18, my mother wanted to get away from New York so she went out to California to live with Cedric and Dolores for a while. They were very good friends with an actor named Richard Barthelmess. He had a boat, and one weekend they went to Catalina on the boat. Gary Cooper was a guest, and that's how they met.

Before he married and settled down, your dad had a reputation as a playboy. Did he talk to you about his early relationships?
No, not at all. Obviously, one reads reams about it and there was a

Maria with her parents in 1961 in Beverly Hills. (Photograph courtesy of Maria Cooper Janis.)

lot of publicity about that at the time, but he just dismissed it.

After working on *The Fountainhead* (1949) with Patricia Neal, the two became quite close and that led to your parents separating for a few years in the early '50s when you were a teenager. How difficult was that time for you?
No kid likes to see their parents go through times like that. But they handled it very intelligently. I never ever heard them fight, although I'm sure they had words, but never in front of me. In spite of being separated, we were always doing things together as a family which totally puzzled the Hollywood pundits and made for some good gossip. During the separation, he went over to Paris to do a picture. My mother and I went over and we all spent some time together traveling around France. So they both handled that period very well and there was never any bad-mouthing on either side about the other person.

Did you do anything to get your folks back together?

No, I didn't even try. Forcing people to stay together for the kids never ends up well. But I knew they always respected each other tremendously and still loved each other despite whatever dalliances went on, so I think the issue of mutual respect was very important. Sometimes people just need to be apart, have their own space, and reflect about what's really important to them. My mother didn't go out and take comfort in drinking, and playing bridge with the girls was not her thing. She had led a very active life, was a beautiful woman, and had a lot of beaus, so she didn't have to sit home and knit. She also understood men and had a European woman's approach to them, more than a typical American woman at that time.

Not surprisingly, you were angry at Patricia Neal. But years later, you and your mother actually became friends with her?

Yes, certainly. Obviously at first I was naturally upset with Patricia, but life throws stuff at you. Many years after my parents got back together, I ran into Patricia accidentally in the South of France where my husband was giving a concert. She was going through a difficult time then with her own marriage and had a lot of health problems. I told her about my close friend, the former actress Dolores Hart, who lived at the Abbey of Regina Laudis in Connecticut. Ultimately, she went up to the abbey and met with Mother Dolores. The abbey helped her come to peace with her own issues, and I think probably saved her life. Part of that was being able to reconcile with my mother. So the two of them got together. Although my mother was house-bound and not all that well at the time, the two of them had a very lovely time together.

Towards the end of his life, your dad became very ill with cancer. In fact, when he was awarded his third Oscar, the honorary award in 1961, he was too sick to accept. Jimmy Stewart accepted for it him and that was when people first realized just how sick your dad was. Was he watching the ceremony on TV?

Yes. My mother, father and I were together at home watching it. I don't recall him saying a whole lot. He adored Jimmy and they were very close, and it was obviously a very moving moment for Jimmy. We didn't know what Jimmy was going to say in his speech. He didn't actually reveal how ill my father was, but the fact that he became quite emotional was a clue to everybody. My father's mother was actually still alive when he died, but she was a very resilient lady. We stayed in touch, obviously, and I think she was 97 when she died. So there was some longevity in the Cooper family genes, but it didn't help my father. I blame the cigarettes — he smoked a couple of packs a day. He tried to stop numerous times, but with the tension on the set and nerves, he just kept going back to it. Then he'd be angry at himself and swear to stop again, and just go back and forth. As I've said before, my father was a private person, so he just kept his illness to himself. He was very low-key about it all, you might say typical Gary Cooper.

Maria Cooper Janis on Gary Cooper. Telephone interview on 10/30/10. *Gary Cooper Off Camera: A Daughter Remembers* is the 1999 biography written by Maria Cooper Janis published by Harry N. Abrams. The official Gary Cooper website is www.garycooper.com.

13

Sara Karloff on Boris Karloff

Unlucky was the co-star who crossed paths with Boris Karloff, who most often portrayed monsters, murderers, and misfits on-screen. Yet by his daughter's account, the real Karloff was a quiet and gentle soul. Born in the UK in 1887 as William Henry Pratt, he took the more exotic-sounding name of "Boris Karloff" long before he became associated with horror films in 1931, when he first portrayed "the monster" in Frankenstein. *Just eight years later, while filming* Son of Frankenstein, *Karloff made his final appearance as the creature, at least on the big screen. No doubt the four hours it took each day to transform Karloff into the creature was grueling for an actor in his fifties. But it was also a time to celebrate. Just a few weeks into production in November 1938, his only child, Sara, was born. Sara Karloff now manages Karloff Enterprises, through which she maintains the personal and professional legacy of her father. Although Boris Karloff died in 1969, Sara says his fans are still fascinated about the life and career of their favorite cinematic villain.*

Your dad played some pretty gruesome characters throughout his career, what was he like off-screen?

He really was a true gentleman in every sense, a warm and gentle person. Nothing negative was ever written or said about him personally — few people in the industry could say that. Nor did he ever complain about anything or speak negatively about anyone he worked with. People who worked with him on- and off-screen just adored him.

It was amazing how effectively he could use his voice and eyes on screen, wasn't it?

He could do anything with his voice — make it terrifying and threatening, or nice and pleasant. In fact, he made many recordings of children's stories for Caedmon Records. But oh, what he could do with his eyes! The

Sara and Boris Karloff on the set of *A Comedy of Terrors,* circa 1963. (Photograph courtesy of Sara Karloff.)

slightest look could terrorize on the screen. As a child, he could certainly give you that look if you said you were going to do something and didn't, but he was a fair father.

He was not a young man when you were born, was he?

I was born on his 51st birthday, which probably made me the most expensive birthday present he ever got! But I don't think I missed having a young dad. He was a good father because he was a good man. My parents divorced when I was seven and I moved to San Francisco with my mother and stepfather, whom I adored. My father lived in Los Angeles, so I wasn't with him all the time. He also married again, and both he and my mother remarried happily and successfully.

How did your friends react to you having the king of monster movies for a dad?

In Hollywood — Beverly Hills — where I grew up, a famous name really didn't stand out. The kids and teachers were all accustomed to it. So it really was nothing special. In San Francisco, I went to a private girls' school where a famous name did attract attention; but what really mattered there were academics and discipline, not your name. We wore uniforms, there was no make-up or jewelry allowed, and it was a sheltered but fairly normal environment.

Did his films scare you when you were young?

When I was little, his movies weren't playing as first-run films in theaters, so I rarely saw them. Besides, girls didn't go to horror movies then. I first saw *Frankenstein* on TV when I was 19. But actually, it was the worst casting in the world, me being Boris Karloff's daughter — I'm the biggest wuss when it comes to scary shows!

That seems rather odd, given the type of roles your father was famous for!

It actually stems from a birthday party I went to when I was five or six. There was a private screening of *The Wizard of Oz* [1939], and it scared me to death! For years afterwards, I looked under the bed for the witch. When I first watched my father in *The Mummy* [1932], it was with Ron Borst, my friend and a historian of classic horror films. He came to my house and had to hold my hand while telling me "Sara, you can do this!" He did the same thing with *The Black Cat* [1934], and I was a grown woman then!

Did your dad know you found it hard to watch his films?

Yes, but he didn't either. Many actors can't watch their own films.

When we think of Karloff, we immediately think of horror films, but he had numerous other roles in film before *Frankenstein*.

Before coming to Hollywood, he learned his craft in British Columbia, working for ten years around theater productions. He painted sets, broke down sets, and moved from town to town, sometimes not even getting paid. He would sustain himself by working on railroads, driving trucks, digging ditches, whatever it took. After he wangled his way down to Hollywood, he spent ten more years playing bit parts, many times in ethnic roles because of his dark skin color and ethnic-looking face. I think *Frankenstein* was his 81st film, and nobody saw the first 80!

Frankenstein was an unexpected hit and so was Karloff, wasn't he?

Colin Clive, who played Dr. Frankenstein, was supposed to be the star, but it turned out to be the creature. My father wasn't even invited to the premiere! After 20 years in the business he literally was an overnight success. Universal couldn't turn out scripts fast enough for him.

Didn't he injure his back when he had to carry Colin Clive?

Yes, but he didn't have the best back going into the film, and lifting Colin exacerbated the problem. He was very bowlegged, and his legs gave him a lot of trouble in later years. He had to wear leg braces and, ultimately, had three back surgeries. But he tried not to let it show in his work. When he guest-starred on the TV show *I Spy* in the late '60s, he had to fall into a muddy gutter in one scene. A double was supposed to do it but he said, "Indeed not!" He was in his seventies at the time and it took several takes, but he still did it himself.

Horror film actors don't win Oscars. Did he want that recognition?

No, he never acted to win awards. But he did win a Grammy for his recording of "How the Grinch Stole Christmas." He was in England when the award was given, and his agent accepted it for him. When he returned to the U.S., his agent was very excited to give him his Grammy statue. My father took it, walked over to the door, and put it down as a doorstop! That's how important most awards were to him. I do think, however, he would have liked to have won a Tony when he played in *The Lark* on Broadway, in 1955, with Julie Harris. He absolutely loved working with her, and when she won a Tony, I think he wanted to win as well, if only to legitimize his acting in his mind.

So he enjoyed his stage work?

Yes, and he especially loved *Peter Pan* when he played Captain Hook/Mr. Darling on Broadway in the early '50s. He loved working with the children — The Lost Boys. He also loved it because kids would come backstage afterwards to try on his hook! But he did suffer from stage fright, at least in the first few moments of a show. But I think that's what makes good actors — the adrenalin rush that keeps them at their peak. If you just walk through a performance, how good can you be?

He only appeared as the Frankenstein monster in three films: *Frankenstein* (1931), *The Bride of Frankenstein* (1935), and *Son of Frankenstein* (1939). Why not more?

He felt the scripts had been developed as far as they could be, without turning the creature into a bad joke. So he refused to do it any more.

Speaking of jokes, what about the two Abbott and Costello films he

appeared in? In *Abbott and Costello Meet Dr. Jekyll and Mr. Hyde* (1953) he played Dr. Jekyll. Did he enjoy those?

(*Long silence*) That's my answer! Let me just say he wasn't thrilled with what was done with the creature in some of those films.

And, of course, *Abbott and Costello Meet the Killer, Boris Karloff* (1949) was a rip-off because he only appears for a few minutes. Were they just cashing in on his name?

It was never intended to be a Boris Karloff film. That's all I'll say about it, except that my father loved every film he worked in.

He actually starred in two films called *The Raven*, the 1963 one being best remembered with co-stars Vincent Price and Peter Lorre. Did he have fun doing that?

Oh yes, they had all reached points in their careers where they could have a good time spoofing their own boogeyman characters and playing practical jokes on each other and the director. I visited the set of *The Raven*, and Vincent Price would tell stories about carrying me around on his shoulders when I was a little girl.

Were there any actors he didn't like to work with?

If there was, no one would have known about it. He just never talked about that sort of thing. But I can tell you George Kennedy was one of his favorites. I met him at a Chiller show in 2008 and was so pleased to tell him how much my father admired him. When he heard that, it brought tears to his eyes. He told me of a time when he was in New York and he wanted to meet my father who was appearing in a play. Dad came out of the stage door and George saw him from across the street. He so wanted to cross over and introduce himself to my father, but was afraid to do so. He said he always regretted that he didn't do it. But he was so pleased to learn how much my father liked his work.

Did your dad have any hobbies?

He adored gardening and was a voracious reader. He thought he'd died and gone to heaven if he could go to a cricket match, which he did whenever he visited England. He would have a beer, and eat smoked salmon and cucumber sandwiches at the match.

Any other unusual foods he liked?

Whenever he would return to the U.S. after being in England, he would have sandabs, which are very thin whitefish, sautéed lightly with lemon and

Sara Karloff at a Thriller convention, circa 2008. (Photograph courtesy of Mel Weinstein.)

capers. And he felt the only proper way to fix Coleman's dry mustard was by mixing it with gin!

Why did he choose "Boris Karloff" as a name?

He repeatedly said Boris just came out of "thin air." And he always said Karloff came from somewhere back on his mother's side of the family. But with all the research I've done on his background, it's not clear where that name came from. I tend to believe Karloff came from a playbill or book he read.

Didn't your father have a role in forming the Screen Actors Guild?

That was one of his proudest achievements. He was one of the first ten members — his card was number nine — along with people like Jimmy Cagney, Frank Morgan, and Jimmy Gleason. They put their careers on the line when they formed the union. Actors worked long hours and were just viewed as "meat" in those days.

Why were they jeopardizing their careers by starting SAG?

The powerful studio bosses and tyrannical directors were very much against it. My mother told me they would go to parties and as the couples danced by each other they would whisper instructions about upcoming secret meetings. When they held a meeting, they would park blocks away and walk to the house where it was held in case they were being followed or watched.

Did he hang out with show business people?

Many of his friends were not in show business. But he was great friends with Jimmy Stewart and Greg Peck. But he was never a name dropper. He liked and admired Peter Bogdanovich, who directed him in *Targets* in 1968. That's my favorite film.

Was there a rivalry between him and Béla Lugosi?

There wasn't any antagonism between the two, as the press claimed. They were professionals and respected each other. But they had different backgrounds and interests and didn't socialize together.

How would he have reacted to all the graphic violence in film today?

He would have been appalled. He understood the value of involving the imagination of the audience and respected their intelligence. He'd be disgusted by the lack of good scripts. He valued the shadows of the black-and-white films and the suspense of what was coming next.

Did you ever have a role in any of his films?

Heavens no! It was not my thing and he knew it. I remember he had arranged for me to fly back East to see him on-stage in *Peter Pan*. He told me that I paid more attention to Nana the dog, than him! He said, "You don't have that fire in the belly to be an actor."

What have been your professional interests?

I've been a licensed real-estate broker in California for many years. I now have the business of Karloff Enterprises which allows me to travel and meet his fans, and to keep his legacy protected and available for the fans.

You had some legal battles with the studios over the use of your father's images. Was that resolved?

They'd have me in handcuffs if I discussed the details! Let's just say it was settled out of court ... and I smiled. I own the rights to my father's name and likeness. When somebody wants to use his likeness as Frankenstein or The Mummy from the films, they need permission from Universal. For all other uses, they have to come to me.

With the Internet, people sometimes just "copy and paste" images to their site without giving credit or payments. Is it a problem for you?

Many do ask for permission, because it lends legitimacy to what they are doing. I just want to make sure that when people use his name and likeness in any project, that it's done appropriately and tastefully.

Do you go to many fan conventions?

Not a lot. Usually around Halloween I will and it's always enjoyable. Never have I met so many painted and pierced people as at these shows! But they couldn't be more respectful of me and my father, and I love doing it. Where else could I go for three days and have so many people say such nice things to me. It's entirely due to the fans that my father's career had such "long legs." He truly felt he was the luckiest man in the world to be paid for doing something that he loved.

Sara Karloff on Boris Karloff. Telephone interview on 7/20/09. Sara Karloff runs the official Boris Karloff website: www.karloff.com.

14

Pia Lindström on Ingrid Bergman

If there was an instruction manual for assembling a classic Hollywood actress of the '30s and '40s, it might have read like this: take a stunningly beautiful woman, add a generous helping of talent, mix in a hint of vulnerability, then blend with a gentle, exotic European accent. Such a recipe could have created Ingrid Bergman (1915–1982). Named after a Swedish royal princess, Bergman collected three Oscars, four Golden Globes, two Emmy awards, one Tony, a BAFTA, and three NYFCC Awards throughout her career. She also produced four children: Pia (with Petter Lindström), and Isabella, Ingrid, and Roberto (with Roberto Rossellini). A respected television journalist and theater critic, Pia Lindström was separated from her mother as a child and, a decade later, reunited with her famous parent.

Your mother lost both of her parents at an early age. Who raised her?

Her mother, Friedel, died when my mother was just two years old and she had no memory of her, expect through photos and some early movie camera films. Ten years later, her father, Justus, also died. She then went to live with an aunt — her father's sister, Ellen — but just a few months later she died, too, in my mother's arms. From there she went to another uncle, Otto, and lived with his family. They had a daughter, Britt Bergman, who was about my mother's age, and they became very close.

Was there one event that influenced her to consider acting as a career?

When she lived with her father, their apartment was very close to the theater. He took her to see the opera and she was very impressed with the singers. She told me that she said to her father, "That is what I want to be!" It turned out she didn't have the voice to be an opera singer, but she wanted a life on the stage.

116

Your mother first appeared in some Swedish films. Is it true that David O. Selznick discovered her?

David Selznick did not discover her. His assistant, Kay Brown, did during a trip to Sweden when she saw my mother in a film and suggested a screen test.

After you were born, your family moved to the U.S. What happened during those early years in America?

I was about two years old when we came to America. My mother went to California to work while I stayed with my father in Rochester, New York. He began studying for his med-

Pia Lindström and Ingrid Bergman, circa 1963. (Photograph courtesy of Pia Lindström.)

ical degree and would go on to become a neurosurgeon. He had wanted to study medicine in Sweden, but his family couldn't afford it, so he obtained a Ph.D. in dentistry and taught at a university, although he never practiced dentistry. While I was in Rochester with my father, I always looked forward to my mother's visits when we would play and go on toboggan rides. After my father graduated, we moved to California and were all together again.

As a child, did you think of your mother as a big movie star?

No, I only thought of her as my mother. Of course I knew that she was an actress, playing a nun in *The Bells of St. Mary's* [1945], or Joan of Arc — I realized that at an early age — but I knew it was just pretend and that she was having a good time doing it. She brought that pretend world to the home, too. She was lots of fun to be around. Like many actresses, she retained that ability to play, and it was wonderful. One of my best friends was Maria Cooper and when we got together we didn't talk about how famous our parents were. I would go over to her house and Gary Cooper would be making hamburgers on the grill like other dads, and we'd swim or play in her room.

How did your dad handle your mother's rise to fame once her career took off in Hollywood?

He had married a young Swedish actress who was just beginning her career, so he didn't marry an international star. I don't think he was prepared for what would happen to her in Hollywood. I have heard that he tried to negotiate some contracts for her, which was a way he thought he could protect her, but that didn't go over well with the Hollywood crowd. They denigrated him, I think, because they liked to deal with the agents they knew. Even though he had become a respected neurosurgeon at a Los Angeles hospital, he was often referred to by the entertainment industry as "that Swedish dentist." It's easy to look back now and say he should have stayed out of it completely and let her find a professional agent, but like many husbands from that period he thought of himself as her protector and took on a paternalistic role. But much of it was beyond his control. There's a momentum to the life of an actor that is almost unstoppable in the beginning, like a runaway train. I'm sure my mother found it a fun ride, but my father wasn't prepared to see us constantly photographed and his family's privacy invaded. He probably tried to control how the publicity was handled. From my viewpoint now, they both did the best they could.

You and your dad were casualties because she left you both behind when she went to Italy to make a film for Roberto Rossellini in 1949. How did you handle it as a ten-year-old?

When she left, she told us she was going to Italy to make a movie. I don't think she knew she wasn't coming back, but she became pregnant with Roberto's child. I'm not sure she thought any of this through and what the consequences would be. For me, there were a lot of emotions like fear, regret, and sadness. I was ashamed when she was denounced, and embarrassed because it was a humiliation for my father. I felt terrible for him. He was always hoping that she would come back to him. The only time I saw her was once in London when my father took me to see her. I didn't see her again until I was 18, when I visited her in Paris.

Did she ever tell you she had regrets about going to Italy and not being around when you grew up?

She was not sorry that she went to Europe. She was very happy that she was doing what she loved. She fell in love and always said she had no regrets. That train I mentioned earlier? It just kept moving on for her.

Instead of being an only child, you ended up with an extended family — she had two daughters and a son with Rossellini. Were the families close?

We never lived together growing up, so I didn't have any brothers or sisters stealing my teddy bear or to fight with! So we all ended up great friends. I actually have seven half-brothers and sisters and have tried to maintain relationships with all of them. My father remarried a physician and they had four children. It's been particularly wonderful that Ingrid and Isabella Rossellini live near me in New York City because we have become a family.

The U.S. public, Hollywood, and the media were not pleased when your mother moved to Italy. Why did they all turn against her?

One problem with fame is that you can be torn down by the same people who build you up. Mama played the "good girl" in many of her films and was perceived as a vulnerable,

Pia Lindström and her father, Petter, circa 1950. (Photograph courtesy of Pia Lindström.)

natural, country beauty, without pretense, not as a seductive vamp who would betray her husband. She was publicized as a good mother and happily married woman with lots of photo layouts at home, posing as a simple Swedish girl. My mother played a nun and a saint in the movies, and received accolades from religious groups. Her fans held her in high regard. She was one of the most admired actresses by the public, and not thought to be a vamp or a seductress. She never wore makeup or sexy clothes. When she became pregnant by Roberto Rossellini, while married to my father, it was a time when that behavior was thought to be highly improper. It was perceived as being personally disloyal and professionally snubbing Hollywood when she left the United States to have an Italian film career and another family. Her fans were shocked when she left my father and her career in Hollywood to move to Italy and make Italian movies.

Despite that, she went on to win a third Oscar for her somewhat brief appearance in *Murder on the Orient Express* (1974). Did that surprise her?

She had already made *Anastasia* [1956] and been received back into the

Hollywood fraternity, but was surprised by that third Oscar. I suspect that was Hollywood doing a "kiss and make up": "We raised you up, knocked you down, then let you come back — not quite as big as you were, but we still love you!"

What happened to her Oscars?

Isabella and Ingrid each had one, but they are now with the Ingrid Bergman Collection at Wesleyan University. I have the other one sitting on my bookcase — I rather like looking at it!

Which of her films do you remember seeing first?

I was too young and not allowed to go to the movies. So besides seeing *The Bells of St. Mary's*, which was considered appropriate, and playing a part as an extra in *Joan of Arc* [1948], I saw my mother at home and not in the movies. As a six- and seven-year-old, I was at home or at school, except going to Beverly Hills to see Saturday afternoon cartoons. I didn't see *Casablanca* [1942] until I was much older. I once took a screenwriting class and they used *Casablanca* as the "text" on how to write a screenplay. So I have looked at every frame now.

What were her thoughts about *Casablanca*?

Unlike other films from that period, *Casablanca* has held up well over the years, but I don't think she thought it was her best work. She was disappointed that so many people would remember her for that one film and focused on it so much rather than her other great films such as *Notorious* [1946]. She said she did not have a pleasant experience making it. It is well known that they didn't have a finished script and changed writers in the middle of shooting. For instance, my mother asked the director, Michael Curtiz, who she was supposed to be in love with, Humphrey Bogart or Paul Henreid? He didn't know then, so he told her to "play it in the middle." For an actor, that was not a lot of help. The audience didn't know who she was going to end up with until the very end — and neither did she! Bogart didn't want to do the film and his wife was in his trailer, mad with him throughout the filming. And Paul Henreid hated wearing the white suit — anyone trying to escape from the Nazis is hardly likely to parade around wearing a white suit, he said! So it was not a particularly happy experience and she was never friends with any of the cast. She never worked with Curtiz again. As for Bogart, she had no connection with him at all. She said, "I kissed him, but I never knew him." Their on-screen "chemistry" was all acting.

Who was her favorite director?

She loved Hitchcock; the two were crazy about each other and he was a close friend of my mother's. I knew him personally, too, and was at his home in Beverly Hills many times. He was the only person I ever knew who had a walk-in refrigerator! He was a charming person, very funny, with a droll sense of humor. But he also had a little bit of a nasty, sarcastic streak that I liked! I remember when I had to interview him, it was very strange because I tried to act as a professional interviewer and not as a person he had known as a child.

Do you have a favorite Ingrid Bergman movie?
    I like Ingmar Bergman's *Autumn Sonata* [1978] for personal reasons. Not because she looked so beautiful in this one — she was older — but because I thought it addressed a theme that runs through many lives. The story is about a mother who has a musical gift, and leaves her daughter to pursue her career. The central question is: if you have an exceptional gift, do you use it and go where that talent takes you? Or, do you stay at home and nurse your children through chickenpox and take them to baseball games? Well, the movie is set in Sweden, so I guess you would be taking them skiing! The story comes from my mother's life, and also director Ingmar Bergman's. He had been married to a musician who traveled to concerts and, by necessity, had to leave her children. I find it a fascinating film because the dialogue comes out of their own personal experiences and applies to everyone who faces that dilemma, man or woman.

Your mother's autobiography was published just before she died. What did you think of it?
    I didn't think much of it because I didn't hear her voice. I didn't hear the intonation in the words or the rhythm of her speech. It just didn't sound like her. I mostly heard the co-author's voice. The only section that I really heard her was in the chapter where she talked about the surgery that Isabella had to undergo for scoliosis when she was 13. I think she had to write that herself because another writer couldn't possibly know what a mother feels like when a child has to go through such an ordeal. And, of course, like anyone who writes an autobiography, it's her interpretation of her life.

You've been in front of the camera, too, as a news anchorwoman, but mostly as a theater and arts critic for various networks. Actors don't have a great love for critics, so how did she feel about you working as a critic?
    I remember she was shocked when she found out. "You're going to be a critic?" she asked. I'm not sure any actor would want their child to become a critic. But it was okay. I've interviewed many actors over the years and she once asked me, "How do you know what to ask people?" I thought that was

a strange question, but then I realized as an actor she was always given the prepared words to memorize. We laughed about that and I told her I just listened to what the other person was saying and hoped a question would come.

Did being Ingrid Bergman's daughter help your career?

People are curious, so it may have helped in the beginning to get a "look-see." But I don't think anyone hires you for 20 or 30 years because you had a famous mother. And there are just as many people who don't like the idea of hiring someone known for having a famous parent. It goes both ways. I remember being told by someone that a news director didn't hire "celebrities." So I was not going to be hired. I was hardly a celebrity myself, just starting out, trying to get a job. There can be a reverse reaction — like nepotism, or someone has an unfair advantage by having a well-known parent. I remember working in a research department at UNESCO and a woman said to me, "What are you doing here, just taking a job away from someone who needs it?" Believe me, I needed it — I needed to work. But the perception was that I was an interloper and just playing around.

In her later years, when the two of you spent more time together, did she reflect on her life?

She didn't talk about the past or the movies she had made, nor did she act like a star. In fact, she liked to clean her house a lot. She never cooked — but loved to clean! When she came to visit, we talked about her health, my career, and her grandchildren. She was a grandmother, and that's what grandmothers do! I never asked her questions like, "What was Cary Grant like?" Besides, I met him! Unfortunately, it was difficult for us to go out in public. If we tried to go shopping, there would be photographers and people pointing and staring when they recognized her. It was uncomfortable. She didn't want to ever appear rude, but we learned to look past the stares and focus on our conversation. If we did go out to a restaurant, we would try to get a secluded table. People are imprisoned by fame. It was daunting as a child, but as I got older I learned to tune out the stares and comments, as she did.

Pia Lindström on Ingrid Bergman. Telephone interview on 12/7/10. Pia Lindström's personal website is www.pialindstrom.com; it contains photos of her mother and family. The official Ingrid Bergman website is www.ingridbergman.com.

15

Paul and Joan Howard on Moe Howard

Physical comedy in early film was often focused on the potential for personal injury, wanton destruction, and perilous situations. It was skillfully executed by the likes of Charlie Chaplin, Buster Keaton, Harold Lloyd, and Laurel & Hardy. But the masters of Hollywood madcap mayhem were undoubtedly The Three Stooges, a trio of turmoil who could flatten their surroundings faster than a professional demolition team. One constant throughout their long film career was Moe Howard (1897–1975), who first appeared on-screen as a Stooge in Soup to Nuts *(1930). With his brothers, Curly or Shemp Howard (or their later replacements), as well as Stooge regular Larry Fine, Moe would go on to appear in 190 shorts* for which the Stooges are best known. *However, the original leader of the gang was vaudeville comedian Ted Healy, who dealt out the punishment to the others. When Healy departed for a solo career, Moe inherited the role of head Stooge in 1933, and for some 30 years was the self-appointed, short-tempered boss of the team. Off-screen, Moe was gentle and quiet. With Helen, his wife of almost 50 years, he had two children, Joan and Paul, who were raised (literally!) with three Stooges for their father and uncles.*

What are your earliest memories of your father performing?

JOAN: I can recall going to see the Stooges' early films, but I preferred the live performances, which were very exciting for me. I have vivid memories of seeing my father on-stage, when I was around eight, while he was doing live shows for vaudeville. He would sit me in the front row, and there was a lot of slapping and hitting going on. What really stood out in my mind was that when he would slap Curly on the face, saliva would fly out of his mouth. After the show, Curly would complain: "Hit me harder so they can hear it in the back row!"

Father and son fool around, 1945. Paul was about 12 years old. The box seen here came from a side-line business run by Moe and a partner. They manufactured, right after World War II, the first "TV table." While the business didn't last long, the concept is still being used today. (Photograph courtesy of Paul Howard.)

PAUL: The very first time I saw the Stooges perform, I must have been about three or four years old, and remember it very clearly. I was in the front of the theater, sitting on my mother's lap looking up on the stage, and a voice introduced them: "Ladies and gentlemen — The Three Stooges!" Then the music began, and my father entered on one side of the stage and Curly came in from the other side with a cigar in his mouth. I don't remember where Larry was. They began to kind of dance together. Then "Pow!" — they smashed right into each other's bellies and faces. At the same time, a big bass drum produced the sound effect as they ricocheted off each other and I noticed Curly's cigar was just flattened against his face. To a four-year-old, it was startling to see my father do such a wacky routine in front of an audience.

What did your paternal grandparents think about your father and uncles going into show business?

JOAN: My grandmother thought show business was a curse. She was from

Lithuania and was very European. She went into real estate and did well until the depression came. When she finally visited a theater to watch the boys perform in an early movie, I don't think she realized the movies weren't real. I remember she was watching one scene with Ted Healy — he was really beating up on the boys — but thinking it was real. She waved the umbrella in her hand and ran up to the front row and began banging on the screen with the umbrella! My grandfather was actually in one of their films. He wanted to see what his sons did, so they took him to the set one day and used him in a scene as an extra in *Disorder in the Court* [1936].

Growing up with a father and two uncles who were Stooges must have been interesting. What did your friends think about your family?

JOAN: I don't think I realized my dad's fame until the press started asking me about him in my later life. Then I realized my life had not been ordinary. Moe was just my dad, and Curly and Shemp were my uncles. You just live your life and don't think about it being all that different. When I was a kid, girls didn't really like that kind of physical comedy at all, so I was actually a little hesitant about telling my friends what my father did because I knew what their reaction would be. They would say things like, "Oh, it's silly and stupid" or "I don't like that kind of comedy." I never lied about what my dad did, I would just be evasive. But my brother would actually lie!

PAUL: That's true! If anybody asked me what my father did for a living, I'd say he was a meter reader for the Pacific Gas and Electric Company! To me, that was a normal job for a typical father. All my young friends had "normal" dads. One owned a furniture store, another was a doctor, and one was an electrician on the railroad. So to me, they were the sort of things a father should be doing. It's hard to explain, but I guess I was just wired that way for some reason. I also worried about whether kids came over to our house to see me or to meet my famous father. So I was just insecure on that level. It lasted from when I was a little kid in elementary school until I was in my twenties when I eventually realized it was a rather non-productive attitude. Now, I celebrate my family connection to The Three Stooges. I go to fan club meetings, and take along my family films and slides and tell stories about growing up with Moe, Shemp, Curly, and Larry. The fans really appreciate it and I'm thrilled when I see them enjoying it.

Did Moe, Curly and Shemp's families spend much time together?

JOAN: I was born in Brooklyn, in 1927, and we lived there for about six months. During the first few years, Dad was working with Shemp, so our families traveled together until I was of school age, about six. At that point, we moved to California, and later built a beautiful home at Toluca Lake in

1940. So apart from those early years, the families were not together socially a whole lot, except for special events, such as weddings and Christmas. Curly was very shy socially and would come over to visit occasionally. He loved to swim and dive in our pool, but there wasn't too much conversation. I didn't see any of them behave like their screen characters around our home. I like to tell people that we ate our pies, we didn't throw them! Dad enjoyed being with people, but he was quite reserved. He rarely socialized with people from the movie business. His friends were my mother's friends, and they were doctors, judges, and people from those types of professions. Shemp, however, loved to throw parties and he did hang out with people from the entertainment industry. Larry enjoyed his friends and co-workers, and his wife loved to do Christmas and would have a yearly open house.

PAUL: Rarely did the brothers goof around at home when they got together. But when my dad pulled out his movie camera, Curly could be quite entertaining. I remember one home movie where he is on the end of a diving board in our swimming pool. He dropped to the diving board and landed on his butt, then went up in the air and landed right on his face in the water. Then he did this outrageous stroke to get to the side of the pool. It was typical Curly. So whether he was on land or water, my Uncle Curly could be an outrageously funny person.

Moe, Curly, and Shemp weren't the brothers' real names. What did they call each other in private?

JOAN: Curly's real name was Jerome. But because he was the baby of the family, the brothers all called him Babe. I used to call him Uncle Babe. Shemp's real name was Samuel. His mother had a very strong European accent so when she said, "Sam," it came out like "Samps." That, of course, sounded like Shemp to everyone, so that's what we called him. Moe's birth name was Moses, but everyone always called him Moe.

There were other brothers; did they do any acting?

JOAN: No. The oldest brother, Irving, died young, then came Jack. Neither of them had any interest in acting, and both of them became Metropolitan Life Insurance salesmen. Being the youngest, Curly got a chance to watch Moe and Shemp act and that looked really exciting to him. He was not a very good student at school, and decided acting would be the best thing for a career.

Did Moe want either of you to get into acting?

PAUL: Dad wanted me to go into films, but I wanted to try and be successful on my own. Once he knew that I was pretty firm in the direction I wanted to go, it was fine with him. His bottom line was as long as I am happy and successful, that was what counted. So I knew I didn't want to go into show business. I looked into commercial art and became an advertising agency art director in Manhattan. Around 2000, I decided I'd rather sell smiles instead of soap, and now have a career as an artist drawing caricatures of people. I don't sell myself as the "son of Moe," but people sometimes realize who I am from my website as I have a small dedication there to my father.

JOAN: I had small roles in about ten films, but was always very afraid I would forget my lines. Dad had a fabulous memory. Sadly, I didn't inherit that from him! My husband was Norman Maurer, a successful writer/producer/director, and in the '60s he wrote and produced several of the Stooges feature motion pictures. I was my husband's secretary for many years and I loved doing research for his projects. After Dad died, I found a great deal of Stooges memorabilia in the attic. I realized their fans would love to see these vintage items, so I put it together in several books that I wrote over the years. I like to think I've been a liaison between my dad and the fans.

Joan, you were actually in one of the Stooges shorts, *Pop Goes the Easel*, in 1935. Do you remember much about it?

It was a small role, but exciting and fun. I was one of the girls playing hopscotch. The other girl was Phyllis Fine, Larry's daughter, who was three years younger than me. I had been in a few other films and thought I was a "big shot" by showing Phyllis how things were done! I actually don't remember going to any of the other sets, although there is a photo of me taken during a photo session. Columbia had a ranch with buildings designed to look like a New York City street, and I always thought that was where this was filmed. In 2008, a fan, Jim Pauley, contacted me because he had found the locations for many of the Stooges' films — the exact spots where they were shot. He said the scene was filmed at a building on Larchmont Boulevard, not far from Columbia, which was used by many studios during the '30s. I met Jim and he took me to the exact spot. He had a laptop with a photo of the scene on the screen and it matched perfectly, so that was definitely the place.

What other films did you appear in?

JOAN: I had small roles in films with Shirley Temple and Humphrey Bogart. The Bogart film, *Swing Your Lady* [1938], was probably the only bad film he was in, but it wasn't my fault! In fact, I didn't have any screen time with him. Even though I've said I have a terrible memory, to this day I can still recall my two lines. I was probably so petrified I'd forget them, that I engraved them in my head.

Did any of the other Stooges resent Moe being the leader?

JOAN: There wasn't really any professional jealousy. My dad just took the leadership role from day one. There was a period early on when Shemp's wife was a little annoyed over Dad being the leader. That was when they were with Ted Healy. But then Shemp left. Larry often had a smaller role in the movies, but I don't think he resented that. He really enjoyed life — much more than my father did. Larry was a will-o-the-wisp and he knew how to relax and enjoy his success. Even on the set he was funny and socialized with the stagehands who were around him. My dad was much more private and worried about things. He was quite reserved off-screen and was quite a serious person. On the set, he would always be thinking about the next scene and how he could improve it.

What was Moe like at home?

PAUL: He was a very protective father when I was young. When I started to walk, he would tape soft sponges to all the sharp furniture corners in the rooms to keep me from hitting my head if I fell. Later, when I was about four years old and before I had learned to swim, he built a swimming pool at our house. In a corner of the shallow end he built a six-foot-by-four-foot slatted, wooden "crib" which was immersed in about six inches of water. I could splash around in it, on a hot summer day, and Dad could turn his back and weed in his gardens without worrying about me drowning. If the Stooges had been the Three Little Pigs, my dad would have been the practical pig who built his house out of bricks! He was a very sensible and cautious person in real life, not at all like his crazy, angry screen character. But he was impatient and did worry a lot. I would see him sitting at his desk at home in the early evening going over his check book and muttering to himself. He would worry about the act and whether or not their contract with Columbia would be renewed each year. Curly and Larry didn't have any interest in that aspect of their careers, so my dad was a worrier for all three of them.

Was family life for the Howard clan pretty normal?

PAUL: Most of the time it was like any other American home. You would often find my dad just working in the backyard. He created wonderful vegetable and flower gardens, and when he was on his hands and knees in the garden he was in heaven. Our families didn't go out a lot as a group. Usually when we got together, it would be in our backyard on a Sunday. My parents did have a favorite Italian restaurant, Mateo's in Beverly Hills, which they went to regularly. When I was older, I remember coming to town on business and we went to this place. The owner greeted my mother and gave her a big hug and he slapped my dad on the back, then sat down to eat with us. My father asked him if he knew how to make Chicken Cacciatore, hunter's style. He said, "No, Moe, how do you do that?" Dad began to explain the recipe, but Matty, the owner, interrupted my dad, turned to my mother, and asked her if he could "borrow" him for a few minutes and the two of them disappeared into the kitchen. About 20 minutes later they returned with the finished dish and we ate it. A few months later, we all went back to the same restaurant again. As we were perusing the menu, my parents' mouths dropped open. There on the menu was dad's recipe, now dubbed "Chicken à la Moe!"

What was Curly's life like?

JOAN: Curly often acted just like a big kid and he liked women, spending money, and drinking. Years ago, I came across a letter from my father. He wrote something like "Jerry"— he was called Jerry then —"is behaving himself." The reference made him sound childlike, like a mischievous kid, which he was in many ways. Dad was really a father to Curly. His intentions were good because he just wanted Curly to have a good life.

PAUL: Dad did treat Curly like both a brother and a son, and did try to look after him. A lot of Curly's life wasn't happy. But he was terrific to me. He'd say, "How ya doin', Paulie boy?" I remember he once gave me a rifle and I was thrilled. But my dad, always trying to protect me from harm, quickly had the rifle's firing pin sawed off. Speaking of guns, you may have noticed that Curly always walks with a slight limp in the films. When Dad and his brothers were in their teens, they spent the warm months on a 110-acre farm, in Upstate New York, during World War I. One day, when Curly was carelessly handling a rifle, it accidentally discharged, and the bullet struck his lower ankle. He refused to have it fixed properly. As a result, he had the limp all his life.

What is the story of the "Moe Checks"?

PAUL: Joan was going through the attic one day back in the '80s and found boxes with thousands of canceled checks our dad had written and saved. When Joan's husband saw them he said, "Wow! And every check, a Moe autograph!" Hearing that, Joan got an idea. She went to *Rolling Stone* magazine and wrote an ad entitled "An Open Letter to Three Stooges Fans From Moe's Daughter." In the ad, she shared that her dad died of lung cancer due to smoking. And for every $10 contributed she would send the donor a Moe-Check and donate the money to The American Cancer Society. Within a few months she had generated over $40,000 and donated the money to the City of Hope Medical Center, in Los Angeles. Nowadays, the checks sell for $200 to $1,000. I kept a few of them, but it was wonderful they could be used for such a good cause. Both Helen and Moe died of cancer. I had my bout, too, and I'd like to believe that our donation to the city of Hope — through the Moe checks — could possibly have saved my life.

Did Moe ever want to do serious roles?

JOAN: He did, from the beginning of his career. Near the end of his life he actually did one straight role as a cab driver in *Space Master X-7* [1958] which my husband produced. As a child actor, dad — using his real name of Harry Moses Horwitz — made his screen debut in *We Must Do Our Best* [1909].

How did Moe get along with Jules White, who directed many of The Three Stooges Columbia shorts?

JOAN: Jules actually lived just around the corner from my parents' home. But I don't think my dad was all that happy with him. Dad pretty much knew his own character and how it should be represented on screen. Jules was very overbearing as a director and was always telling my dad how to move and how to react, and I think Dad resented that. With Jules, if something was really violent he loved it, but gratuitous violence was something my dad didn't care for.

Of course, there was a lot of comic violence in their films. Did the Stooges suffer any serious injuries during filming?

JOAN: Well, of course, all the hammers, wrenches, and tools they used to hit with were made of rubber. The sound effects were just amazing and matched the action perfectly. With the famous eye poke, Dad would hit them right over the eyebrows. It was like a snake strike, it was so fast. Occasionally, one of them would get gunk in the eyes when they got a pie in the face. The dark-colored pies that were supposed to be something like blueberries actually contained lamp black [soot] and it could be irritating if it got in the eye. In one film, they had worked out a scene where Larry was supposed to get hit in the forehead with a quill pen. The point was supposed to go into a protected area on his head. But it missed and the pen ended up sticking right out of his forehead. I imagine that didn't feel too good! Then, another time, Dad was climbing on to a table which was supposed to break when he fell on it. A special-effects man had cut the table so that when he hit, the table would easily break in two. But he didn't cut it deep enough. The table didn't break, but Dad broke a rib.

How much did Moe contribute to the production side of The Three Stooges films?

JOAN: When they began to work for Columbia [in 1934], they did eight shorts a year. They also worked for 12 weeks a year in vaudeville. Dad got

Pick out the dummies in this photograph taken in 1982 at the Hollywood Wax Museum with wax figures of the Stooges. Gary Owens is at the far left. Joan Howard is at the far right; to her left is her son, Jeffrey Scott. (Photograph courtesy of Joan Howard.)

into writing and the creative part of it all. I don't think Larry or Curly did much of that as they were just having a good time. Dad loved what he was doing and wanted each performance to come out perfect.

How did they come to use "Three Blind Mice" as the theme music to the shorts?

JOAN: I think it was one of the pieces the music department had that was in the public domain so the company wouldn't have to pay for it!

Were any props from their old films saved?

JOAN: Not many. The only thing I have is a clapper board that was used on one of the films. Although it's not from a film, one interesting piece I have is a weather vane of The Three Stooges made out of wrought iron. It's a silhouette of the Stooges doing their "stuff" and has been on my house for about 50 years. It shows my dad poking Curly and Larry, and my mother had it made for Dad back in the '30s or '40s.

PAUL: I, personally, have no props. However, my dad had a fondness for collecting trinkets that conformed to a frog theme. Drawings, a magnifier, paper weights, ceramics, etc. I still have a few of these frog icons.

There's plenty of Three Stooges memorabilia on display in a Pennsylvania museum called The Stoogeum. Have you been there?

JOAN: I've been to The Three Stooges conventions in Philadelphia several times and visited the nearby Stoogeum, which is fabulous. The man who put it together, Gary Lassin, is related to Larry by marriage. He had a huge collection of Stooges-related items and decided to build this museum for his collection, and did it with such great taste. I heard that even people from Disney went to see it to get ideas for setting up a new museum they were working on.

Any thoughts on Joe Besser and Joe DeDita, the later replacements for Curly and Shemp?

JOAN: I've seen all the Curly shorts, because that was during my childhood, but I haven't seen all the Shemp ones because I was raising my family at the time. I've probably only seen a half dozen of them. So Curly is still my favorite "other Stooge." Joe Besser didn't allow Moe to hit him and that changed the whole feel of the comedy in his films. It really messed up their timing. Joe DeRita had good comedic qualities and I liked him, but many of the fans didn't care for him.

PAUL: I didn't know Joe Besser. I was busy in college, in my separate world, at the time. Joe DeRita was a humorous, pleasant man. Aside from a pleasant chat now and then, I didn't get to know him well. I soon moved to New York and was away from the Stooges scene.

Shemp, Curly, and Larry all had children. What became of them?

JOAN: Shemp had a son, Mort, who died in his early forties from a form of blood cancer. Shemp's wife always felt chemicals caused their son's illness. He loved to play golf and chew his fingernails. Mort's wife, Geri, felt he could have picked up chemicals that were sprayed on the grass. He also owned several gas stations and was around a lot of petroleum products. I don't know if that's correct, but that's what Shemp's wife and daughter-in-law thought. Larry had a son who was killed in a car crash in his thirties. Larry's daughter, Phyllis, was a dear friend of mine. She died in 1989. Larry's wife was a heavy drinker, by the way, but Larry barely touched it. Curly was married several times, and his early marriages were not happy. One of his daughters lives on the West Coast; the other on the East Coast. The two never met until the '80s, ironically at a Three Stooges convention.

What about your mother, Helen. Did she support your father's career?

JOAN: My mother always wanted to go on a trip to Europe, but Dad keep telling her "after we finish the next short." Well, that went on for 190 films! But my mother was very supportive of his work. She was a wonderful foil for him. He was very nervous and uptight, and worried all the time, whereas she had a way of laughing things off. He was ready to quit after Curly died, and then again after Shemp died. But she encouraged him to continue because she realized he would not be happy if he gave up acting. Finally, in 1955, they did take that trip — not only to Europe, but around the world.

Do you think there is much interest in the Stooges now?

PAUL: I still get letters almost every day from Three Stooges fans. I remember getting an email from a soldier who had returned from Iraq. He told me how he and his fellow troopers watched the Stooges regularly while preparing to go on missions and how their "make-believe mayhem" kept the soldiers sane. So it's wonderful to know that my dad, uncles, Larry, and the others still make the world laugh, so many years after their passing.

Paul and Joan Howard on Moe Howard. Paul: Telephone interview on 6/14/10; Joan: Telephone interview on 6/4/10. Paul Howard's personal website is www.caricatures-bypaul.com and contains information about his father. The official Three Stooges website is www.threestooges.com.

16

Denise Loder–DeLuca on Hedy Lamarr

Although she only appeared in about two dozen Hollywood produc-
tions, starting with Algiers *in 1938, and ending just 20 years later with*
The Female Animal, *Hedy Lamarr (1914–2000) needs little introduction*
to fans of classic film. Her instantly recognizable picture-perfect face dazzled
Hollywood after appearing in several European films as Hedwig Kiesler,
her birth name from her native Austria. While she never acquired the leg-
endary status of a Garbo, her stunning screen persona, very respectable acting
ability, and mild Austrian accent produced a legion of devoted admirers
who christened her "The Most Beautiful Woman in the World." Just ask
Victor Mature's character in Samson and Delilah *(1949), who was*
enslaved—and shaved—by her allure.

For decades, "Hedy Lamarr" has also been the answer to surely one of
the oddest Hollywood trivia questions of all time: "Which actress had a U.S.
patent for a method of blocking enemy torpedoes during World War II?"

Though she had no formal training in science or electronics, young
Hedy had a keen mind. From her first marriage in 1933 to Fritz Mandl,
an Austrian arms manufacturer, she developed an interest and knowledge
of weapons, as well as a hatred of the Nazis. Later, after moving to America
and divorcing Mandl, she befriended American musician George Antheil,
in 1940. Antheil had lived in Europe, too, before returning to the U.S. to
become a film composer and columnist for Esquire *magazine in the '30s,*
and had an equal dislike of Hitler and Mussolini's goal of world domination.
The unlikely partnering of Lamarr, an actress, and Antheil, a composer,
yielded U.S. patent No. 2,292,367 for a "Secret Communication System"
which the pair believed could help make U.S. guided munitions immune
from enemy jamming by employing a system of constantly changing radio
frequencies ("frequency hopping"). Similar patents had been issued to others
earlier, but the technology to put their idea into practice wasn't available

in the 1940s, so the U.S. government buried the idea. It reemerged 20 years later and was used successfully in U.S. Navy torpedo guidance systems. After another two decades, the concept was applied to commercial radio and became the basis for "spread-spectrum broadcast communications technologies" used today in such familiar applications as wireless Internet, cell phones, and defense satellites.

Married six times, Lamarr had two children (Denise and John) with her third husband, actor John Loder. Daughter Denise Loder-DeLuca lives in Seattle and acknowledges her famous mother as not only as a fine classic actress, but as an important inventor.

Some early Hedy Lamarr biographies were mostly panned as being inaccurate and sensationalistic. It must be tough to read that stuff.

I've been dealing with this all my life, and I've never gotten used to it. For instance, with the book *Ecstasy and Me*, she trusted her business manager and signed a release as co-author to allow it to be published. But it was full of lies and she absolutely hated it — particularly all the sexual references. I remember Mom telling me it wasn't worth reading, so I never did. She said, "Why would I write a book like that and dedicate it to my children?" She has been mentioned many times in general books and articles about Hollywood and actors. There was a 2009 *Vogue* article about her which I thought was really insulting and full of factual errors. I wrote a letter to the editor defending Mom, never thinking they would publish it, but they did. Probably the best book about her is *The Films of Hedy Lamarr*. It's a beautiful book filled with photographs, although out of print now. In 2010, Stephen Shearer's book, *Beautiful: The Life of Hedy Lamarr* was released. He consulted with me, visited me, and I gave him photos to use. It is an honest book about my mother's life, yet parts of it were difficult for me to relive.

Is it true that she never liked the way Americans pronounced her name?

I don't know about that. But I think with an Austrian accent her name sounded more like "Hay-dee," and with an American accent like "Heddy."

Actresses of her day copied your mother's look, such as the way she parted her hair down the middle. That must have been flattering?

Not only actresses, a lot of other women, too! But that's not uncommon. Like Jennifer Aniston — everyone wanted her haircut when she was on *Friends*.

And Bette Davis was your godmother?

Yes, but I don't think I ever saw her again after the christening when I was a baby. She would have been a trip to hang out with!

What about the oft-repeated story that Hedy Lamarr met or knew Hitler. Did she really meet him?

No, but she did talk about meeting other influential people, such as Edith Piaf and Jack Kennedy. She admired people who had talent, charm and intellect.

Hedy Lamarr and daughter Denise, circa 1950. (Photograph courtesy of Denise Loder-DeLuca.)

So growing up, was the house full of movie stars?

Well, she was working a lot so we were sent to boarding schools, which I didn't like at all. But at home, she was more into the arts than movie-star hype. The people who came to our home from the entertainment world were more likely to be musicians, composers, or artists, than actors. It was those creative people she admired and surrounded herself with. I remember one day when we were living in Texas she made us come home from school to have lunch with a musician. It turned out to be conductor Leopold Stokowski. She thought it was important for us to meet creative people like that. Well, I wasn't impressed at the time — being dragged out of school to meet some old composer! But now I can look back and appreciate it.

Is it true that the Hollywood Wax Museum removed the "Hedy Lamarr" figure?

Yes. My brother is in the 2004 documentary movie about my mother, *Calling Hedy Lamarr*, and actually visited the museum to look for her. But they had just taken her down. I guess they have to keep up with the times. Honestly, most young people would probably say, "Hedy Lamarr — who's that?"

Robert Redford's daughter, Amy, was actually planning to make a biopic of your mom at one time. Do you know what the focus of the story would have been?

Yes, it was in the works for a while. They consulted me and my brother on and off for a couple of years. The film would have actually focused on the years of her invention, which was before I was born. So it would have looked at the years during World War II when she actually came up with the invention, then gets turned down by the U.S. government, and how it all came about. Instead of her whole life, they were planning to focus on that aspect of it and it's definitely an interesting story. So, hopefully, a movie about her will come out some time, so that people will finally know that her contribution to science and technology will outlive any of her movies. It's so much more important.

That film seems to be on hold indefinitely. Who would you like to see play your mother if a film of her life is ever produced?

I don't want to mention any names. But, obviously, someone who could portray her intelligence and amazing screen presence.

Given her interesting life, why do you think a feature film about Hedy Lamarr wasn't made years ago?

People today just don't have that much interest in stars from the '30s and '40s. Just like I don't know who all the silent screen stars were, even though they were huge in their day, most young people probably don't know who she was, unless they're film buffs.

Did she talk much about her invention?

When I was young, she would tell us about this anti-missile device she had invented. But you know, I barely believed her. I'd say, "Yeah, right, Mom!" like any kid probably would. Then, when I was an adult, a professor sent me a copy of a science magazine that had her on the cover and had an article about what she had done. So I called her and said, "So you really *did* invent that!" She said, "I've been telling you that for years." Very few people really knew what she had done. When she died, the articles written about her mentioned it, and it was really the first time the press had talked about it.

Did she consider the invention one of the major achievements of her life?

The achievement she was most proud of was having children. I'm not sure how much the invention or the movies meant to her. I never really asked. When it's your parents, you don't think like a reporter would and ask that sort of question. We usually talked about normal things, like any mother and daughter. I'm sure she was proud of all her accomplishments, we just never talked about them a lot. But it was an important invention. I have a book of famous inventors on my coffee table. They are mostly elderly men; then there's my glamorous mother among them!

Hedy Lamarr and daughter Denise, circa 1950. (Photograph courtesy of Denise Loder-DeLuca.)

But without a background in science, how could she really comprehend the technology she was proposing?

She came up with the idea and her partner, George Antheil, figured out how to do it. For her, it was more of a case of logical thinking. She was very smart and had learned a lot about weapons from her first husband. It reminds me of the American Indian Code Talkers during World War I. The Choctaws were enlisted to use their native language as code to send messages, but the Germans had no way of understanding it. I don't know a lot about the technology, but Mom's invention changed the frequencies of the signals used in radio transmissions to control torpedoes, and the enemy couldn't understand the code.

Is it true that your mother and Antheil never made any money from their idea?

Nothing, not a penny. The government didn't use it and then the copyright expired and she never extended it. Her original idea was simply to produce a piece of technology that would help the war effort during World War II.

A lot of actors worked to support the government during the Second World War. Aside from her invention, did she do anything else?

She made millions of dollars during the war effort for various patriotic foundations, such as the War Bond tours. She also worked at the Hollywood Canteen where she served the G.I.s who were heading off overseas. In fact, I believe that's where my mother and father met.

She was one of the most photographed actors of her day. What are some of your favorite images of her?

There's a picture of her on the cover of a 1997 magazine, *Invention & Technology*, that I love and have framed. It's a gorgeous photo of her with the headline "Hedy Lamarr, Munitions Inventor." I also like my own "Hedy paintings" that capture her glamour. My favorite is the one with a yellow peasant blouse, where she has a white flower in her hair from *Tortilla Flat* [1942]. I just love that one. I still have the original painting, and that's a popular one with the reproductions I sell.

Who owns the rights to her image?

I own the rights to her name and image and the official website is hedylamarr.com run by CMG Worldwide who maintains the site. My brother, John, also has a site, hedylamarr.org.

Do you sell many of your paintings of her?

I don't really promote my art, but there is a link to it on the website. I've sold some through the website and at various art showings. But during the recession that started in 2007 or 2008, I don't think a lot of art was flying out of galleries!

What is your background in art?

I've been painting all my life, and Mom was an artist, too. When I was little, she framed everything I drew. I majored in art at UC Berkeley, and was an art teacher K through six for a year in Seattle. Then I became a regional training make-up artist in the cosmetic division for Nordstrom, where I worked for 28 years. After retiring, I went back to doing what I always wanted to do — painting canvases, not people's faces! Mom died two weeks after I retired, so she never got to see any of my paintings of her.

She is often quoted as saying her beauty was a curse. Did she really say that?

I have heard that she said that, and she probably did. It's hard to imagine being so well known for your looks all your life, then having to face growing old. For most women it's tough, but to be known as the most beautiful woman in the world — that's a lot of pressure.

She certainly had a presence on the screen. It's noticeable, for instance, in Boom Town (*1940*) with Clark Gable and Spencer Tracy. And in her last film, The Female Animal (1958), she was in her forties but still looked pretty stunning!

Yes, she doesn't come on until half way through *Boom Town* and when she does, the whole film picks up. Even in her eighties she was always super sheik. We were once out in New York when she was in her late seventies and she was wearing a scarf, sunglasses, cool jeans and a beautiful coat. People didn't know who she was, but they would come up to her and ask, "Who are you? You must be *somebody!*" She just had a natural flare about her that people noticed — a persona like Sophia Loren — not just a beauty but a presence that was spectacular. And she had that wonderful, soft, Austrian accent.

Was there a resemblance between the two of you?

I remember some people once picking me up at the airport — they knew my mother, but had never met me. I had a shawl and threw it over my shoulder. One of them said that the minute I did that, he knew I was Hedy's daughter. Some people actually guessed that I was her daughter without knowing anything about me. In fact, my husband did, just from looking at me. I think I have her eyes, hair, and some of her mannerisms. Now that I'm older, I think I'm aging quite similarly to her.

You actually have an extremely youthful voice. I mean, you really sound like you're in your twenties!

You know what? Mom sounded very young right up until the end, so we both have that in common. I'm pretty young at heart, too.

She didn't appear in many television shows, did she?

Back then, the big stars just didn't do a lot of TV. But she did make several guest appearances on variety shows, like *The Steve Allen Show*, and game shows like *What's My Line?*

According to the author of *The Films of Hedy Lamarr*, her favorite leading men were Jimmy Stewart and Clark Cable, but she found Spencer Tracy an ordeal to work with. Do you remember her talking about her favorite co-stars or what her favorite movie or director was?

I really have no memory of conversations about her favorite actors. But *H.M. Pulham, Esq.* [1941] was her favorite film and I think DeMille, who directed *Samson and Delilah*, was probably her favorite director because he was so interesting.

So do you have a favorite Hedy Lamarr film? And how do you feel today when watching her films?

My favorite Hedy film is *Come Live with Me* [1941], with Jimmy Stewart. I'm really proud of her films. She had more than just beauty — she had class, intelligence, and charm — and the camera loved her.

Denise Loder-DeLuca on Hedy Lamarr. Telephone interview on 1/22/10. A shorter version appeared in *Films of the Golden Age*, Spring 2010. Lamarr's daughter, Denise Loder-DeLuca, has a website about her mother: www.hedylamarr.com.

17

Kiki Ebsen on Buddy Ebsen

Like many actors who starred in a popular television series, Buddy Ebsen (1908–2003) is yet another who will forever be associated with one role: the country bumpkin turned millionaire, Jed Clampett, who starred in 274 episodes of The Beverly Hillbillies *which ran for nine seasons from 1962 to 1971. Or maybe two roles: Ebsen got his second series wind a decade later playing the milk-slurping private eye Barnaby Jones for another impressive eight seasons. Like so many actors of the classic film period, his roots were in vaudeville. Gradually, the six-foot-three Ebsen inched his way into small film roles in the 1930s, often as a tap dancer, and worked up to mostly supporting or co-star roles in many of his 30 or so movies. Born and raised in Illinois, the ten-year-old Ebsen moved with his family to Florida, where he later briefly attended college before pursuing acting. He was married three times and had seven children. The youngest of six daughters, Kiki Ebsen is a successful musician and invites you to "set a spell" with a plate of "vittles" as she shares fond memories of her father.*

How did your father develop an interest in dancing?

My grandfather was a dance and swimming instructor, so he taught my father to dance. However, my grandfather taught ballet, so my father picked up a lot of dance steps in the alleys of Chicago from the black tap dancers who couldn't perform in clubs. He had four sisters, and one of them, Vilma, formed a vaudeville act with him. It was an all-dance act that was a combination of tap, jazz, and acrobatics called "eccentric dance."

Is there any film footage of Buddy and Vilma performing together?

There are a lot of still photographs and articles about them, but sadly there's very little film of the two. The only movie they appeared in together was *Broadway Melody of 1936*. They reunited some 20 years later on a TV show called *You Asked For It*, where people would write in asking to see certain things. Someone wanted to see Buddy and Vilma dance again, so they pre-formed a dance called the Shim Sham Shimmy. My family has a copy of the episode and it's really a precious performance.

Is it true your dad wanted to study medicine, but his parents encouraged him to go into show business? Usually, it's the other way around!

He did start pre-med in college, then dropped out. I think the family ran out of money and he ended up going to New York on his own hoping to break into show business. Once he got some work, he sent for his sister, which was about a year later. They eventually went to Hollywood, and he even had a meeting with William Morris who personally told him: "You're not going to make it in Hollywood. You're a good dancer; you've got a cute act with your sister, but it's different out here." Well, if someone had told me that, I probably would have quit. But he didn't. He had an amazing amount of confidence in himself which carried him through those dark years. Vilma quit the business and he had a rough ten years in the beginning. He did some not-so-great movies, and his dry spell lasted from around 1938 to 1948. But then he got work with Disney in the 1950s as Davy Crockett's sidekick, and a role in *Breakfast at Tiffany's* (1961), which were fantastic for him and a boost to his career.

He was originally hired to play the Tin Man role in *The Wizard of Oz* (1939), but became very ill from inhaling aluminum dust used in the make-up and had to be replaced. Did he talk about how much of a disappointment that was for him?

He never talked about his involvement in the film when we were growing up, and we only learned about it later. He was tremendously disappointed, although he was very stoic about it. Initially, he was promised the Scarecrow role, but Ray Bolger had a better dance act so he was given that part, and the role of the Tin Man went to my father. When he became ill, Jack Haley was given the Tin Man role while my father was recuperating in hospital. The callous way the whole thing was handled really upset him. The rumors are that some of the long shots in the final film are actually of my father as the Tin Man. There are still photos of him as the Tin Man and audio recordings of him singing "If I Only Had A Heart," but I'm not aware of any film footage that clearly shows him from the movie. Despite being so ill from the aluminum in the make-up, he never received any compensation for the damage it did to his lungs — they just didn't have any provisions for that sort of thing back in the '30s. However, he always believed that the aluminum affected him and he had respiratory problems his whole life, including a cough that never went away. But my father was never one to get depressed about things like that and

Buddy Ebsen and daughter Kiki, six, having fun at a church function in Newport Beach, 1964. (Photograph courtesy of Kiki Ebsen.)

he pushed on. I can see now these sorts of disappointments are where his little sayings came from. For instance, "Every day is a new ball game," was one he would tell us when we were growing up.

What was the life like in the Ebsen household?

We first lived in Hollywood Hills. Then my father wanted to be close to his boats so we moved down to Balboa Island in Newport Harbor and we lived a very bohemian lifestyle there. A few years later, we moved to the 36-acre rural ranch in Calabasas where I still live. So we had two extreme lifestyles—one near the water that revolved around sailing and swimming, and the other on a very isolated rural ranch. We all got a very good dose of nature and were encouraged to pursue whatever we wanted. I developed an interest in horses and music. My father was not a Hollywood person and didn't hang out with other actors away from work, except in the local community theater.

What were those theater performances?

We did family shows that were like vaudeville acts. My father taught us how to tap dance and he and my sister danced, I sang, and we would do short skits. We did this at local theaters and at colleges. In the late '70s and early '80s, around the holiday season, we also would visit places in the area such as veterans hospitals, the El Toro Marine base, and the Motion Picture & Television Country House and Hospital in Woodland Hills and put on short shows.

Your parents were together for four decades. How did they meet?

My mother, Nancy, was an amazingly talented person. She was an actress who got her degree in theater from Vassar. They met in the Coast Guard while stationed in Seattle. She traveled with him while he performed in summer stock theaters up and down the East Coast. She was a great support during his career in those early years by taking over the household duties and managing the family. Their first child was a son, Christian, who died of complications from an ear infection in the first few months of his life. Through their marriage they collaborated on several theater projects together. She went on to have her own community theater and travel worldwide as an ambassador for the California Theater Arts Council. They raised five children and managed to stay together for 38 years. The complications of trying to raise a family and fulfill the needs of two extremely talented and creative people took its toll eventually, leading to a less-than-amicable divorce. Even though we were adults when they split, it was a sad day for the family. Our parents never spoke again and our relationship changed as well, as he went into his new life with a new wife. I choose to think lovingly of both my parents and live my life the way they would have wanted me to — fearless, taking risks, and, most of all, being happy with my choices.

Did you meet many stars when you were young?

The only time I got to meet celebrities growing up was when I visited the sets he was working on. I remember going to the Disney set and seeing Kurt Russell and Goldie Hawn when they were teenagers. I was pretty shy as a kid and didn't gravitate towards acting. I liked animals more than anything else, so whenever I went to *The Beverly Hillbillies* set, I used to hang out with Duke, and Elly May's animals.

It's hard to imagine "Jed Clampett" as being anything other than a kind father. What was Buddy Ebsen like as a dad?

He gave us a lot of freedom as we grew up, so we didn't want to challenge his trust too much because it would have been almost impossible to get it back if we let him down. He was basically very easygoing, but he was also very conservative. I remember sneaking out of the house one night with my girlfriend and we were gone the whole night. When he found out we were not at home he was not pleased. Being so tall, especially to a little kid, he only had to look down sternly at us and we knew we were in trouble. He didn't have to yell or wave his arms in the air; he would just silently stare at us and shake his head. He would say very little, but that was all we needed, and we knew we were in pretty big trouble. He was also a great story teller and would sit on our beds before we went to sleep, tell stories, sing songs, and play the guitar.

What kinds of stories did he tell you?

He created a whole series of stories with the same character called Mr. Gilfrump who was an old man living in the woods. He was always having adventures and getting himself into trouble. Then there were these little elves in the forest who Mr. Gilfrump couldn't see, but they would always come and help him out. I remember one story where Mr. Gilfrump went to bed with a toothache. When he woke up the next morning, the tooth was gone. During the night, the elves had tied a long string around his tooth, then 40 of them got together and yanked on the tooth, pulling it out. It was so cute because it was all done to music — he'd play chords on the guitar — then tell some more story, and sing a little. Another character he invented was a little girl called Angelica who was always getting into trouble. My father had six daughters, so Angelica was basically a combination of us and all our mischievous mistakes were wrapped up into the one little girl. These stories just became part of our growing up and were very comforting for us when he would put us to bed. I'm sure there was a message in those stories to just behave, do our chores, and listen to our mother!

You were only about four when *The Beverly Hillbillies* was first broadcast. What did you kids think when you first saw him on TV?

It was a big deal, every Wednesday night at eight o'clock on CBS. We were all required to sit down and watch because Dad was coming on. My brother and I both thought it was pretty cool. But I don't think we had a clear concept of what it meant for him to be on television, which was still kind of new to us at that age. We thought that everyone's parents must have been on TV — that's what parents did — so we didn't understand when other people made a big deal out of it. My brother and I would look for him on other shows, too. In fact, any time he wasn't at home we would turn on the TV because we figured he must be on there somewhere. I remember we would see a show with someone who kind of looked and sounded like him, although the guy sounded a little different, but we convinced ourselves that it was him. One day our mother came in and asked what we were doing and we said: "We're watching Dad on the TV." She said, "That's Lawrence Welk!" You have to remember, we were only three or four at the time!

What do you remember from visiting the *Hillbillies* set?

I loved going to the set and sitting in the Clampett truck, hanging out with all the animals, and going into the dressing rooms. This was in the old studios on Las Palmas Avenue

Buddy Ebsen and daughter Kiki around age 30. (Photograph courtesy of Kiki Ebsen.)

and there were bungalows that still had that smell of Old Hollywood. Dad had a valet named George L. George. He was the sweetest old black gentleman who looked after my father's dressing room, and we young kids when necessary. I've gone back to the studio as an adult for various projects I've worked on, and it's like going back to my childhood. I can smell the Triscuits and ginger ale that George always had on hand. The *Hillbillies* cast members were always nice to me. Donna Douglas was always so sweet. I remember meeting Raymond Bailey one time, who played Mr. Drysdale. He was out of make-up and I wouldn't speak to him because I didn't recognize him. My mother thought it was funny and explained that I had been taught never to speak with strangers! Granny, Irene Ryan, was such a darling and so funny and wiry. She also looked totally different out of make-up and I remember she had curly red hair. Max Baer, Jr., who played Jethro, was very animated, and I always thought he was kind of crazy and a bit of a loose cannon.

You must have been popular with the other kids having a TV star for a dad?

Initially, it was a big deal, especially as the show was so popular with audiences. It was kind of cool, but I really couldn't understand what all the fuss was about. Everyone wanted to be our friends and we did get a lot of attention. Kids were always wanting to come around to our home. However, our home on the island was kind of a hub anyway, so there were always tons of kids around. My dad always made himself accessible to people and never denied autographs to anyone or turned people away if they wanted to talk to him, although it did get tedious for him at times. In many ways, there was a lot of "Jed" in him with his friendly, easygoing, laid-back nature.

There's an interesting website called The Buddy Ebsen Museum (buddyebsenmuseum.com). On the main page, there is a photo of his large home, not unlike the mansion in the Beverly Hillbillies. When did he live there?

That's the house in the Pacific Palisades where he lived for the last 15 or so years of his life after he married his third wife, Dorothy. I think she was involved in creating that website. His lifestyle shifted a bit after the marriage and he moved to a more upscale home, unlike the ones we grew up in. I never lived there, but would visit him. It was very fancy — "don't walk on the carpet" sort of thing. It was a change from the rural ranch house he raised us in where we had tons of dogs and were a little more like down-and-dirty cowboys!

What did he think about *The Beverly Hillbillies* movie remake from 1993?

He never said whether or not he liked it. But I guess he liked the idea since he had a cameo role as Barnaby Jones. I never saw the movie because it was too weird for me and I knew I wasn't going to enjoy it.

Your dad had many hobbies and interests outside of acting, but sailing was on the top of his list. What type of sailing did he go in for?

Most of his sailing was off the Pacific Coast, although he did take a boat to Florida and another over to Europe and did some sailing there. He was a very competitive sailor and entered a lot of races, including the Honolulu Transpac which is a race from San Pedro to Honolulu. It's a pretty prestigious race and takes about two weeks to complete. He actually won the race in 1968 in his 35-foot catamaran, the *Polynesian Concept*, which was the smallest boat in the fleet. Growing up, the family would go sailing every Sunday and he taught us how to sail and crew for him. My sister and I would crew for him on some of his three to four day races.

What are your main interests?

I do a lot of work with horses at the Healing Equine Ranch at my family's old ranch home in Calabasas. I teach natural horsemanship and equine-assisted growth and learning programs using a herd of rescue horses. It's a program that not only helps people, but the animals too. I showed horses as a youngster, and my sister raised quarter horses. My dad rode occasionally, and had done some riding in a few westerns back in the '50s, but he didn't take to it the way the kids did. His outlet was sailing rather than riding. But he loved the life on the ranch, being outdoors, cutting wood, and fixing fences.

How important is it for you to still live in your parents' old family home?

Extremely important. I owe so much to them because I still get to live there. I feel led to help and heal others through an appreciation of art, music, nature and animals as part of their legacy. I am reminded of my father every time I light a fire in the fireplace. The warmth of the flames and the wood smoke remind me of when we sat around at night as a family, reading in our respective chairs or couch in the living room: Dad smoking a pipe; me dozing on the couch with three cats; and a few dogs scattered around me, exhausted from hours with the horses up in the mountains. Such a simple, fulfilling life.

When you're not riding, you're a singer and musician. How would you sum up your professional career?

I'm a singer/songwriter/keyboardist and much of my music is pop-jazz or pop-rock and I have made four CDs. My father had old-fashioned tastes in music and would have liked me to sing more of the jazz standards, which I actually do more of now. I'm also a freelance keyboard player and have worked with some great acts, such as Chicago, Boz Scaggs, Al Jarreau, Christopher Cross, Tracy Chapman, and Peter Cetera. Also, a lot of R&B artists like James Ingram and Geoffrey Osborne. And I've played in house bands for everyone from Glenn Campbell to Take 6. My dad came to many of my performances over the years. From high school rock bands to larger venues as an adult playing with name artists. He appreciated my success; but mostly, he enjoyed me singing music from his era. After he passed away, I recorded one of his songs, a jazz ballad called "Missing You" for my CD *Kiki*. He would have enjoyed that one.

Were you in any of your father's TV shows or movies?

I appeared as a pianist in a TV movie with my sister, Bonnie, that my dad wrote called *The Paradise Connection* [1979] and was filmed in Hawaii. But really, I've only had a few, mostly uncredited, parts. For instance, I was an extra in *Back to the Future* [1985]. It was in an early scene with Huey Lewis when the bands are being auditioned and there were a bunch of musicians standing around. I was one of them.

How much influence did your father have on you as a performer?

He influenced me in a lot of ways as I was growing up. He was very "old school," and I don't think I appreciated everything he tried to teach me when I was younger. We had that generation gap, maybe even two generations, because he was 50 when I was born. So in some ways he was like a grandfather as well as a father. I was a typical rebellious teenager and probably thought of him as a bit of an old fogy at times. But now I can appreciate what he was trying to teach me about performing. When we did those vaudeville-like family shows, I learned that it was all about entertaining and connecting with the audience. By watching my father, who was so light-hearted and relaxed on-stage, it also helped me to get over the fear of performing. I also learned that you don't have to be perfect when you're on-stage. Even if you make a mistake, you can laugh about it with the audience and move on. He had such a warm, inviting way that it allowed people to connect with him in all the roles he played. The audience may not have thought his acting ability was amazing, but they knew he was real. He was charming and likable in the same way that actors like John Wayne and Jimmy Stewart were, by putting so much of themselves into their characters. Once your audience likes you, you've won them over. Buddy Ebsen made that look easy.

Kiki Ebsen on Buddy Ebsen. Telephone interview on 11/9/10. Kiki Ebsen's main website is www.kikiebsen.com; the site for her healing equine ranch is http://thehealinge-quineranch.com. The Buddy Ebsen Museum website is www.buddyebsenmuseum.com.

18

June Lockhart on Gene Lockhart

Although she was best known to TV audiences for her roles in three popular '60s shows, Lassie, Lost in Space, and Petticoat Junction, June Lockhart' was in some three dozen film roles, from 1938 to 2009. In fact, the Lockhart family may very well hold a record in the world of entertainment: five generations of entertainers! Her father, Gene Lockhart (1891–1957), was one of Hollywood's most recognizable character actors. He appeared in over 125 films, including such classics as A Christmas Carol *(1938),* Algiers *(1938),* His Girl Friday *(1940),* Meet John Doe *(1941),* Going My Way *(1944),* Miracle on 34th Street *(1947), and* Carousel *(1956). June's mother, Kathleen Lockhart (1894–1978), was an actress, and appearing in 40 films during her 26-year movie career. Gene and Kathleen even appeared together in about 20 films. But it doesn't stop there! June's grandfather was a concert singer and voice teacher, and her daughter, Anne, has had an extensive career with over 200 film and TV credits and is best known to sci-fi fans for her role as Sheba in the '70s series* Battlestar Galactica. *Both of Anne's children (Carlyle and Zane Taylor) have appeared in a few TV roles, too. Anne was also married to the late Adam Taylor, who worked on the production side of filmmaking, and Adam's dad (Buck Taylor) and grandfather (Dub Taylor) appeared in many films. June's other daughter, also named June, had a few small TV roles in the '60s and '70s, then moved into the business world.*

What's the history of the Lockhart family?

My father's family originally came from Scotland. My grandfather, John Coates Lockhart, was British. I didn't know him well, but remember him as a jolly man. He was a concert singer — a tenor. He moved to Canada, where my father was born in London, Ontario, on July 18, 1891. In his later years, my grandfather lived in Chicago. My mother was born in Portsmouth, England, and her parents were English and Irish. She and her family immigrated to Canada when she was a young girl.

Did your grandparents influence your father's acting career?

My father's early stage experience as a little boy was with his father in The Kilties Band of Canada, in which he did the Highland Fling and also sang. He toured the United States and Canada. My father also had a lovely tenor voice and sang on-stage in many musicals, including Gilbert and Sullivan operettas. My mother had a beautiful voice, too. She had trained in England as a singer, dancer, and pianist, and was a member of the Dickens Fellowship. The Lockharts did shows in which my father played the piano, and they would sing and do comedy sketches written by him. In the '30s and '40s they did a lot of radio, too. They were both versatile people and my father also directed stage productions.

Is it true your parents were introduced by Thomas Edison?

Yes. For several years, Thomas Edison had a cross-country train tour every year to showcase his latest inventions. It was called the Edison Dealers Convention Caravan. Today, dealers participate in trade shows in cities such as Orlando, Florida, or Las Vegas, Nevada, and the dealers travel to see the new products; but nothing like that existed in the early 1920s. Edison knew how to promote his new inventions by taking his product to the dealers. To entertain the dealers at stops in the large cities as the train traveled west, Edison presented full entertainment productions in large theaters of these towns. Performers included singers from the Metropolitan Opera House, motivational speakers, and actors in plays with music. My father was in one of the plays in 1922, and again the following year, when my mother was hired in June. Edison introduced my parents to each other in his office in West Orange, New Jersey, before rehearsals got underway. They started in New York, went to Chicago and St. Louis, then across the southern half of the United States and up the Pacific coast to Banff, Canada, where I believe the tour ended. When they got to Lake Louise, Daddy made his move! They were married the following year, in 1924, in Chicago, in June. I was born the following year, also in June. They were expecting a boy who was to be named Gene, Jr., so my being a girl was quite a surprise. My birth certificate reads "Female Lockhart!" They later chose June as my name because it was a significant month in their lives.

Kathleen, June and Gene Lockhart in Thurstonia Park, Ontario, circa 1930. (Photograph courtesy of June Lockhart.)

What were your father's other interests when he was young?

He was quite an athlete at school. He was captain of his hockey team and played football for the Toronto Argonauts during World War I when he was in the Canadian ROTC. He also played tennis, water polo, enjoyed golf, and was a fine swimmer. He swam the mile in Hamilton Bay, Toronto, faster than anyone at the time and his record stood for many years.

What were his artistic interests?

He had a remarkably long, active career in film and the theater. As I mentioned, in the '20s and '30s he and my mother did concert recital revues together, which my father wrote. At the same time, he was writing radio shows. In 1933, he played Uncle Sid in a production of *Ah, Wilderness!* written by Eugene O'Neill, and starring George M. Cohan. When I was seven or eight, I went to visit him one night during a performance and I stood in the wings with my father, watching the scene on-stage. Mr. Cohan came up behind us, and Daddy quietly introduced me. Cohan patted me on the head and said to my father, "Enjoy them while they're young, Gene — they leave you so soon!" It was such a tender moment. It was my father's successful run in the play which brought him to Hollywood, under contract to MGM, in 1934. He was a versatile man and composed music all his life. He was one of the first teachers of acting at the Julliard School of Music where he was a drama coach and taught acting in opera. He believed that the opera singers of the day should learn how to move on stage rather than just stand, planted on stage, facing front. He said that they needed to learn how to sustain scenes, and move across the stage. Two students of his who I remember were Gladys Swarthout and Risë Stevens. Ms. Stevens, many years later, was in the movie *Going My Way* [1944] with Bing Crosby and my father. He was also very involved with the Metropolitan Opera and several times a year he would write and direct comedy sketches for their special gala performances. He was good pals with the management and opera stars, who were also involved in charity events, and they were frequent visitors to our home. At the same time, I was studying ballet at the Metropolitan Opera House and made my debut there at the age of eight in a pantomime scene, opening the season in December 1933 in *Peter Ibbetson* by Deems Taylor. It starred Edward Johnson, Lucrezia Bori, Lawrence Tibbett and Gladys Swarthout. I think I was paid $2.50!

It must have been an interesting home to grow up in. What was family life like?

I grew up on Long Island, before I moved out to California in 1934. It was certainly an entertaining and English-style household. For the most part, when my father came home for dinner, he didn't talk much about the day's work. He was more concerned about politics, world peace, music, and the arts. So it was not all show business at home. My mother's parents and her sister also lived with us. We would all sit down for dinner, daddy would select the music, and there would be records playing the classics, or symphonies, or music from the Metropolitan Opera. After dinner, he would go to his study and learn his next day's dialogue or continue writing radio scripts, which he did for years. Every day, at four P.M., tea was served for those who were home.

It was in the dining room, with a linen tablecloth, silver service, china cups and saucers, and some sweets — a grand British ritual! In Los Angeles, I was a five-day boarder during my last two years at Westlake School for Girls, which meant I came home on Fridays and spent the weekend with my parents and returned to school Sunday nights. From 1939 to 1965, we also had a home at Lake Arrowhead, about 100 miles east of Los Angeles. Our time there was terribly important to all of us and we spent every holiday and all summers up there. My father would finish work on Friday nights, and he'd drive up there for the weekend. Being from Canada, he had to have all those tall trees and a big lake! I had a 1939 Chris Craft Runabout boat, and helped form the Lake Arrowhead Water-ski Club. On weekends, when we were at our home in Los Angeles, many English character actors who were in town and many famous singers and musicians like Nelson Eddy, Lawrence Tibbett, Rosa Ponselle, and Meredith Wilson would come over on Sundays. Others guests were authors, columnists, publishers, musicians, composers and conductors. We would play badminton, swim, then have a buffet, and play charades. Each Christmas, we would have friends over and put on a performance of *A Christmas Carol*. This was prior to the three of us doing the film. We read from a script that my father had prepared from the original story. We would have wonderful actors like Doris Lloyd or Walter Kingsford playing parts. Leo G. Carroll was my "Uncle Leo" and a close friend of the family and he would play the role of Scrooge. It was marvelous! I had an "education" from all sorts of people during my teenage years. And, by the way, our dogs were also a great part of the family. We had a pair of wire-haired terriers named Panda and Monium, which I named, and later one called Wacky. My father adored them!

Did he have any other jobs that were unrelated to acting?

In the early '30s, we were living in New York. During the summers, when he was not in a play, my father would go to Europe where he conducted travel tours in Britain, Scotland, Spain, middle Europe, and the Holy Land. He spoke French and some Italian. The tour company was called Cuthbert Lockhart Tours, and originated out of Toronto, Canada. He did this for several summers and would be gone for four or five weeks. He always found a way to make money to support his family.

Your father also composed songs. What's the story behind the hit song "The World is Waiting for the Sunrise," to which your father wrote the lyrics?

He wrote that in 1919. Ernest Seitz composed the music, which was originally a slow ballad. Paul Whiteman wanted to record it in 1922, and wanted it jazzed up to be dance music. So my father talked with Seitz; but Seitz, who was a successful, talented concert pianist, didn't want anything to do with pop music. So Daddy rewrote the music as a foxtrot, but always gave Seitz the shared credit and royalties. In the mid–'50s, Les Paul and Mary Ford had a big hit with the song. Willie Nelson also recorded it on his album, *Moonlight Becomes You*. I called him up to tell him I was so pleased that he recorded my father's song. Willie said, "I didn't know that was Gene's song!" Later, when he came to LA for a concert, he invited me to come on-stage and sing it with him. I was thrilled! The song has had an extraordinary history and amazing influence on others. In John Lennon's autobiography, he wrote that the Les Paul version was the first song he learned on the guitar. I still get royalties from around the world, from countries you couldn't imagine — Uzbekistan, Trinidad and Tobago, among others. It's amazing!

Wasn't it played to the Space Shuttle astronauts?

That's right. NASA played wake-up music to the Shuttle crew. So I called NASA one day and spoke with astronaut Ken Reightler and told him I had a good wake-up song for them to use. They loved the idea. So, on October 27, 1992, I went to Mission Control in Houston and at around two A.M. they played the song for the crew of the Columbia mission. The announcer told the crew that I was there, and that my father had written the song. Then a voice from space came over the speaker: "Some of us up here want to know what Lassie's mother is doing in Mission Control at two o'clock in the morning!" That began a wonderful, long relationship with NASA that still exists today.

What's the story about a song he wrote that appeared in *Mrs. Miniver* (1942)?

During the time before the United States joined Britain in World War II, my father produced a Sunday night show at the Hawthorne School in Beverly Hills. It was called "Gene Lockhart's British Revue," and many British actors appeared in it. He wrote the lyrics and melody for one of the songs that was called "A Midsummer's Day," and it was performed by a group called the Worcestershire Wassailiers. It was rather a naughty song — at least for the time — about having a good "lay in the hay" on a midsummer's day. *Mrs. Miniver* was about to be produced, and the producer chose to use it in the garden party scene. The Wassailiers sang the song in the background during that scene.

How bawdy were the lyrics?

They were mild by today's standards. My father always thought that no one ever really listened to the lyrics because, in those days of the Hays Code of censorship, it's hard to imagine the lyrics would have been given the okay. So if you watch *Mrs. Miniver*, all these character actors are lined up on-stage in special costumes of the period, singing "A Midsummer's Day." And, I still get royalties for that whenever *Mrs. Miniver* airs!

Did your parents want you to follow them into the entertainment profession?

They were perfectly happy with whatever I wanted to do. They encouraged me with music, dancing and the arts because they knew it would be a good background for whatever I did. There was no pressure, and the opportunities unfolded easily.

Your first film role was in *A Christmas Carol*. You had the unique opportunity of appearing in it with both your parents. That must have been a great experience.

It was. I thought my parents were wonderful as the Cratchits, and it was just great fun to see how a film was made. When MGM made the movie and my parents were hired, they asked if I wanted to be one of the children. I said of course. It just seemed a natural thing for me because my family had been performing it at home for years. Even "Uncle Leo" would be in it as Marley's ghost. I also really loved wearing the Victorian costumes, the petticoats, etcetera. And that's something that stayed with me all my life because I always loved doing westerns and period shows. One thing I do remember was feeling quite nauseated on the set one day from something I had eaten the night before. Then they placed a bowl of mashed parsnips in front of me during the Christmas dinner scene. The stench made me so ill, the prop man had to replace the dish with potatoes. I've avoided parsnips ever since!

Do you remember your first line in the film, when your dad brings in the food for Christmas and asks the kids to guess what's in one of the packages?

Of course. My daughter, Junie, and granddaughter, Christianna, have never let me forget that the first words I ever spoke in movies were: "I know, I know — sausages!" It's become a family joke and we all shriek with laughter when we watch it now. Watching the film has become a family tradition each year. And now, to be able to watch it with my grandchildren — well, who gets to do something like that?

Did you get to visit many sets when your father was filming?

Not really. My first time on a set was when he played Joan Crawford's father in *The Gorgeous Hussy* [1936]. She was the first movie star I ever met and she was charming. She invited me to visit her on many of her movie sets in subsequent years, and was always kind to me.

Your father was nominated for a Best Supporting Actor Oscar for *Algiers* (1938). You were around 13 at the time; do you remember that?

I went to the premiere and, later, the Academy Awards dinner. But we knew before the awards were handed out that he had not won. The man taking the tickets at the door told him, "Sorry, Gene, not this time!" That was actually good, because we were all prepared. But the nomination itself was wonderful because it stays with you forever. My father took the loss well. It was great to see him handle it with grace and that was a good example for me to see even at that early age. He lost that year to Walter Brennan. My mother, however, wasn't too happy because Walter had won in a previous year.

Hedy Lamarr was also in *Algiers*, and your dad had a big role as her older husband in *The Strange Woman* (1946). Did he talk about working with her?

I don't remember him talking about her and I don't recall ever meeting her. My mother was also in *The Strange Woman*. She later told me about a scene daddy did with Hedy Lamarr, in which Hedy was sitting up in bed with a nightgown on. After they filmed the scene, Hedy had to do it again for the European version but with her gown dropped way down. Apparently, my father was terribly embarrassed. Hedy lowered it as far as she could, and the European version was shot. In the American version, the censorship of the Hays Code prevailed so you see mostly her back in that scene, as I remember. Charles Boyer was also in *Algiers*. A couple of year later, I worked with him in *All This, and Heaven Too* [1940] and played his daughter. I went to school while on the set, of course, and one day had some French reading to do for homework. He came over and sat down at the table and I did my French homework with Charles Boyer! That's when I learned he could speak perfect English without a French accent if he wanted to, because he was able, by example, to demonstrate to me how I had mispronounced a French word by showing me my error.

In *Algiers*, your father played a role which became fairly typical for him — villains who were treacherous, sneaky, or shifty types of characters. Did he like those roles?

He did at first and he was really a wonderful villain, but he got sick of playing them later in his career. Often he wasn't evil, just crooked, like the sheriff in *His Girl Friday* and the mayor in *Meet John Doe* [1941], who were not high-class guys. He often found a way to bring some humor into many of his characters, whether they were villains or not. Speaking of humor, in *Miracle on 34th Street* he played the judge. Oh my, what he did with that part. If you listen to his dialogue in the courtroom scenes it's just regular courtroom terms and his dialogue is not necessarily funny as written. But he found a way to make them subtly humorous with his gestures and looks. It's just marvelous.

Your parents were in many films. Do you still come across their movies which you have never seen before?

My father made so many movies that I have never seen them all. So when one comes on television that I haven't seen, it's a wonderful treat. I remember watching Turner Classic Movies and saw my mother playing Rosalind Russell's mother in *Roughly Speaking* [1945], which I had not seen before. She was absolutely wonderful. To wake up in the middle of the night, and turn on the TV and see my father or mother's face, how cool is that? Something interesting happened a few years ago when I was visiting New York around Christmas time. I read in the newspaper that Macy's had a *Miracle on 34th Street* display in their windows. So on my way to the airport before leaving, I got the limo to stop outside the store. They had animatronic displays of various scenes from the film, including the courtroom scene. The driver waited as I got out and went up to the window, and to my astonishment they were playing the soundtrack from the film and my father's voice was coming over the speakers onto Broadway! I couldn't believe it, it was just such a surprise that I burst into tears!

Did your dad experience any accidents on a set?

There was a scene in *Androcles and the Lion* [1952] where he was supposed to fall backwards down a flight of stairs and the stunt man was going to catch him to ease the fall. But the stunt man missed him, and he fell backwards, all the way down the long flight of stairs. They printed that take and used it in the film. Whenever I see Alan Young, who was in the film, he always says, "Oh my God, I thought Gene was dead!" My father wasn't a child when this happened and was quite heavy, but I guess his athletic past kicked in. He just relaxed, went with it, and didn't break a bone.

Did your father have a favorite film that he appeared in?

I never heard him mention a favorite, but *Algiers* was probably one. I think he loved *A Christmas Carol*, too, because it had been such an important part of our family.

Gene, Kathleen and June Lockhart in 1953. (Photograph courtesy of June Lockhart.)

In addition to his many film roles, he appeared on Broadway in more than a dozen shows. Do you have a favorite stage performance?

He replaced Lee Cobb as Willy Loman in *Death of a Salesman* in 1949. He was brilliant in that. Apparently, Arthur Miller wanted my father to play Willy in the initial production, but Elia Kazan wanted Lee Cobb. Cobb was superb, too, but when he had a heart attack and had to leave the company, Miller said to Kazan, "Now can I have my Gene Lockhart?" That's a true story, not apocryphal.

You also appeared on Broadway. In fact, *Life* magazine published some interesting photos of you and your father in 1947 after your Broadway debut in *For Love or Money* and for which you won the Tony Award for the Outstanding Performance by a Newcomer. Your parents must have been proud.

They were so pleased for me. After the show on the first night, I went to a couple of parties and when I went back to the hotel I called the newspapers to see what the reviews were from the show, and they were wonderful. So I had to go out and get copies. My parents were already in bed, so I got my father up and we went down to Times Square. We bought lots of copies of the *Herald Tribune* and *New York Times* and took them back to the hotel and read the reviews to my mother. We later recreated that evening for the *Life* photographer who followed us around and took the pictures for the magazine.

You worked with some big names over the years. You played Rosie York in *Sergeant York* (1941). Do you remember Walter Brennan and Gary Cooper?

Oh, what an experience! Walter Brennan was just a lovely, authentic, real guy, and a colleague of my father's. It was so much fun doing the scene where he sang "Give Me That Old-Time Religion." Gary Cooper was grand. I was into flying kites between the Warner Bros. sound stages and he would help me fly them. I remember one long scene when Gary Cooper, as Alvin York, is sitting with his mother at a table in the foreground and telling her how he's going to get himself a "piece of bottom land" so he can marry his girl, Gracie. I was lying in the background, in bed. They had to get me out of school each time to do that scene and all I did was lie there, and I had no dialogue. I was facing the wall, away from the camera, so they really could have used anyone in the scene, or even just used a lump of blankets. Anyway, the shooting went on for hours. Finally, Gary Cooper turned to me just as the director called "Action!" and jokingly asked, "Know your lines, June?" Well, I started to giggle — it was just such a silly thing to ask, and we laughed and laughed. I was giddy and couldn't stop; it was a great release. I shur luv'd talkin' that southern drawl, too! I also had a lot of scenes without dialogue and just looked lovingly at my big brother, Alvin, who was going off to war. "Ma, what are they a-fightin' fir?" I remember asking. "Don't rightly know, Rosie," she answered. Many years later I met the real Rosie York at a reception when the Defense Department was introducing a tank they named the "Sergeant York." They brought out the surviving members of the York family for a ceremony, and Rosie was one of them. The following day, the tank was brought out onto a military base for its debut display in front of a bleacher full of military dignitaries and civilians. But when they fired the tank, the missile came out of the turret, and just plopped onto the ground. It was like a Laurel and Hardy movie! It had no fire power at all, and the order for the tanks was canceled. It was shown on the news and all the newspapers carried the story.

And what about working with Judy Garland in *Meet Me in St. Louis* (1944)?

I loved that film, and, again, I was able to wear period clothes. We rehearsed for many weeks to learn the choreography for the dance in the Christmas scene. Working with Judy was fine — when she showed up. The whole cast would come in at six o'clock in the morning for make-up and to get dressed, and be ready to shoot by eight A.M. Then Judy wouldn't show up. So we'd wait, and wait, and wait. Around 12:00 or 12:30 P.M. we'd hear that Judy had just come through the gates and we were told to go have lunch and to be back by 2:30, ready to work. Well, when we came back, we would find out that Judy didn't want to work that day, so we were sent home. That happened often. But when she finally showed up and did her scenes, she knew her lines, she was terrific and funny; she was just grand. She was very tiny and only weighed about 85 lbs. We heard much later that she wasn't sleeping at night and, so, would sleep in late. Then they would give her pills to wake her up so she could come in to work.

Did your father help you get film roles?

I doubt it, the business doesn't work that way. But he had so many friends in the business, I was probably treated very nicely because of being Gene's daughter. I was not exposed to some things that I've heard other young actresses were.

What sort of acting advice did he give you?

When we would go to a movie, he would often write me notes about the actors' performances. I guess I absorbed that advice over the years. When I was preparing for my first role alone, as Isabelle in *All This, and Heaven Too*, with Charles Boyer and Bette Davis, I found a wonderful letter from my father on my bed on the first day of work. It's dated February 8, 1940:

> *Dear Junie,*
>
> *Tomorrow you start what Mommy and I hope will be a career which will bring you happiness, security, satisfaction, and success in the same order of their importance to your life.*
>
> *It will be an interesting and eventful day for you because you are starting your race to success in what the bookies call fast company.*
>
> *There are one or two things I might say which may be helpful and I will jot down so that you may, if you care to, think about them at your leisure. You are now on your own.*
>
> *First impressions mean a good deal to one's progress. Your first day, your first week, and your first picture will start you in the right direction if you impress your superiors as being earnest, sincere and intelligent.*
>
> *Keep ahead of your story, know your lines, know what the others have to do, be ready for your scenes, have your makeup, wardrobe, and hair in good order so that you can step into the scene when called.*
>
> *Live your character, think as she would, not just at the moment when you go*

into the scene but in your dressing room beforehand. You are Charles Boyer's daughter and Bette Davis is your new governess. Ms. Davis and Mr. Boyer really no longer exist. She is your new and charming governess and already you're curiously beginning to like her. You watch her, you study her. She is a lovely person. He is your father, so kind, so thoughtful, you love him so much. But somehow you realize that he is not as happy as he wants you to think he is. Read the scenes that your governess and father have together. If possible, watch how they play the scenes. Notice their concentration, their control, the tone of their voices, the way in which they sustain their characterizations. Note how they fill in their lines with looks, gestures and pauses. It will seem so natural to you, but this embroidery of the lines with thought which they express with looks and pauses is what makes them real and shows what is going on in their minds.

The camera always shows what you are thinking and all you have to do is think how Isabelle would.

Ask Mr. Rapper, the dialogue director, when he rehearses you to please get every bit of meaning out of what you do. He will help you tremendously. He's a splendid director. Naturally, you will not ask him this favor when others are around.

After Mr. Litvak [the director] sets your business in the scene rehearsals, there is always a little time off where lights are set. During this time, get your business set well in your mind so that it comes naturally and simply. Any moments you are doubtful about, practice them in your dressing room. When in doubt about how to do a bit of business, always take the simplest and most honest way of doing it. Isabel is well read, nicely spoken, friendly, sincere, and vital. She means what she says. Be Isabel on and off the set. Mean what you say and you cannot possibly do anything out of character. You will be in scenes where you have nothing to say, but the camera sees you. Never let down.

Love, Mommy and Daddy.

Now that's an acting primer, isn't it? It's absolutely how to perform. It shows you what a good writer he was.

So you worked with your dad in *A Christmas Carol*. Did the pair of you ever work together in any other productions?

Not in any more films. During later years, we worked together in some theater, live TV, and TV panel shows. We did a play, a version of *A House of Seven Gables*, for *The Robert Montgomery Playhouse*. With my mother, we also did a play with Art Carney that was a period piece. For many years during the early '50s, I did a current events news quiz show called *Who Said That?* with the White House Press correspondents. I was the only regular woman panelist. The format was that we were given a quote from the news and the members of the press, and I as the only "civilian," told the story and would try to identify "who said that." It began a long association for me with the White House Press, which exists to this day. I am a member of the White House Press News Photographers Association. My father was sometimes on the show, and it was great fun because he was as big a news buff as I have always been. He, of course, held his own with the White House correspondents. A highlight of my life was doing a play with my father called *John Loves Mary* for the occupying Air Force in Germany after World War II. Constance Bennett produced it so that she could be with her husband, General John Coulter, who was based in Germany at the time. It had a cast of actors from television and films, and we toured all of West Germany for four to six weeks, playing in recreation halls and theaters. We also played in a theater in Berlin that hadn't been bombed, the Titania Palast. We flew into Berlin during the Russian blockade, and flew out again on swept-out coal planes. The trip was profound because this was 1949 and the cities of Germany were still in shambles from the bombings. We also took a tour to the concentration camp at Dachau. It was horrendous. I can't speak or think of it today without becoming emotional.

What about some of your father's personal characteristics? What was his personality like off-screen? What foods and drinks did he like?

He was sweet, funny, always smiling and chuckling. I never saw him pass my mother in a room without patting or hugging her. He was very affectionate. He was also a journalism buff, he read everything, and was an occasional columnist and a prolific writer. He enjoyed a cocktail, and wine was always served with dinner. He liked salads, but also apple pie and Canadian bacon! But he had to give those up later in life when he went on a diet. My mother was always trying to get him to diet. Towards the end of his life he had a couple of heart attacks and then had to lose some weight. He lost some, but not a lot. He just loved his sweets! He also smoked all his life, then one day in the late 1940s he just quit.

So how would you sum up life growing up in the Lockhart family?

There were always projects going on, and it was a sweet home. There was a lot of laughter, music, singing, entertaining, great Parcheesi, and parlour games. It was a happy British-American household and I was given lots of guidance, attention and affection.

June Lockhart on Gene Lockhart. Telephone interview on 2/26/10. A shorter version of the interview appeared in *Classic Images*, July 2010. June Lockhart's official site is www.junelockhart.com.

19

Brooke Tucker on Forrest Tucker

> *Few actors looked down on Forrest Tucker (1919–1986). Towering over stars and co-stars alike at six feet, five inches, "Tuck" was a strapping Plainfield, Indiana, farm boy who made it to Hollywood. His memorable first role was in* The Westerner *(1940), in which he tangled with Gary Cooper, himself no shrimp at six-three. Tucker went on to appear in some 80 movies and 70 television shows, and starred in the '60s sitcom* F-Troop. *His best-known stage performance was in the long-running* The Music Man. *Off-screen, Tuck was a bit of a rascal. Yet his daughter, Brooke, says it was impossible not to love him.*

Who were the early influences in your father's career?

I would say the first was Jimmy "Carnation" Lake, who ran a burlesque theater in Washington, D.C. He was a vaudevillian, a comic and dancer, who hired my father to work in the theater. He was the reason my father always wore a carnation in his lapel. But most importantly, a man called Herman Sartorius, who played a huge role in helping my dad get to Hollywood. He was his mentor and was very wealthy. His father owned Sartorius Pharmaceuticals near New York City at the turn of the century. Uncle Herman, as I called him, was my godfather. And he truly was my father's "godfather" because he paid my father's way to California, and even bought him his first home there. He was always in my life until the late '50s, and my father was devastated when he died in the '60s.

Your dad was a tall man. Was he six feet, four inches or six feet, five inches? It varies in different sources.

Both my parents were tall. My mother was five feet, ten and three quarter inches and my dad was six feet, five inches. I guess I inherited that, because I'm six feet. My dad would always tell me, "Stand up straight and be proud of it!" He also wore a size 14D shoe — huge! He actually had worn size 12½ shoes for a long time and always had trouble with his feet. When he was working on *The Music Man*, they realized his shoes were too small and had the larger pair made for him.

Forrest and Brooke Tucker. (Photograph courtesy of Brooke Tucker.)

Being tall and famous, he must have been hard to miss in any situation. Was he recognized a lot?

All the time. I remember we'd be eating in restaurants and people would come up, but he was never rude. He'd stop eating, answer their questions, and sign items for them. He was always gracious and one of the kindest people you could ever meet. He thought a lot about his fans. He would always dress up when he went out or if he was doing a show. And whenever we would go to the theater, he expected me, my mother, and later my stepmother, to dress formally, too — no scarves, and definitely dresses, no pants. He always felt that if he was going to meet fans out in public, they deserved to see a performer dressed nicely. He believed entertainers should be "glamorous," and he always wore a three-piece suit made in England, handmade shoes, and a carnation in his lapel. And since his fans might meet his family, they too had to be well attired. He would say, "If they want to see people in hair curlers, they could go to the local supermarket!" When he was flying, and waiting for the plane at an airport, he would go into the lounge. People would recognize him and say "Hi, Tuck" and he would buy them a drink and chat. Another example of his attitude towards fans was when he would do theater-in-the-round. At the end of the show, he would take his bows and launch into an after-piece. His valet, Carl, who had been with him for years and years, would bring him a drink — Scotch on the rocks — and a sweat towel, and my father would start talking with the audience. He'd be there for an hour, absolutely beguiling, telling stories and jokes and mesmerizing the crowd. I don't think a lot of actors took the time to do that. I'm not making him out to be a saint — he was a complicated man — but he always felt he owed his fans a lot.

Was he accessible to fans backstage after the shows?

I was on the road with my dad and stepmother for a year, so I was around him a lot. If people from the audience had a backstage pass, he would warmly greet them — in his boxer shorts! That may sound strange given what I just said about him dressing up, but he wanted people who came backstage to get a look at the real, behind-the-scenes life of an actor. So he would often greet them in his shorts while taking off his make-up. I'm sure some little old ladies were shocked to see that, but imagine the stories they could tell: "I got to see Forrest Tucker in his dressing room, taking off his make-up, and in his underwear!" Eventually he would get cleaned up, dressed, and head out the stage door wearing a cape, with a carnation — bigger than life!

He had four wives. What do you know about them?

Sandra Jolley was my mother, his first wife. They were born ten days apart and died ten days apart! She was an Earl Carroll show girl and was absolutely beautiful. Even though they divorced after ten years, they remained friends their entire lives. I attribute that to both their characters. I never heard either one of them utter an unkind word about the other — ever. I feel they never wanted to put me in the position where I would have to choose one over the other, or take sides. Marilyn Johnson was his second wife. She was originally a dancer, but had to give it up due to her health, and became a talented interior decorator. They lived in a rented duplex that was very large and quite lovely, and Marilyn did a wonderful job decorating it. There was a small den with a card table and four chairs they brought over from France, two big club chairs, and an unusual bar that was created from a hole in a wall. The space behind it was a closet, so the only access to it was through the closet. Marilyn was 37 when she died. She had a hole in her heart, and not much could be done for that in the 1950s. His third wife was also named Marilyn — Marilyn Fisk. She was a dancer in *The Music Man*, which is how she and my father met. They were together three years during *The Music Man*, then married and remained married for 25 years. She is only five years older than me and we've been friends since I was 14. Dad's last wife was Sheila Forbes, and we don't talk about her!

You mentioned he was complicated. In what ways?

He had a few vices. He cheated a lot — and I don't mean cards! He really was quite a womanizer, even when married. He felt that there was nothing wrong with that, although none of the relationships were long or serious, and he was very discrete. As I got older, my mother explained about his dalliances and I thought it was appalling. My mother told me she was not the type of person to put up with that, and they divorced. He and I would argue all the time about it and I would say to him, "I'm going to meet someone in my life who will be absolutely faithful to me." He would look at me, almost with pity in his eyes, and say, "Baby, it ain't going to happen! Men are not monogamous." And you know what? So far he's been right! I still adored my father, and he was a wonderful man in many ways, but that's just the way he was.

Apparently, he was also fond of drinking. How did it affect him?

He could hold an enormous amount of alcohol without becoming drunk. My dad played the role of Harold Hill in the Original National Company of *The Music Man*, which opened at the Philharmonic Auditorium, Los Angeles, on August 18, 1958. He appeared in over 2,000 performances as the show traveled the country. When it opened, he set up a bar in his dressing room but the producer, Kermit Bloomgarden, thought that was inappropriate. However, after the great success of the opening night, Bloomgarden sent him a case of Scotch, which was essentially Bloomgarden giving his "blessing" to the drinking. My father had a loud, booming voice, but he was always a gentle man and, in his own way, quite shy. When he drank, he just became bombastic and bigger than life, which is the way people expected him to be. I'm not sure there was any one thing that started him drinking, other than it was something that all the actors did in those days. It really only affected his work in the last eight years of his life when it started to show in his performances. When he was doing a lot of TV work, I would sometimes get a call to come and collect him from the studio. Marilyn and I joined Al-Anon, the support group for the families of alcoholics to find out how to help him. We did have an intervention with him, although he would often look at us like we were crazy because he didn't think he had a problem. But there were other times when he would admit that he did.

Did his parents have a drinking problem?

His mother was definitely an alcoholic. She was a brilliant woman, but alcohol took over her life. Long after my parents divorced, when I was living with my mother in a small two-bedroom apartment in North Hollywood, my grandmother got a bit out of control and needed somewhere to stay. My mother said she could come and live with us, but told her the first time she picked up a drink, "You're gone!" She stayed with us for a month or two and, inevitably, smuggled a bottle of something into the house. True to her word, my mother kicked her out. She didn't end up on the street, but went to her own apartment. However, she did later set her bed on fire, due to smoking!

You mentioned *The Music Man*. Robert Preston did the original on Broadway, and in the film. How do you think your dad compared?

Robert Preston was a singer and did a fine job. For the film, I think they wanted to go with someone who could sing and had a bigger name recognition at the time. Dad wasn't a singer and did a talk-sing version, like Rex Harrison in *My Fair Lady*. In some ways, I think my father was better suited to the character. I actually joined the show in 1960, and I remember watching him singing "Trouble" and he really nailed the beat: "Ya got trouble, my friend, right here, I say, trouble right here in River City." You were mesmerized from the time he opened his mouth. Dad was bigger than life and could spin a tale and make you believe anything. He was the Music Man, someone people would follow.

Of course, he was also in around 80 films. Do you recall him talking about other actors?

He did tell me that in his last movie, *Chisum* [1970] with John Wayne, it almost killed both of them doing some of the fighting scenes. My father was a great rider and did all his own riding in film and television — he'd never let anyone ride for him. He had been in the last horse cavalry in the U.S. army, so it's somewhat ironic that he is so well remembered for *F-Troop*! He and John Wayne were good friends and drinking buddies. I know dad disliked Charlton Heston, and thought he couldn't act. There's another story about sitting next to Joan Crawford at a banquet. She made a pass at him, but he wasn't having any of it — she wasn't his type. He let her know it and she got quite mad at him.

What's the first movie you saw him in?

I don't know if it was the first, but I have a vivid memory of seeing him in *Bugles in the Afternoon* [1952] when I was about seven. He played a cavalry guy and was shot in the heart with an arrow. I lost it and went berserk. My mom had to take me out of the theater and when we got home, called my dad to come over — they were divorced at this stage. I thought he had been killed in front of me and wasn't consoled until I saw him, and he explained that it was all make-believe. I probably wasn't entirely convinced, because a few years later I became very jealous of Margaret Lockwood, who was with him in *Trouble in the Glen* [1954]. I thought he seemed to care for her too much, like a daughter. I was horrified and thought that he liked her more than me!

On the set of *F-Troop*, Forrest Tucker and family. Left to right: son Sean, daughter Brooke, Tucker, daughter Cindy and wife Marilyn Fisk.

Orson Welles was also in that.
Really? I don't remember; I was too busy being jealous!

He played a doting — if short-lived — husband to Rosalind Russell's Auntie Mame. Didn't you have a hand in him taking that role?
I should have been a casting director! When I was ten or 11, I was spending the summer with him, and at dinner one evening told him: "I've just read the most wonderful book about the most wonderful woman. If they ever make a movie about her, you should play her husband." Well they did, and he did. It was *Auntie Mame*! I still love that movie and watch it every couple of months. Rosalind Russell's character actually inspired my life: I also believe in fun, bling, and craziness. That may sound odd, but it's my take on life. I created AWGO —*Amazing Woman, Genuine Original*— a website for happy, snappy people, like Auntie Mame. I would have given anything to meet Rosalind Russell. But when my dad was making the film, I was away at a Catholic convent school where my parents had sent me for some discipline — I'd run away from home as a teenager, and was a handful. They didn't exactly have an open-door policy, and wouldn't let me out just to visit with Auntie Mame!

Rosalind Russell wasn't the only actress to play Auntie Mame; Greer Garson did, too, on the stage.

She was another idol of mine. I've loved her since I was ten years old and, over the years, was determined to meet her! I would ask people if they had a connection to her, without luck, and my father didn't know how to find her either. In 1994, I was working in Dallas teaching a class of 35 students in my work as a miniaturist. I had read that Greer Garson lived in Dallas, so I told my class no one was leaving until someone told me where she lived! Later, one of them came up to me and told me Greer Garson lived on a long-term care floor at the Dallas Presbyterian Hospital — the woman was a nurse, and breaching confidence by telling me, but I didn't care. So I sat down with a girlfriend who helped me write a long letter to Miss Garson. We took the letter to the hospital, along with some flowers, and they allowed me to take the flowers down to her room, but not go inside. I was shaking, a complete wreck! I could see her in the distance, sitting by the window, and thought I was going to faint. I could not believe that the woman I had idolized was just 15 feet from me. I begged the nurse to give her my letter, which just explained how she had influenced me, and I wanted her to know that she was still important to somebody and hadn't been forgotten. The nurse said she would pass on the letter and I went out and sat in the car, crying with my friend. When I got back to the hotel, there was a phone message — to call Greer Fogelson! That was her married name; her late husband, Buddy Fogelson, was an oil and cattle man and had donated money to build a wing at the hospital. It seems the nurse had tried to find me after I left, and they tracked me down from the hotel stationery the letter was written on. When I called, she said, "Well, hello, Brooke dear!" I could barely speak. Over the next two years, she allowed me into her life in small ways. We would talk on the phone and have short conversations. Eventually, I went to see her and spent two hours with her. Believe it or not, I was the first person the nurse called when she died, because the nurse knew how fond I was of her and she didn't want me to turn on the news and hear it that way. She suffered from congestive heart failure and lived for several years in a wing of the hospital.

And you probably bumped into quite a few other interesting people over the years?

Oh, yes. I remember Tony Curtis visiting us when I was little. He and Janet Leigh came to the house for dinner, when my dad was married to Marilyn Johnson. Janet was pregnant with either Jamie Lee or her sister, I can't remember which. The adults were settled in the living room for drinks before dinner and when dinner was announced, Janet couldn't get out of the couch as she was so pregnant. She sunk so deep, it took Dad and Tony to pull her out! Very dignified, to say the least, and I have never forgotten.

More than anything else, your dad is best remembered as Sgt. O'Rouke, in *F-Troop*. It looked like one of those shows that the cast would have had fun making.

He had a wonderful time with Larry Storch and Ken Berry and the crew. Dad lived in Toluca Lake, which was about three minutes from the Warner Bros. lot where *F-Troop* was filmed. He had a golf cart to drive back and forth to the studio and he got Carl, his valet, to decorate it with flower boxes, bugles, flags and a bar, of course, at the back where the golf clubs usually go. It had an ice chest, bottles and glasses. Then he had a TV installed. He got all his friends to sign the cart and had it glossed over so it wouldn't fade. After shooting all morning and breaking for lunch, Larry and Dad would jump in the cart and head over to Lakeside Country Club, which was also just a few minutes away. They'd drink their lunch, and return for the afternoon shooting. Well, they got very little done some days because they would be ad-libbing all over the place. You can see that if you watch some of the episodes. Larry had the same sense of humor as my dad and was very talented. Norma, his wife, was a real snob and very controlling. She took over his life and told him what he should wear and where he could go. He seemed okay with it, as long as he could still do his thing. When she died, none of us thought he'd ever survive: we expected him to turn up wearing a pink sock with a blue sock. But he did just fine and his socks even matched.

Was your dad good at learning his lines?

He was "one-take Tucker," quite an amazing study. He had a great memory and could go through seven pages of dialogue with ease. He could also cry on cue, totally believable tears. But he got to the point later in his career where he thought crying was some great emotional response that he had to put into all his roles. I think the tears came easier when he was drinking more. Everyone I've talked to has said he was a wonderful actor and very believable.

You did some acting on stage but never really pursued it?

Forget about my acting. I was not destined to be an actress. When I did *Charlie's Angels*, I was scared to death that I wouldn't hit my mark or would flub my lines and shame my father. Most of my life, I have built miniature models, which I call 3-D paintings, of room settings. Around 1970, Dad and I were at the Drury Lane Theater, in Chicago, and I wanted to build a little memory box. I visited a miniature store and got the bug. I happened to be good at it, at a time when nobody was. They've sold for up to $16,000, but there was a lot of expense to prepare them. After 35 years, I just became burned out. Now, I work in the fragrance industry.

Your mother's father, I. Stanford Jolley (1900–1978), was a most prolific actor. He appeared in hundreds of films from the 1940s to the 1970s — one of those character actors whose face is instantly recognizable. He always seemed to play the villain. What was he like?

He was a true gentleman, and a gentle man. There was not a person who met him, that I know of, who did not love him. When he talked to you, he made you feel like you were the star in the room. He listened intently and just made people feel good about themselves. My young friends loved to be around him. He died in the Motion Picture Home (and so did his wife, my grandma Emily, in 2003, at age 103).

Wasn't that where your father also died?

My father also died there, from throat cancer, not emphysema, as some sources say. I know, because I was there every single day. My father spent two months in the ICU at St. Joseph's Hospital in Burbank, and was then moved to the Motion Picture Hospital where he died only a couple of days later. When we were trying to encourage him to wean himself from the respirator, I promised that I would go out and get him a bottle of champagne if he did. His eyes lit up! So I got a bottle, and the patient label that was attached to it was for "Frank Parker" September 3, 1986 because he was under that alias in the hospital so that the *Enquirer* and other [tabloids] couldn't find him and plague the family. I still have that very bottle downstairs on a shelf with a note for my daughter to be sure it is never thrown out when I am no longer here!

So, despite your father's difficulties, was he a good dad?

He was a super-nice guy and had a larger-than-life quality about him, and not just his physical presence. He would never let me go to bed without kissing me goodnight — ever. Even if we had just had a spat he would always end the day with "Goodnight baby, I love you!" I talk about my parents all the time and every so often I tell myself, "I'm not ready to be an orphan!"

Brooke Tucker on Forrest Tucker. Telephone interview on 1/15/11. Brooke Tucker's website is www.brooketucker.com.

20

Jackie Elam on Jack Elam

If ever an actor deserved to be charged with wanton larceny, it was Jack Elam (1920–2003). Whether flashing a malevolent scowl as the epitome of screen villainy or bantering with the hero as a lovable sidekick, Elam could "steal" any scene he wandered into. He stole from Charles Bronson in Once Upon a Time in the West *(1968), from James Garner in* Support Your Local Sheriff! *(1969), and from John Wayne in* Rio Lobo *(1970). But no one objected; any film featuring Jack Elam — the man with the wonky eye — could only be elevated by his presence. Named after her dad, Jackie Elam recalls her father's dual good guy/bad guy screen image.*

What is your dad's family background?

He was born in Miami, Arizona, to Millard Elam and Alice Kerby Elam. The song "Moon over Miami" was a long-running family favorite, even though the song was based on Miami, Florida. His mother died when he was very young and I know that it was a tough time growing up in the Great Depression. He had an older sister, Millie, with whom he maintained strong ties, and he was especially close to his grandfather, Hiram "Hi" Elam, and Hi's wife, Elizabeth. Hi had been a sheriff and had even been shot once or twice in the line of duty. I think Dad always got a kick out of the fact that he made a living playing villains, when his role model was a man of the law!

What were some of his jobs before turning to acting?

He started out as an accountant, then left it for good when he began acting. We had a tax accountant when I was growing up, but Dad remained a meticulous bookkeeper. He was always both right and left brained — an ambi-brain! He was also controller for Hopalong Cassidy Productions for three or four years, and he was instrumental in handling the finances when the Bel Air Hotel was built. Another job that stands out to me was, in his early teens moving the life-sized chess pieces at the Phoenix Biltmore's outdoor chessboard.

How did he get into acting?

He agreed to arrange the financing for three westerns in exchange for a small part as a "heavy" in each film. Then, Darryl Zanuck was looking for an actor to play a "heavy" in the picture *Rawhide* [1951], with Susan Hayward and Tyrone Power. Mr. Zanuck saw these pictures and hired my dad to play the part of Tevis. It was the break he needed, and the beginning of a long career.

What are some of your memories of growing up with Jack Elam as a dad?

I found him fairly laid back. He was 50 when I was born, so there was a large enough age difference between us that he didn't over-react to my shenanigans. Dad's first wife of 20 years, Jean, passed away in 1961. She was mother to my siblings, Jeri

Jackie and Jack Elam, around New Year's Eve 1997.

and Scott. I'm the sole child from his second wife of 40 years, Jenny. He loved restaurants, so we had a lot of fun eating out together. Two of his all-time favorite restaurants were Barones and Le Petite Chateau, which are still alive and well in Los Angeles. He was also the best Easter egg hider, possibly of all time. There was always a very difficult hunt for the adults and an easy hunt for the kids. I remember actor Gene Evans and Dad spending an evening carving out oranges, still on the tree, in the garden and hiding orange eggs. It was masterful. And we also shared a love of horror movies. Really, anything that jumped out of graves — moldering corpses, or flesh-eating zombies — we loved it.

Where did you grow up?

I grew up in a couple of places: Laurel Lane in Studio City, a section of Los Angeles, as a little kid; and Santa Barbara as a teen. We also spent a lot of time on location as a family. Dad liked to travel with my mom and me, so we spent a lot of time in interesting little towns that were conducive to locations, places near swamps and deserts.

When did you realize your dad was an actor?

When I was around five, I remember watching him get shot on television, probably in an episode of *Gunsmoke*. He was sitting with me at the time. We both found it pretty amusing. I will say that I remember being on a set before I remember ever seeing him on film or television, so I understood the process and "movie magic" before I ever saw the end product of all that work.

What was he like off-screen?

Dad was a card, very funny and smart. He was also a gentleman. He was gracious to everyone — waiters, studio execs and fans alike. Poker was one of his true passions and many in Hollywood fell prey to his bluffs. He was a good teacher, too. He was pretty pleased when I could finally hold my own at the poker table, and playing at the same table as my dad was the best. Most people don't know about his range of artistic talents. He designed modern furniture and we still have the bedroom set that he designed. He painted, wrote, and had a very imaginative approach to home-improvement projects. At our home in Studio City, he built a "virtual" tropical rain forest, by rigging sprinklers over the outdoor bar — a little nugget of Hawaii in the Valley; he loved Hawaii. When guests were coming over, he'd have me run out into the yard and "turn on the rain." He was also a big supporter of animal charities, especially Dogs for the Deaf, and he was very partial to the Federation of the Blind.

Does anyone else in the family act?

A large number of Elams are interested in the arts, in one form or another. My half-brother, Scott, has acted professionally in films and television, and he's really good. He also makes beautiful wooden percussion instruments. My half-sister, Jeri, directs a workshop in Portland called Astrodrama, in which she uses performance to teach people about astrology. My cousin, Star Herrmann, is a very gifted and respected stage actress on the East Coast, and is married to film/television/stage actor Edward Herrmann.

Do you prefer to watch your father playing the good/funny guy or the villain?

I like watching it all. I love the early "film noir" stuff, just because he's so young and saucy. *Kansas City Confidential* [1952] is a personal favorite. It's nice to be able to watch his later work, as that was filmed in my era. I really enjoy watching any movie directed by Charlie Pierce; the locations were very special experiences and his cinematography is gorgeous. *The Winds of Autumn* [1976] is pretty amazing. I also love some of the obscure TV stuff like *The Texas Wheelers* and *Struck by Lightning.* They were brilliant shows, I think, that were ahead of their time.

How easy was it for him to make the transition from villain roles to the comedic ones?

Comedy became easier for him as he got older, because of the physical demands of westerns. At a certain point, you just don't want to do the hard, manual labor of an action film. In terms of material such as villainy or comedy, I don't think he had a preference. He just liked to work, and he really enjoyed the camaraderie of the set. In general, he preferred film to live-tape, such as sitcoms. He was very good in front of a live audience, but it made him nervous. He felt most comfortable one-on-one with a camera.

Your dad worked with some great actors over the years. Can you share some of his stories?

He loved working with Mickey Hays in *Aurora Encounter* [1986]. He thought that little dude had a great spirit, and I think their on-screen chemistry reflects that. He worked with Walter Brennan, whom he liked a great deal and respected, on *Support Your Local Sheriff!* [1969]. I remember the story of Mr. Brennan saying to my dad, "Sonny, one of these days I'm going to die and then you'll work regular." We have a portrait of Mr. Brennan, painted by his son Andy, in my dad's office at home. In *High Noon* [1952], he worked with Gary Cooper. After the shooting scenes of *High Noon* were finished, the studio thought they might need some comedic relief from the long gunfight. They spent a couple of days shooting additional footage of my dad in the bar drinking everyone's abandoned drinks. However, when they premiered the original *High Noon* in Santa Barbara, it was a big hit so my dad's bar scenes ended up on the cutting-room floor. *Rio Lobo* [1970], with John Wayne, was my first "location," and I was just nine months old! I do remember hearing the story of when my dad was in Durango, Mexico, on Sam Peckinpah's *Pat Garrett & Billy the Kid* [1973]. While in Durango, the Wayne company was also shooting *Cahill U.S. Marshall,* and John Wayne was sending his actors and crew home for Christmas. He kindly let my dad join them. Dad was worried about not getting back to Durango for his picture, so Mr. Wayne offered to fly him back on his private jet, if necessary.

Who were his favorite directors?

Charles "Charlie" Pierce and Burt Kennedy. He worked several times with both, and they established a true family atmosphere on set. There was

Jack and Jackie Elam, Christmas, 1994. (Photograph courtesy of Jackie Elam.)

mutual loyalty. They liked that Dad was low-maintenance and, usually, not in need of a lot of direction. Charlie's sets were especially fun for me; he let me run errands and pretend that I was working. In reality, I was probably getting in the way, but he was very good-natured about it. Dad also really enjoyed working with Sam Peckinpah. They clicked artistically and liked each other personally.

Who did your dad hang out with?

Dad had a close circle of friends that included actors such as Gene Evans, David Huddleston, and Don Galloway; directors Burt Kennedy and Don Siegel; road manager Al Hassan; and costume designer Luster Bayless. One of his actor friends, Morgan Paull, transitioned to becoming his agent. And director Robert Totten was married in our backyard in Santa Barbara. Dad had a lot of friends, everyone from gaffers to producers, and basically anyone with a sense of humor, his primary criteria, and who had an affinity for Liar's Poker. And whenever we were in Los Angeles, we stayed at the Sportsman's Lodge in Studio City. Chuck Connors always drove in from his ranch in Tehachapi to join my dad for breakfast. After Dad formally retired, he still worked. He had a circle of friends in Ashland, Oregon, with whom he liked to play poker and go out to dinner.

It's often reported that he was blind in his left eye. Could he see at all?

The party line, that it was a childhood accident when he was around ten or 12, is true. He could "see" light, but not objects. Although I imagine it bothered him as a young person, once he made it as an actor, I don't think he cared.

Did he want you to go into acting?

Dad was very supportive of anything I wanted to try. I dabbled with acting briefly in my early twenties, but ended up taking a different job path and am now an academic administrator at an arts college, CalArts.

How would you say your father influenced you?

I think I've got my dad's common sense and ability to approach things analytically. And bad teeth! Dad and I could never catch a break with the dentist. I'm definitely a film nut, and I think that comes from having great experiences watching films, both in the process of production and on the screen. Before working at CalArts, I worked at the American Film Institute. Both have great film schools, and it makes it more fun to go to work when you love what you do. Once in a while I spot one of my dad's films on a class syllabus — and it's great to know that these films are still being watched and discussed. He remains a very cool dude.

Jackie Elam on Jack Elam. Email interview on 10/29/10.

21

Judy Lewis on Loretta Young

*"Elegant" is perhaps the best word to describe Loretta Young (1913–2000). Known by her birth name, Gretchen, in her early films, she radiated beauty, talent, and elegance from the silver screen, dazzling movie audiences from 1917 to 1953. A 1948 Oscar winner (*The Farmer's Daughter*), Young went on to shock Hollywood studios my making the successful transition to television in 1953 with* The Loretta Young Show, *which ran for eight seasons. Married three times, Young had two sons with second husband Tom Lewis. But five years before her marriage to Lewis, she gave birth to a daughter, Judy, who for much of her life believed she was adopted. Eventually, she would learn that not only was her real mother Loretta Young, but that her father was one of Hollywood's most famous leading men.*

Your mother began acting in the silent era. Did she talk about that period much?

She had a few stories. Her first starring role was in *Laugh, Clown, Laugh,* in 1928, when she was just 15. She played a circus tightrope walker and had some romantic scenes with Lon Chaney who was much older than her, but he was a sweetheart of a man. On one occasion, director Herbert Brenon was giving her directions that she really didn't understand, so Lon took her aside and offered some advice. He asked her, "Gretchen, do you like milkshakes?" She told him she did. He asked what kind of milkshakes and she said, "Vanilla." So to help her feel more comfortable about their scenes, he suggested that every time she looked at him, she should think of a vanilla milkshake! So that was the delicate way Lon Chaney, who was a big star at the time, helped a young actress. She was terrified of the director, however. He threw a chair at her one time, and if she hadn't ducked, she said it would have "taken her head off." So she realized at that early age, she would have to learn to take care of herself. Also, a lot of stars didn't survive the transition from the silent period to talking pictures because their voices didn't match their good looks. But my mother's did.

She had three sisters who all acted, and they even appeared in one film together?

Yes, the four girls played sisters in *The Story of Alexander Graham Bell* [1939] and it's wonderful for me to watch. They were all drop-dead gorgeous. Georgiana was the youngest, and this was her first film. Polly Ann was in over 30 films, mostly in the 1930s. Betty Jane took the stage name of Sally Blane and did a lot of westerns with Tom Mix. There was also a brother, Jack, who didn't go into acting. He became an attorney.

Is it true your mother got her break in *Naughty But Nice* (1927) by accident?

That's right. Director Mervyn LeRoy called the house for Polly Ann and my mother answered the phone. He wanted to cast Polly Ann in the movie, but she was out on location. My mother said, "Polly isn't here, but will I do?" She told him who she was and he invited her to come down to the studio to try out. So she caught the streetcar to the studio and was given a contract at a very early age — she was only 14.

When did she first take you to a movie set?

That was when I was about four and a half and she took me to the 20th Century-Fox Studio, which no longer exists — it's now Century City, a residential and business district. I remember sitting in the screening room with my mother as she was viewing the dailies, although I don't remember which film it was. There was a scene in which my mother, larger than life up on the screen, was crying. I was too young to realize that she was just acting, and I became upset and had to be taken out of the room. But I did enjoy my visits to the studio. I remember spending my tenth birthday on the set of *The Stranger* [1946] which she made with Orson Welles, who was her favorite director.

There was a point in her career when she ran afoul of the studio head. What happened?

Well, Darryl F. Zanuck, head of 20th Century-Fox, wanted her to do certain films but she refused. So he blacklisted her for two years. In those days, Zanuck and the other studio heads would get together and play poker once a week. All he had to say to the others was "Loretta's misbehaving. I don't want her to work for a while" and she was blackballed by all of them. It was a difficult time for her. The studios had enormous power over actors. In those days, actors were under contract and had to do several films a year. There was also a morals clause in the contracts and the studios controlled what movies their stars were in, who they went out with, where they lived, and even what clothes they wore. They played a very paternalistic role in all of their stars' lives.

After working on more than 100 films, your mother made a successful transition from movies to television, and was one of the first big movie stars to do so. Aside from some TV movies, she never did another feature film. Why not?

Loretta Young and daughter Judy Lewis pose for a portrait around 1940. (Photograph courtesy of Judy Lewis.)

She loved the freedom of having her own successful television show. I remember she told me, "I couldn't pick my own roles in movies. When I had my TV show, that's when I really had a good time." So she became her own studio and could play the roles she really wanted to play. *The Loretta Young Show* ran for nine years, a half-hour show with 30 to 35 episodes each year. Each story had a moral to it which she addressed at the end of each program, and it was one of the trademarks of the series. Another was her clothes. At the beginning of each show she would come through the door wearing a different glamorous gown, then talk to the audience about the upcoming show. She loved clothes and wore them beautifully. And she got to keep them — it was her show!

She worked with some of the top leading men of the time including Jimmy Stewart, Douglas Fairbanks, Jr., Tyrone Power, Spencer Tracy, and Clark Gable. Apparently she fell for most of them?

In those days, everybody fell in love with everybody else! The movie stories often involved leading men falling in love with their leading ladies, and visa versa. So yes, she admitted it herself, she fell for most of her leading men and dated every single one of them. As strange as it seems now, that was the normal thing to do then. It was a very romantic period. The studios promoted such romances between two leading actors, if they were unmarried. They would send the couples out on the town, all dressed up and arrange for the PR people to follow them around for good publicity. That's the way Hollywood worked. It was a small town in the '20s, '30s, and '40s. Then it began to change in the '50s with the decline of the studio era. But even today, relationships between entertainment couples rarely seem to last. You basically have two narcissistic people living together who are always working, so it's a strain on the relationship.

Some have called your mother a controlling person. Would you agree?

I think when your own life has been out of your control, as it was for much of her film career when she was a product of the Hollywood studio system, you compensate for that when you are able to take more control of your professional life. So that's how I would interpret any reference to her as "controlling"—she learned how to take control of her life and make important choices about her career. I remember in the '50s, many of her associates in the film business thought she was a traitor because she went into television and had her own show. In those days, television was viewed as an "upstart" by the motion picture industry; one they didn't think would last. She told me, "I've won the top award in my field of motion pictures. I want to begin in a new industry." And that's what she did, going on to win three Emmy awards. So she had great vision.

Some actors don't like to watch their movies. Did your mother?

By that time she was retired and living in Palm Springs, we would watch them together, and she did critique her acting. Some of the films, I had never seen. *Laugh, Clown, Laugh* was one that I first saw with her. As we watched it, I remember her telling me that she was very thin at the time and the producers wanted her to be more sexy-looking. So they built a whole body suit for her to wear to give her more curves. So watching that film again made her laugh.

How would you describe the relationship between you and your mother?

Mother-daughter relationships are always complicated at best. In my case, I didn't have an identity because my mother had always told me that I was adopted, even though she really knew that she was my mother. In fact, she never publicly acknowledged me as her biological daughter as long as she lived. Nor would she disclose who my father was, although she obviously knew. I carried my stepfather's name, but he never adopted me, so "Judy Lewis" did not legally exist. So, for their sake—and mine—I had to tell my

life story by writing about it in my book, *Uncommon Knowledge*. There was
a period when we didn't speak for 12 years when she thought I was writing a
book about her, which I wasn't at the time. So she asked me to leave her
house one day, and I did. I didn't start writing the book until three or four
years later. Then the book came out and thank God both of us said a lot of
prayers and we reconciled three years before she died. So we had three good
years together.

Did she read the book?
    She actually never mentioned the book to me again. I think she read
some of it, but I'm not sure if she read it all.

**So which was the bigger shock: learning that Loretta was really your
mother, or learning who your father was?**
    Instinctively, I always knew there was some secret surrounding me. So I
was not too surprised to learn who my mother really was. But I was surprised
when my fiancé told me, two weeks before we were married in 1958, that my
father was Clark Gable. He and my mother had met on the set of *The Call
of the Wild* [1935] and fallen in love. But to avoid scandal, my mother told
everyone, including me, that I had been adopted. It seems it was the worst-
kept secret in Hollywood because everybody had known about it all my life —
Hollywood people, childhood friends, even total strangers — everyone but
me! They were protecting me and my mother. When I found out, I called
Jack Haley, Jr., who was an old beau of mine, and I was upset with him
because he had known. I said, "Jackie, where were you? Why didn't you tell
me?" He said it wasn't his place to tell me — it was my mother's responsibility
and he had assumed that she had told me when I was younger. I think that's
what a lot of people thought.

**So you learned in 1958 that Clark Gable was your father, but you weren't
able to meet with him before his death in 1960. That must have been terribly frustrating, especially since you had actually met him before you
knew he was your father.**
    I went through every type of emotion you can imagine. I found some
good therapists along the way, and writing the book was very therapeutic for
me, too.

**Your mother was 21 when she met Gable on the set of *The Call of the
Wild*, then they reunited for a second film, *Key to the City*, in 1950. Do
you like watching that film?**
    It's a wonderful film, a comedy. My father had a talent for comedy and

won the Academy Award for *It Happened One Night* [1934] in which he was wonderfully relaxed and easygoing. Mom didn't have much of a sense of humor, but in that film his comedic timing really brings her's out. So to watch them together is a lot of fun for me because she has an element of playfulness with him that she didn't ordinarily have. But I don't recall ever watching the film with her. However, it was after filming of *Key to the City* that he came to our house and I met him.

What happened during the meeting?

Throughout the filming, Mom kept asking me to visit the set. I was 15 and already had been to a lot of movie sets. I had my own life, so I told her I wasn't interested in going. I came home from school one day and there was Clark Gable standing in the living room. That was the first time I met him, but at the time I didn't know he was my father. My mother was also there. You've got to keep in mind that they were both actors, and actors like drama. My guess is that the two of them had fun planning the meeting. So when I walked in, he was just standing there. I had just seen *Gone with the Wind* and I said, "Oh, you're Clark Gable!" He was very tall and looked down at me and replied, "Yes, and you're Judy." Then my mother came 'round the corner and said, "Oh, I see you two have met." I'm sure it was all staged. I started to leave the room and she said, "Judy, why don't you stay and talk to Mr. Gable for a while." So I obeyed. It was a very large living room and we went over to one of the couches and sat down. He put me at ease and engaged me with questions immediately, and I answered. He asked about my life, and I told him about taking dance lessons, dating Jack Haley, Jr., and about school. Then, after a while, I realized Mom had left us alone. We must have talked for a couple of hours. Then I walked him to the front door, he leaned down and kissed me on my forehead, turned around, walked down the steps and out of my life forever.

Have you had any DNA testing to confirm you are his daughter?

No, it's been suggested to me and my answer is that my mother's word is all I need. I was also born with the huge Gable ears! But when I was seven my mother made me have plastic surgery on them. It was very painful and they were literally pinned back. A lot of people have commented over the years that I look like my father — and my mother — not bad genetics! I've been very blessed.

Clark Gable also had a son, John Clark Gable, with his fifth wife, Kay Williams. Are the two of you close?

No, but I'd like to be. I met John once some years ago; we had a nice

Loretta Young and Clark Gable in *The Call of the Wild* (1935).

dinner together and I gave him a copy of my book. He grew up knowing that Clark Gable was his father and I'm sure it's been difficult for him living in the shadow of such a famous actor.

Despite all the difficulties you have had, or maybe because of them, you ended up becoming a professional psychologist and have helped others deal with difficult situations. But you started out in acting?

I went to a Catholic finishing school for girls in New York City — and it finished me alright! So I didn't go to college then — I went right to work on my mother's TV show for two or three years. Then I had a long career as an actress, had my daughter, and ended up behind the camera. Finally, in my forties, I asked myself what I wanted to do with the rest of my life. I decided the one thing I had missed was a college education, so I put myself through Antioch University, which caters to people in mid-life who want to change their careers. I wanted to be a marriage and family therapist, so I obtained an undergraduate and a graduate degree in clinical psychology in three years. I was always fascinated by people. As a child, I was surrounded by all these stars that were bigger than life. But I was a very quiet child, and I observed them quietly and was always curious as to what made them tick.

And the experience you had with your own parents influenced the way you have treated patients?

Absolutely. Life experience is one of the most important elements you can bring to your practice. I deal in family assistance and have to work with the entire family, so coming from the kind of family I did, I am always intrigued by people's stories. I have even helped people who were children of actors, although I obviously can't say who. When you have a parent who is in the limelight all the time, it can be very difficult for that second generation. It's not an easy role as you have to carry the persona for your parent — publicly and privately. I remember my mother once saying to me, "Remember, you're a reflection of me!" That's a heavy responsibility for a child who is also struggling to find his or her own identity. I was fortunate to find therapists who helped me through difficult periods, and I'm glad I can now use my experience to help others.

Judy Lewis on Loretta Young. Telephone interview on 12/6/10. Judy Lewis's website, http://judy-lewis.com, has links to information about her mother, as well as her 1995 book, *Uncommon Knowledge*, published by Pocket Books. There's also the www.loretta-young.com site which is authorized by her family's estate.

22

Sam Gilford on Jack Gilford

> *Soft-spoken, rubber-faced Jack Gilford (1908–1990) was a successful vaudeville and nightclub comedian and Broadway entertainer before his career was torpedoed during the sinister McCarthy-era blacklistings. Like many others actors, including his wife, Madeline (1923–2008), and good friend Zero Mostel (1915–1977), Gilford rebounded and went on to have a long and successful career in Hollywood. His familiar face popped up on TV commercials, in record-breaking Broadway shows, and in popular films such as* A Funny Thing Happened on the Way to the Forum *(1966),* Catch-22 *(1970), and* Save the Tiger *(1973), as well as numerous television sitcoms. Gilford's son, Sam, reveals that despite their affection for each other, life with this great comedic actor wasn't always full of laughs.*

What do you know about your father's early life?

Jack was born in New York's lower East Side, and he grew up there before the family moved to the Williamsburg section of Brooklyn. His father's name was Jacob Aaron Gellman; the family was basically Jewish, from an area originally called Bessarabia, in the eastern part of Moldavia, which is in Romania. We think there is some Mongolian ancestry in the family, because my brother was born with what's known as a Mongolian Blue Spot, which disappears after birth. My mother came from the same area and her family's background was Polish, from Warsaw. Jack's mother's name was Suska, which is a Russian-Jewish version of Sofie. In fact, I was supposed to be named Suska if I had been a blonde, blue-eyed girl. The family spoke fluent Yiddish, which is a European Jewish dialect, and was raised kosher. In fact, when my father bit into his first ham sandwich when he was 21, he really thought lightning was going to strike him! It didn't, and we always had ham. Jack's mother was also quite strict religiously. He was very close to his mother, but I don't know how close he was to his father. His father was a furrier of some sort, I'm not sure exactly. His mother was really quite a woman, and had several jobs, including

188
188

The Gilfords — Madeline, Sam, and Jack — at home, 1965.

running a restaurant for a while. She was also a bootlegger at one point and Jack would deliver the booze for her. There's the story of how one customer forced Jack, who was 13 at the time, to test it to see if it was the type of bootleg hooch that could turn you blind. So young Jack took a few swigs and got pretty loaded from it! Jack lived at home for many years. This reminds me of the old joke that explains how to tell if someone is Jewish: he lived with his mother until he was 30; he went into his father's business, and his mother thought he was God!

Jack had several jobs growing up, including working in the garment business and in a pharmacy. But he was a sickly kid and was tormented by an older brother, Murray. He also had a younger brother, Nathaniel, whom he really loved. All three brothers died from heart attacks; the other two were only in their sixties, and I think their mother and father did as well, at relatively young ages. I'm not really sure what Jack wanted to be when he was young, but he did like to make people laugh from an early age. At the same time, he came from a background of incredible poverty and was extremely deprived. His parents were socialists/communists and I don't think they got along too well and used to argue a lot, although I'm not sure if it was about politics. Although they didn't get along, they stayed together because Jews did not divorce. So there was a lot of fighting in the house, and Jack just didn't like that. He came from quite a dysfunctional family and nobody comes from that background unscathed.

Where did the family name Gilford come from?

My father was named after his father, Aaron Gellman. Milton Berle is
the one who changed Jack's name. Milton thought it should be spelled Guil-
ford, but Jack refused to have the "u" put into Gilford because he knew that
would have sounded like some kind of English WASPy name. Milton and
Jack were the same age, but Milton was his mentor.

What was your father like around the home — funny?

People always ask that! And the answer is definitely no. He was very
intelligent and sophisticated, and a loving father, but quite complicated. While
he could be easygoing, he could also be quite temperamental and reasonably
neurotic. He suffered from extreme depression and I, unfortunately, inherited
depression from both my parents. It's a strange illness that can leave a person
immobilized. But on the other hand, he was able to make millions of people
laugh through his work in theater, film, and television. However, at home he
was a very quiet fellow, in fact, quite a shy person. But he could take control
of a room just by telling a story. He obviously had a tremendous ego, which
is an interesting mix. He had to have that in order to get through all the other
stuff. One story told to me about his insecurity was about the time he performed at a party in front of comedienne Fanny Brice, and he was upset
because she wasn't laughing. Afterwards, Jack went up to someone and asked
what was wrong and was told that she actually thought he was very funny,
but she just didn't show it. Well, comedians are not always a good audience.
But there were times at home when he had to be "on." Other times 'round
the house, he'd just do mundane things and putter around for ages. I can
remember him fussing with the thermostat for hours, and working with the
chemicals in our pool in Connecticut. He would put so many chemicals in
the water that it would make your eyes red and sore. I'd say: "That's chlorine,
Pop, don't put the whole bottle in!" I figured we'd come out like skeletons if
we went in the water! Then he would fuss for hours trying to get the colors
of the chlorine test kit just right. Jack was quite generous, and could be very
sweet, kind and loving, but had a temper at times. I remember we were going
up to camp one time and my parents were having an argument. Jack just got
out of the car and walked away.

So what was home-life like for you in general?

I had a brother and a sister. It was a Jewish home that was traditional,
but not religious. It was a very socialist home, very atheist, very liberal, and
progressive. In fact, my parents lived together for about six months, which
was pretty revolutionary back in 1948. I was born in New York and grew up
in Greenwich Village when people like Jimi Hendrix and Bob Dylan just

walked around. When I was 15, I left home for a farm community school in rural western Massachusetts. I fell in love with the area and still live there today. Growing up in New York, I knew a lot of theater people but not necessarily the Hollywood crowd, because my parents were not in any way Hollywood people. But Jack had to go out there to make a living.

How did you and your father get along?

I personally had a difficult relationship with him most of my life. I just could not get along with him. Some people thought it may have been competition over my mother, or that Jack and I were very similar and that's why we didn't get along. When I was very young we had a close relationship, but it just turned sour when I was about eight years old. And from that time I was just alienated from him. Even though we didn't get along well, we loved each other and I was still one of his biggest fans. Also, he was often away from home because of work. Later on, before he died, I got along much better with him. It was only in his last three years that he understood my great love of all that was passed on to me that he loved as well. He was kind of a straight-laced fellow and uptight, even though politically he was very liberal. My mother was much more permissive and flexible, so as a parent Jack was the stricter one. But he loved his children dearly and I think he was one of the great comedians of all time. He had some very special talents that were so subtle that most people probably didn't appreciate through his movie and TV work.

How did he get into the entertainment business?

He started in local amateur shows. I actually still have a trophy cup from 1935 that Jack won for an amateur contest, which dates how early he started in show business even thought he had other jobs, too. One person who was also in the competitions with him was Jackie Gleason, who grew up in the same Brooklyn neighborhood. Jack was also working in a drug store and somehow Milton Berle came upon him. Milton took him under his wing as a kind of a protégé and that went on throughout the '40s. I don't know all that much about his relationship with Milton, but I do remember Milton turning up at Jack's funeral and it made me incredibly furious! There must have been 400 people at the funeral, but Milton wasn't invited and just showed up. We had prearranged about ten people to speak over one hour, so everyone just had a few minutes to talk. Then Milton shows up, decides he wants to speak, and took 20 minutes to do a whole routine. His opening line was "I never liked Jack Gilford; I loved him." I was so angry — to get up and do an entire 20 minutes shtick without asking anyone was terribly rude, and an egocentric thing to do, but that was Berle; he was a difficult man. The people who were going to speak were Jack's friends, not necessarily performers. So Milton was taking away time from other people. I actually wasn't going to speak but I did get up. One of the things Milton talked about was all the hand signals he used to give Jack off camera when they worked together on his show. So when I got up, I sarcastically pointed out one signal that Milton forgot to mention — and I did the finger as a knife across the throat signal for "cut!" People gasped when I did that; it was not something you did to Milton Berle! Normally, I wouldn't say anything at a funeral, but I just didn't think it was very tasteful or respectful of Milton to just come in and take over like that.

Your father spent some time in the service during World War II. Any stories from that?

He was in the USO for a while. There was one show that he did and thought he'd be funny and go out on stage with his hands hidden in his cuffs, as if he had no hands. But almost the entire audience was made up of amputees. Ouch!

What's your earliest memory of seeing your father perform?

That was probably on some of the early TV commercials. I recall he first did an Accent commercial. Another was for a Rambler car and I think we used to get a car as part of the payment for the ad. Then he did the Cracker Jacks commercials, for which he's best known. But we would always get excited when we saw him on TV, although his TV career started off slowly, with a couple of ads. When I was growing up he was always in a Broadway show, and even before I was born he was doing that and vaudeville. He also had a nightclub act for about 40 years. But then things went bad during the blacklisting years and he couldn't get any work.

What happened to him during those years of the Hollywood blacklisting?

It was a very bad time for my parents. There were these terrible right-wing Jewish reactionaries running Hollywood, like Sam Goldwyn and Louis B. Mayer, who hated unions. They liked things the way they were and thought it was great to have a non-union Hollywood back in the '30s and '40s. So along come people like my parents who were involved with organizations like the Screen Actors Guild — my father was a member for 12 years and my mother for a year — so it was no wonder they got nailed. My parents weren't Russian spies or Stalinists, they were just American socialists and were part of a movement that was trying to get peace, and integration, and organized unions. Jack was blacklisted for something like ten or 12 years, and just could not make a living. Because of the heavy socialist backgrounds my parents came from, they were intensively active politically, so I guess that was the price they had to pay for it, although I really don't think they did anything wrong. It was a real struggle for them to get through that period without any work in Hollywood. A lot of people couldn't handle it and basically "jumped out the window." When Jack was called before the House Un-American Activities Committee (HUAC), he had a great line — a classic. One of their usual questions was: "Is it your intention to overthrow the government by force or violence?" Jack's answer was: "No, just gently." That didn't go over well! J. Parnell Thomas was the HUAC chairman, and he had no sense of humor whatsoever.

And what happened to your mother?

She was blacklisted, too. In fact, the person who named her was Jerry Robbins, the choreographer of movies like *West Side Story* [1961], *The King and I* [1956], and *Fiddler On the Roof* [1971]. Jerry was an incredible genius and I personally loved his work. But no one enjoyed working with him. At one rehearsal, the show's dancers allowed him to rant and, as he was backing up, let him fall into the orchestra pit! As far as the blacklisting was concerned, people were just scared and did things like Jerry did to save their own careers because the people who did name names were spared to a certain extent. I felt sorry for Jerry that he was just that weak. It's like being a prisoner of war — people break under different conditions. I guess Jerry was scared. When my mother was subpoenaed to appear before the committee, she gave them a real hard time. In those days, when a subpoena was served on a person, they would ask your name then would actually touch you with the subpoena. Then you would have to come and testify. My mother actually hit the lady from the HUAC who was serving the subpoena, and told her to get off her property. She had groceries in one arm and me in the other, raced the other two kids inside, and just lost her temper. She told me that my head actually collided with the subpoena lady's. So you see, I was made subversive at an early age! But my mother's worst enemy was Joe McCarthy's chief aid, Roy Cohn, who was just out to get her. He was one of the most evil, dangerous people who was ever put on earth. He's the one who nailed the Rosenbergs and put them in the electric chair. The story was told in the TV movie *Citizen Cohn* [1992].

Zero Mostel didn't fare too well during that period, either. And according to the 2009 play, *Zero Hour*, didn't he also give the committee some grief?

Zero refused to rat on anyone. When he went before the committee they asked if Zero was his given name. And he answered, "No, 'zero' is the amount of money I've made since you got involved in my life." They asked him if that was supposed to be funny. And he said, "Yes, I make my living as a comedian."

How did your father get back into acting?

Some people escaped the blacklist like Milton Berle, Danny Kaye, and Sid Caesar and they were successful during the '50s with the rise of television. My father was prevented from working on TV or film, so that was why he did so much Broadway work. As the blacklisting lifted, one of his first roles was in *Car 54, Where Are You?* in 1963. Things picked up in the '60s and he appeared on many shows such as *Here's Lucy*, in which he was a driving instructor. What really broke the drought was an Allan Sherman special on NBC. Sherman said if he couldn't have Jack Gilford on the program, he wasn't going to do the show.

Jack and Zero worked together in the Broadway production of *A Funny Thing Happened on the Way to the Forum*, which ran from 1962 through 1964. That must have been interesting because Jerry Robbins worked on that too!

Jack did not want to do the show. But Madeline reminded him that Jerry had only named her to the HUAC. She told him, "He named me, not you. The show's going to be a big hit. You're going to do this show!" So Jack did it and they opened in Washington, and it was a big hit. When Jack and Zero turned up for work and saw Jerry for the first time, Zero couldn't resist commenting. He said something like, "Hey Jerry, remember Jack Gilford and his wife, Madeline?"

So did Jack and Zero get along with Robbins on *Forum*?

Well, they managed to work together. I went with my brother to see the play on opening night. Before we left for the theater, our mother had actually lectured us not to use the words "rat" or "fink" if we saw Jerry Robbins! So we headed off to the theater and it was a pretty bad area, like many of them back in the early '60s with the stage door opening out onto an awful, dirty alleyway. As we walked down the alley we had been told to stomp our feet to scare off the rats. I mean, real rats. Well, as we walked, there were all these little shadowy figures scurrying up the fire escapes! We had actually grown up in the Village, but we had never seen rats before so we were kind of excited. When we got inside, Jerry was standing next to my mother and we said, "Hey, Ma, we just saw a rat!" After six hours of lecturing about not using the word "rat" or "fink," we forgot!

Were your father and Zero friends off stage?

Jack and Zero knew each other from back in the late 1930s. They were really close friends in real life, which is funny because they had such different personalities. Jack was more of a straight-laced, quiet, introverted person. Zero was the opposite — completely extroverted and demonstrative. He once actually threw Jack up against a wall because Jack was very upset when his younger brother, whom he adored, had died. They had a performance that night and Zero thought that, in this case, the best thing for Jack to do was to go through with it. So Zero physically pushed him up against a wall and told him, "You'll do the show tonight and that's that!" And the show went on. There's a scene in *Forum*, both the play and the film, where Jack is supposed to play a dead virgin and Zero puts his finger in Jack's mouth to hold down the veil and Jack's supposed to be pretending to bite Zero's finger. During one performance of the play, Zero was stepping on a laugh of Jack's in the show and Jack decided to really bite Zero's finger. It certainly taught Zero a lesson about stepping on Jack's laugh again!

Zero was well known as a painter, but your father also did some painting, didn't he?

Jack used to dabble in watercolors and I still have a couple of his paintings, which are quite good. But Zero was a very serious artist. Jack once signed one of his own paintings as Vincent Van Gilford. And Zero, being extremely serious about art, thought that was very tasteless. This time, Zero did not have a sense of humor! But Zero was quite a character. His real name was Sam, his father was a Rabbi, and his parents disowned him when he married Kate, who was a tough Irish woman and a former Rockette. Zero had a very serious accident, where his leg was run over by a bus and crushed. He never really recovered from that and always had a bad leg.

Most people only know *Forum* as a film. Was the original play good?

The original was an incredible musical play by Larry Gelbart and Burt Shevelove. Larry went on to become very famous, and did the *M*A*S*H* series. But Burt died young. I went to see *Forum* over 20 times. It was quite racy stuff for the early '60s. But of course, most people didn't see the Broadway performance and so we are left with the film, which Jack and Zero were also in. They went to Spain to film it in 1966 and it was directed by Dick Lester who did the Beatles films and he had a huge career. Dick was a darling fellow, but he ruined the film as a musical and he knew it. He messed with the text of the play, took out all the good songs, put in his own stuff, and made it into a chase film. My parents loved Dick and were often in London and would run into him occasionally. Every time he saw my mother, he would apologize to her profusely for what he did to the film. Unfortunately, no one will ever see the original play because it was never filmed. There were union rules up

until the 1970s which did not allow Broadway shows to be filmed, so there is
no film record of the early Broadway shows. The movie is very different from
the play. Of course, there's additional, wonderful stuff you can put into a film
that you can't in a play, but you can spoil the original, and that's what happened.

**Most people probably think of Jack as a comedic actor, but did he do
some serious roles?**

Jack did an incredible number of Broadway shows throughout his career
such as *The Tenth Man,* and *No, No, Nanette.* He was actually fired from *No,
No, Nanette* for standing up to the stage manager, who was an awful woman.
The cast got together and gave him a purple heart! My parents wouldn't let
me see *The Tenth Man,* the Paddy Chayefsky play, which was about the
"Dybick" and the ten Jewish men who formed a covenant to exorcize this evil
sprit from a young, redheaded woman. He also appeared in about 25 films,
like *The Incident* [1967] and *Save the Tiger* [1973], with Jack Lemmon, where
he played serious roles. I felt those roles were more like the other, real side of
Jack at home. *Anna to the Infinite Power* [1983] is an obscure science-fiction
film he was in, and it was the only time I saw Jack play a part where he was
actually an evil scientist. He was kind of like Karloff in *The Body Snatcher*
[1945]—wonderful charm, while at the same time being very malicious. That
takes a special talent, so that was an interesting part for Jack to play. He did
a lot of other obscure films, too. But mostly people remember him for his
comedy roles in films like *Forum* and *Cocoon* [1985], which gave him a lot of
recognition later in life. He also did the rounds of TV sitcoms such as *All in
the Family, The Golden Girls, Get Smart,* and *Taxi.* He was in two episodes of
The Golden Girls and in one he actually married Sophia. In the *Taxi* episode,
"Like Father, Like Son," Jack played Judd Hirsch's playboy father who long
ago abandoned the family and shows up in his life again. It's a cute 24-minute
episode. In the *All in the Family* episode, Jack ends up dying. Someone told
me they never saw anyone die as well as my father! Jack was even offered a
spin-off series from *All in the Family* where he would play a rabbi. But he
didn't want to be typecast forever in that role.

Were awards important to him?

Not really. He was nominated for several Tony Awards, and was up for
an Academy Award once, as Best Supporting Actor in *Save the Tiger,* although
he didn't win. But the following year he won an Emmy for *The Big Blue Mar-
ble,* a kids program. He used to put his awards in the bathroom and used
them as door stoppers. "Pop, is that an Emmy in the bathroom?" I asked him
once. "Yeah, it holds the door well," he answered.

Your mother also worked in the entertainment business. What are some highlights of her career?

She had been a radio actress when she was a kid and was pushed into show business by her mother when she was very young. Later, when the acting tapered off, she became more involved with producing and raising money for shows, and for a while she was a casting director. She was very active in the theater and that side of show business. Many times when Jack did a film, my mother would edge her way into a small part, like she did in the *Cocoon* sequel. She also wrote a book with Kate Mostel, Zero's widow, called *170 Years of Show Business*. It's filled with stories about the two families, and the blacklisting days. In fact, back in the '90s, Marlo Thomas had an interest in doing a TV movie of the book and there was talk that she wanted Billy Crystal to play the role of Jack. But nothing came of it. My mother did the TV rounds, too. She made some commercials, and was on *Law and Order* and *Mad About You* in the 1990s. She also had two very interesting sisters. One of them, Fran Lee, was the person responsible for bringing about the pooper-scooper laws in New York City in the 1970s! She was a crazy consumer advocate.

At your mother's funeral in 2008, a poem was read that had been written by lyricist E.Y. "Yip" Harburg. What do you recall about that?

Yip was my godfather and is best known for writing all *The Wizard of Oz* songs, like "Over the Rainbow." I read the poem at my mother's funeral and it was meant to be bouncy and funny — a great tribute to her. Then at the memorial service, it was decided to let someone else read it, a well-known actress, but she couldn't make it there so her husband read it. It was a simple poem, but he read it like a cross between Margaret Hamilton, as the Wicked Witch from *The Wizard of Oz*, a pirate, and Edgar Allan Poe! It was just awful, and I think he even scared some of the guests. People's jaws just fell open. Here's the poem:

"The Ballad of Madeline Lee" by E.Y. "Yip" Harburg

She dwells in the Village
In Abingdon Square
The beautiful Madeline Lee
All telephone wires converge
On her there
The sweetheart of AT&T
You ask who she is?
She's the soul of the city,
committed to every committee.
The wife of Jack Gilford, the funny, the witty....
The bountiful Madeline Lee.

She solves all your problems
Allays all your fears
And sets all anxiety free.
Just call her collect and
The next voice you will hear
Will be that of our Madeline Lee
"Does your friend need a job? Or a script? Or vasectomy?
Does your wife need a maid, or a quick
hysterectomy?
Call me back in an hour...but don't send a check to me"
Fabulous Madeline Lee.
Loathers of women's lib
Freedom and sex
Don't dawdle when Madeline smiles.
When she pickets the White House.... They run for the ex-
It to cover & lock up their files.
If you're planning a strike, or a parade, she'll gung-ho for you,
Bus you to Washington-raise all the dough for you,
And while she's in prison-produce a new show for you,
Improbable Madeline Lee.
When Joe [sic] McCarthy
Came down from the heights
To investigate Madeline Lee
She appeared in her tights
With the whole Bill of Rights
Tattooed on her plump potpourri.
She's the blonde Joan of Arc ever rallying masses to strike against war & political asses.
Men who never clink glasses with Jackie Onassis make passes at Madeline Lee.
There's no saddlin' Madeline Lee.
So here's to the girl of this wild half a century.
Fabulous, fearless & free!
This nation will not be a fed. penitentiary
As long as there's Madeline Lee.
So let's tear a herring & toast it in wine for her, Let Barnum & Bailey design a gay
shrine for her,
And the zodiac light up a new neon sign for her,
Lovable, laudable, bright & applaudable.
And audible,
Madeline Lee.

After your mother died, weren't there were a few problems with the estate?

This was the estate battle from hell and almost killed me! Sometimes when you lose your parents, it can bring family closer together, but in our case there was a real battle. The problem was that there was little money left in the estate. My mother had done some of those stupid, too-good-to-be-true refinancing deals on her apartments in the West Village and in Connecticut, and died with a huge debt.

Many people remember your dad as "Simon the Likable" in an episode of *Get Smart*. In fact, that was the premise of the whole show: he played a character who had such a distinctive face, no one could hurt him. Jack was definitely one of those character actors whose face is immediately recognized, but only film fans could probably name him. Did that bother him?

You have no idea what it's like growing up with somebody who had such a famous face. It was impossible to go anywhere without people staring and pointing. But at the same time, few people could put a name to the face. Some could be really rude and would come up and say things like: "Do you know who you are?" Others sometimes thought he was Soupy Sales or Sid Caesar. He was insulted when they didn't know his name.

Your father could do some unusual impressions. Can you give some examples?

Jack had this face of rubber, with which he could do remarkable things. For instance, he did an impression of a fluorescent light bulb going on in a dark room. Unfortunately, there are no video copies of that. He would do it with his face, blinking his eyes for the light. Then there was his imitation of thick pea soup coming to a boil. That was actually used in the "Like Father, Like Son" episode of *Taxi* from 1981. Like the fluorescent light bulb, he just did this stuff with expressions on his face. A lot of people do impersonations, but Jack's impressions were quite obscure yet funny routines. He did a lot of animal imitations, too. I loved his camel. He also did an eagle, owl, and a Russian wolfhound. Others were a racehorse that fell upon bad times, and a conductor leading an orchestra. His specialty was obviously pantomime and he was influenced by the early silent comedians from the 20s like Buster Keaton, Charlie Chaplin, Harold Lloyd, Harry Langdon, as well as Harpo Marx. He loved all the early silent clowns.

What's one fact about Jack that probably no one knows?

Jack actually made up the phrase, "The butler did it!" In the '40s he did a routine spoofing movies, and he came up with that line.

What was the best thing about having parents in show business?

Often, I'd get to see how things worked behind the scenes. Jack had a non-singing role for 15 years in *Die Fledermaus* with the Metropolitan Opera. He played the drunken jailer named Frosch. After the performances, I was

Sam Gilford and his mother, Madeline, at home, May 1997. (Photograph courtesy of Sam Gilford.)

allowed up on the stage and it was amazing to see how things really looked and worked. It was always a bit disappointing, however, because you would see that everything was fake. For instance, in *Die Fledermaus,* Jack used to wear padding because he had to fall down steps when he came in as the drunken jailer. To the audience, they looked like stone steps, but behind them was a slide. As Jack came in he would slide instead of stepping down the flight of stairs, and everybody would laugh. But I got to see how that was done and I thought it was great to be able to see those things as they really were.

You didn't go into acting. How has your career unfolded?

I live in a very small village with lots of farms and stables in a semi-rural area in western Massachusetts. But I can go back to NYC any time I want, as it's only three hours away. I've never fitted well in society and I never did all the things that everyone else did — never went to school, got married or had kids. But I've still had a very interesting life. Even though they were both actors, my parents certainly didn't encourage me to go into show business. They were very liberal, progressive parents and encouraged me to do whatever I wanted to. I have a few talents — I can play almost any instrument by ear, and I've done all this artwork which I used to peddle on the street for years. I think I have one of the largest collections of music and film in the entire country, and have a 24-hour radio station on Pirate Radio. Other things I've done include: creating and producing public access TV here in the Greenfield, Massachusetts, area for six years; playing piano in several local clubs over the years; creating several original programs called "Let's Learn About Astrology"; creating a one-hour-forty-five-minute-long DVD as a tribute to my father; producing a series of about 130 half-hour shows called "Sammy's Video College," which was a local experimental alternative video music collage program; and I was on college radio at the University of Massachusetts Amherst for 15 years. I've also had some rough times and once tried to kill myself in 1981 over a love affair. That night, Jack had a taping of his own TV special and I had completely forgotten about it — I was not thinking about Jack's taping that night. But Jack had to do the show, even though he knew that I was possibly dead. So he did it, and then came up to the hospital afterwards. Of course he was concerned but, as they say, "The show must go on!"

How would you define Jack's comedy style?

Jack was one of the great comic geniuses who made it in Hollywood, Broadway, nightclubs, and television. Most people know him through his movie and TV work where he was doing other people's material. But early on, he did do his own club act. He had a lot of material he created that was very interesting stuff. When you see the old material that he wrote, then you can understand where his real genius lay. Some of it was pretty obscure and not like any of the standup comedy now, but he didn't believe in blue humor to get a cheap laugh. He had his own style which may seem old-fashioned to audiences today. But he was very physical and into pantomime with a long tradition of influences under his belt. His humor was often very esoteric. For instance, when I was a kid — and I used to hate this — he would put me on his knee like we were posing for a picture and he's say, "Look, Father and Sam!" I never understood it when I was a kid. I'd love to see an *American Masters* featuring Jack Gilford. A lot of people don't know about his life, so I hope my information and inside stories will help people understand more about my father and also what it can mean growing up with a famous parent. It can be a curse as well as a blessing, but despite the difficulties, we always loved each other very much.

Sam Gilford on Jack Gilford. Telephone interview on 9/23/10. Sammy Gilford's website is www.live-artist.com/samsart.

23

Braden Barty on Billy Barty

He may have been small in size, but Billy Barty was never overshadowed on-screen even when working beside such superstars as Tom Cruise, Michael Landon, Mickey Rooney, or Elvis Presley. Born in 1924 with dwarfism, Barty was determined that his height would not prevent him from achieving his career dream as an actor. And it didn't. He appeared in close to 200 movies and television shows throughout his 70-year acting career, and his presence was always captivating. Barty died two days before Christmas, in 2000, and his son, Braden, says his father also worked throughout his life off-screen to promote the rights of "little people," the generally accepted term for adults of small stature. Barty founded the Little People of America organization to promote public knowledge and social acceptance of people with small physical stature, and was an inspiration to many people, both big and small.

What's the history of the Barty family?

My father's grandfather emigrated from Italy around 1880 and settled in the Pennsylvania coal region. My relatives had many different jobs, and some of them were miners. My grandparents had three children, and my father, William John Bertanzetti, was the middle child. He had two sisters, Evelyn and Delores. In 1927, when my father was three years old, my grandfather moved the family to Los Angeles and changed the family name to Barty, which was my great-grandfather's nick name. We think the name was shortened to Barty because vaudeville acts were charged by the number of letters in the name on advertising marquees. So, Barty was cheaper than Bertanzetti! My father and his sisters traveled the vaudeville circuit as "Billy Barty and Sisters." In the act, Evelyn played the piano and the younger sister, Delores, played the violin. Billy played the drums and did a comedy routine. They traveled for about three or four years with the act.

Your father was born in 1924 to parents who were of average height. Was it tough for the family knowing they had a child who was going to be small?

He was born in a period when not much was known about dwarfism. It wasn't until he was around two years old that the family realized he wasn't growing much and they took him in for tests and found out he did indeed have dwarfism. His two sisters were of average height, as were their parents. And I'm five feet, eleven inches! So it's just a random selection of genes that produce dwarfism and there was just no way to test for it back in the early days. As far as difficulties, there were the standard things like finding clothes that would fit, so his mother made most of his clothes. But he was determined not to let his dwarfism prevent him from having a career in entertainment. He actually lived at home until he was married when he was around 38, which was not unusual in Italian families.

How did he get his start in show business?

He used to do this trick to get the change out of his pocket because his arms were short. It began with him standing on his head, so the change would fall out. Then that evolved into spinning on his head. His father was very mechanically inclined and had a lot of jobs that involved constructing and inventing things, and worked at the film studio. One day, when he was three years old, he was walking down the street in Hollywood with his father and they passed a set where there was some filming taking place outside the studio. My grandfather went up to the director on the street and told my dad to spin on his head to see if it was something the director could use in the film, and the director liked it. I've heard that the director was Jules White, but I'm not sure if it was or if they used his spinning in the film. But the director became interested in my father and his film career was off.

Jules White is best known for his work in the Three Stooges films. Did your dad ever work with the Three Stooges?

He had a bit role in *Soup to Nuts*, which was the first film the stooges appeared in. He also worked with the Marx Brothers on *Monkey Business*, although his scene was cut out of the final version. However, I have a still photo of him with Harpo Marx, and Harpo is dressed up as a female nurse on a ship, holding my dad as if he were a baby.

What was his first significant role?

He was cast alongside Mickey Rooney in the Mickey McGuire comedy shorts in the late '20s and early '30s that were similar to the Our Gang comedies. He played the role of Mickey's brother, Billy McGuire. The series was

Billy Barty and his son, Braden, age 9, in 1979. (Photograph courtesy of Braden Barty.)

not as successful as *Our Gang*. That was because producer Hal Roach would shoot a lot of footage to make *Our Gang* movies, but most of it was just ad-libs that he pieced together. The Mickey McGuire stories were more rehearsed, more contrived, and didn't seem quite as natural. Probably the most natural character in the series could have been my dad. He was the youngest in the show, and a cute little kid. He stayed friends with Mickey Rooney and they kept in contact for years. They would joke and say they "grew up" together. When my father passed away in 2000, Mickey showed up at the funeral even though he was just out of triple-bypass surgery. When I walked in and shook his hand, I remember he had sweaty palms. My dad had many other roles in the 1930s, and appeared in films including *The Gold Diggers* of 1933, *Footlight Parade* [1933], *The Bride of Frankenstein* [1935], and *A Midsummer Night's Dream* [1935].

Why wasn't he in *The Wizard of Oz?*
When *The Wizard of Oz* was shot in 1938, he was just 14 years old and was too young: you had to be at least 16 to work on the film. And even then, they weren't really looking for youngsters; they were looking for mature little

people for the Munchkin parts. He was also pretty small and you had to be a certain height.

After the 1930s, he gave up acting and didn't resume until the 1950s. What happened?

He went to college when he was a teenager. He actually left acting and wanted to become a journalist and sportswriter. He graduated with a journalism degree, but also loved sports and even played football for L.A. City College, as well as basketball and track. I think he played half-back on the football team. They even had a play called "The Billy Barty Play," where he would be close to the end zone and he'd wave his arms to ask for the ball. They would throw him the ball and he'd go out of bounds with it. He was three feet, nine inches tall for most of his life, but was very muscular for his size. World War II came along and obviously he wasn't selected for the draft, so he went right back into acting.

How did your father meet your mother?

In the 1950s, he was acting in various films and TV shows. He knew a couple of other little people who were also actors and one of them was Gerry Maren, who was the Lollipop Guild member of the Munchkins in *The Wizard of Oz*. So my father got together with Gerry and a few of the others to form an organization. They planned on getting people together from several states to have a convention of little people. They chose Reno, Nevada, which is known as "The Biggest Little City in the World," to hold the convention. So they had their first convention in 1958 and about 50 people turned up, which was a moderate success. It took them a couple of years to get the second convention organized, which was in Las Vegas. My mom was living in Los Angeles at the time, where she did graphic design. One day she was waiting at a bus stop and a lady named Debby Dickson came up to her, and said, "Hey, you're a little person; we have a convention in Las Vegas — do you want to attend?" Well, my mother, Shirley, had never hung out with little people before, but decided to go. However, she had a funeral to go to in Idaho on the same weekend of the convention, which was over several days in Las Vegas. With her older sister, she drove out to Idaho for the funeral, but then my mother didn't feel like going to the convention. However, she did eventually go. They had a fashion show there and she wore the dress she took for the funeral. My dad was emcee for the fashion show, and so that's where they met for the first time. Back in Los Angeles, they began to date. The relationship was on and off for a while, and the second time he proposed to her, she accepted.

Your mother was a Mormon. Were there conflicts for your father between religion and acting?

My mother was a Mormon and my father was converted to Mormonism in 1968, shortly before I was born. So he had to begin living a clean life and be an example to everybody. In 1975, he did *The Day of the Locust* and he had to say things like "bastard" and "son-of-a-bitch," which by today's standards aren't that bad. So he talked to his bishop at the time and asked if he could say these things. The bishop told him to "do what you got to do." So it wasn't a major problem for him. Besides, he was always very concerned and conscious about his demeanor on TV and in film. And overall, he was pretty morally well-rounded anyway.

Were there any challenges for you growing up with a father who was much smaller than you?

The house I grew up in was in Studio City, California. It was a fairly normal home. He didn't hang out with the Hollywood crowd. In fact, I can't think of any celebrities who would come around to our house, not even Mickey Rooney. Mostly, he hung out with his own friends who were involved in his career like his manager, and friends from his college days. As a father, he was very gentle but stern — when he spoke, you listened! He added on one bedroom and bathroom to the house and also modified it for their comfort by lowering all the kitchen cabinets and counters, the counter in the bathroom, and lowering the light switches in some rooms. Even though I was much taller than my father, it was just something I didn't think about until we were actually in public. He wasn't just a little person, he was a *famous* little person. So whenever we went out in public, people would look at him because of his size or they would recognize him because of his fame. Sometimes you could have fun with it, but other times it could be annoying. I left home when I was 19 and went to college, then moved back for about a year. But I was always close to my family.

Did your parents ever talk about not having children?

No, it never occurred to them even though there was a 50:50 chance that their children would be of small stature. There are over 200 types of dwarfism, and my parents had different types.

There were several little people who were well known actors in movies and TV. Do people confuse them with your dad?

A lot of people say to me "Oh, your dad was in the old TV show, *Wild Wild West*." So I have to tell them, "No, that was Michael Dunn." Other people think my father was in *Time Bandits*, but that was David Rappaport.

Did he ever talk about working with Elvis?

He did two films in the 1960s with Elvis, *Roustabout* [1964] and *Harum Scarum* [1965]. My dad was older than Elvis by a few years, and all I really remember him telling me was how Elvis would bring a Bible to the set and he would talk a lot about his spirituality.

Your dad did a children's show in the '60s called *Billy Barty's Big Show*. Do any recordings of that survive?

The shows were all shot live, and nothing was ever recorded. It was a kid's show that ran in Southern California on KTTV for four years. Dad would come out dressed as a circus ringleader and would sing "Hello, hello, welcome to the show." I think he also played games. I now meet people who are in their fifties and sixties and they tell me, "I was on your dad's show!" They all seem to remember what they won on the show because every kid left with a toy. I have several still photos from the set. One shows a police officer reminding viewers to always lock their car doors. I think security was a big thing in the '60s!

He was a frequent guest star on a lot of TV shows, both variety shows and series. Why do you think he was so popular?

He was always busy working and had a great sense of comedy and was very good at ad-libbing and being spontaneous. He had bit parts on all sorts of shows and as recurring roles. He was on the early variety programs like the *Milton Berle Show* and *The Steve Allen Show*. He was very good at doing impressions and did a wonderful impersonation of Liberace singing "I'm in the Mood for Love," with a miniature piano that had a candelabra on top, like Liberace's did. He'd get about a quarter of the way through and say, "I can't go on any further without my brother, George!" Liberace's real brother, George, was his sidekick. Then another actor, Earl Bennett, would come out playing a character called Sir Frederick Gas and accompany him with a stick, which he played like a violin. Sir Frederick would also play a little whistle in his mouth. Then the candelabra on the little piano would start shooting out shaving cream that was supposed to be melted wax. Sir Frederick would try and clean up the "wax" and wipe it off my dad, who would be brushing him off. The two would get into a fight and start throwing the "wax" at each other. It was a specially rigged miniature piano. Someone behind the curtain would be pumping the shaving cream up through the middle of the piano and out the candelabra.

There was an episode of *The Love Boat* in 1978, in which your father poked fun at himself. So he must have had a good sense of humor?

He did have a good sense of humor, and he was a character. When we got a video camera in the '80s, he would always be "on" whenever the camera was on. You can see his sense of humor in *The Love Boat* episode where he worked with a good friend of his, Patty Maloney, who was a well-known female little person. They also worked together on *Little House on the Prairie*. In *The Love Boat* episode, every time someone said "little," he'd say, "Who said 'little'?" In a way, I suppose you could say the story was about our family because it was about two little people and their average-height son! The son was played by Edward Albert, the son of *Green Acres'* star Eddie Albert. In fact, there's a photo of my dad in his *Billy Barty Big Show* outfit with the cast of *Green Acres* all dressed up in their outfits with the Green Acres car.

How did your dad influence your career?

I don't like acting but I do like to be involved with story making and have been a director/producer for most of my career. I grew up on movie sets since I was 12 years old, and thought making movies and TV shows was really cool. So just being on the set with my father, and seeing how things worked, really influenced me from a young age. Apart from my dad's influence as an actor, my mother was a graphic artist, and my grandfather was an inventor, so I think I inherited all of their creative genes. One of the sets my dad took me to — and it was the biggest movie set that I've ever been on — was a movie called *Legend* that my dad shot at Pinewood Studios in England, in 1984. It starred Tom Cruise. I was 14 and the whole family was in London for the whole summer. I was in heaven going to the set and seeing everything being created. I was even an extra in the background. Tom Cruise had just finished *Risky Business* and his next film was the one that really launched his career, *Top Gun*. We were on the set every day and I got to hang out with Tom — he liked to play backgammon. So I sort of knew who he was, the guy from *Risky Business*. Hopefully, one day I'll meet him again. He won't recognize me since it was so long ago, but I'll ask him, "Do you remember driving to Heathrow Airport doing 110 miles per hour and changing out of your armor to catch an airplane?" And he'll probably look at me and say, "How do you know that story?" and I guess I'll have to tell him who I am!

How important was charity work to your father?

He never turned down charity work and would go anywhere to help a good cause. I think his biggest love was charity work. He founded the Little People of America in the 1950s, which is still active today, and the Billy Barty Foundation, in the 1970s, which helped little people both psychologically and scholastically. He loved golf, and also had an annual fundraiser which was a golf tournament in various places. For his work, in 1992 he was honored in Washington, D.C., with a National Victory Award, which honors people who had an impact on society. The award was presented by President George Bush, Senior, who he met several times. In fact, he actually helped campaign for Bush and was at the National Republican Convention in 1992 with the California delegation.

Speaking of honors, were you with him when he got his star on Hollywood Boulevard?

That was in 1981, right after *Under the Rainbow* came out, and I was there. The star is right across the street from the Chinese Theater. We all drove up in a limousine and it must have looked like a circus troupe getting out the car because Lou Ferrigno was with us. We have photos with him and Dad together. They also gave him a wood-framed star with a gold plaque inside with velvet backing, and a smaller plastic replica. I have them here somewhere.

So he liked golf and charity work. What else did he like to do off-screen?

He loved all kinds of sports and, as I said, almost became a sportswriter. He was a favorite guest at the Hollywood Dodgers Star Night where the stars would play baseball and he would go out and hit the ball, or go to the mound and coach fellow actors like Tom Selleck on how to wind up the pitch. He and a friend were into harness horse racing, and bought horses that raced at Los Alamedas, Hollywood Park. He also played the trumpet and the drums.

He was cast in many of his roles because of his size. Did he ever resent that?

If you're good-looking, or tall, or small, or have some unusual features, you are going to be type-cast by Hollywood. That's just the way the business works. When you're cast as a little person in a movie or TV show, it's because there's a reason for that little person to be in the show. So he didn't have a problem with it. Dad was very disciplined, but also well-rounded, and just thrilled he could have a successful career as an actor and that audiences appreciated him.

Braden Barty on Billy Barty. Telephone interview on 9/17/10. Braden Barty's business website is http://shadowstormproductions.com.

24

Carole Ita White on Jesse White

When he first set foot on Broadway in the 1940s, Jesse White (1917–1997) could never have imagined that the new medium of television would bring him fame and fortune three decades later doing washing-machine advertisements. Beginning in the late '60s, White portrayed the melancholy Maytag repairman, destined to be idle due to the company's high-quality appliances, according to the commercials. But White's career was far from being a washed-up pitchman. He amassed over 160 film and TV roles as well as appearing in many Broadway productions throughout his career. Aside from his commercial work, White is best remembered for the playing the gruff asylum attendant in the film and stage versions of Harvey, *with Jimmy Stewart. Daughter and fellow actor Carole Ita White says that even though he was frail towards the end of his life, her dad was delighted to appear on-screen one last time, in a 1996 episode of* Seinfeld.

Your father came from a poor family. How tough were his childhood years?

He was born in Buffalo, New York, and raised in Akron, Ohio, during the depression. He was one of seven children and the family was dirt poor. His father was a junk dealer who traveled around with a horse and cart, and his mother made bathtub gin which my dad and his brothers would sell when they were shining shoes. The family was so poor they didn't have enough money to feed everyone, so his two youngest brothers were sent to live in an orphanage during the depression. My father was always very enterprising when it came to finding jobs to help support the family, and he also sold newspapers in front of a theater in downtown Akron. My grandmother would put his baby brother on a bus and tell the driver to drop him off at certain places where my father would be so he could deliver a hot meal to him. After the depression, when he graduated from high school, he sold beauty supplies with an older brother. He was popular with the ladies at the beauty shops because he always had a joke or good story to tell them. Then, when he was 20, he moved out to Hollywood. He changed his name from Weidenfeld to White because he thought Weidenfeld was too long for the theater marquees. Some of his brothers, who were musicians also, changed their name to White.

How did he get his start in show business?

He came to Hollywood in 1936, and his first job was working for Mae West who had a legitimate theater in

Jesse White, publicity shot for "Bedtime for Bozo," 1951.

Hollywood. In fact, she helped many young actors and playwrights, and gave them their first break. Anthony Quinn got his start in Mae West's theater. Initially, my dad was just selling popcorn and cleaning up, then she gave him occasional walk-on parts in some of the plays, and that was his first experience acting and he loved it. Mae was about to make her first movie and was going to give my dad a part in the film, but he couldn't do it because his mother and eldest brother wanted him to come back to Akron to sell beauty supplies. My dad was heartbroken, but he respected his mother's wishes and went home. But he wasn't there for long!

What happened when he returned to Akron?

He was champing at the bit to get back to Hollywood, but his family wanted him to forget about his dream of being a movie star. So they suggested he go visit his brother Al, who lived in New York. Well, he did, and there he discovered Broadway! That's where he met and married my mother. They met in a theater group of young actors. But things didn't go well for them at first. Dad wasn't having much luck with work because every time he'd get a role in a play, it would flop. So he began to think he should give up acting and move back to Ohio. Then a remarkable thing happened. They were literally packing their car to move back to Akron when my dad got a phone call from Brock Pemberton's office. He was a big theater producer. Apparently, he had seen my dad in a walk-on role in one of the plays that had flopped, and he had been well received by the audience. Pemberton wanted my dad to come over to read for a play. So he landed the role of Wilson in *Harvey* which ran for four years with Frank Fay as Elwood P. Dowd.

Which was then made into a film with Jimmy Stewart as Dowd.

Yes, and my dad continued his role and in 1950 moved back to Hollywood, where he was put under contract with Universal, and that was the beginning of his film career. I was just six months old at the time, so I never saw the original Broadway production of *Harvey*. But I did see the revival in 1970. Jimmy and my dad had their same roles, and Helen Hayes was in that. My dad just adored doing *Harvey*, and theater in general, because he loved the instant response from the audience. He was also very good friends with Mary Chase, who wrote *Harvey*, and he stayed in contact with her all his life. The original Broadway production of *Harvey* was directed by Antoinette Perry, for whom the Tony Awards are named, and she passed away during the show's run. In addition to the film and Broadway, versions my dad appeared in performances of *Harvey* around the country. I think it was in Denver where he co-starred with Gig Young, who had some drinking problems and was a very angry man. In fact, my dad and Gig came to blows in a fight one time, although I don't know the details.

Your dad had some great scenes in the movie, like when he dragged Josephine Hull up to her room to be mistakenly committed instead of Stewart. Do you have a favorite scene from *Harvey*?

The film is just such a classic now, a delightful picture and my dad was always proud to be associated with it. It was a perfect fit for his style of humor. I love his reaction in the scene where he's looking through the dictionary for the meaning of "pooka" — such a magical moment. He and Jimmy always got along well and I think my dad was instrumental in getting Jimmy to do the Broadway revival.

After *Harvey*, your dad began doing a lot of TV shows. Which gave him the most recognition?

Probably his work with Ann Sothern and Danny Thomas. He actually did two shows at the same time. He had a recurring role on a show called *Private Secretary*, where my dad played Cagey Calhoun, Ann Soutern's nemesis. He played Danny Thomas's agent on *Make Room for Daddy*. These shows were hugely successful and he was recognized everywhere he went. We would go places and people would call out to him, "Hey, Cagey!"

When did you know you wanted to act?

I always wanted to be an actor; it looked like such an exciting life.

Although my mother would keep my sister and me away from my father when he was learning his lines at home, it was the greatest thrill for me, as a kid, to be able to rehearse his lines with him. When I would go out with my dad, people welcomed him warmly everywhere he went — I liked that. Being an actor seemed like a way to be loved! It's a cliché, but that's the truth. I learned at a very early age that people want you around if you can entertain them and make them laugh. So I became the class clown. I was constantly begging my dad to take me to the studio when I was young, secretly hoping to be discovered. He took me to the sets of *Beach Blanket Bingo* [1965] and *The Ghost in the Invisible Bikini* [1966]. I wanted to go professional, but my dad didn't go for it. He wanted me to have a regular childhood before I got into acting. He had seen how show business affected kids, and didn't want that for me. He also knew that actors, even kids, can have good days and bad days. But when you're on a set doing something like a commercial when there may be millions of dollars on the line, you can't have bad days. He felt it was hard enough being a kid without having to be a working professional. So it wasn't until high school that I did my first play at Beverly Hills High. I went to school with many well-known show business celebrities, including Richard Dreyfus, Rob Reiner, and Joey Bishop's son, Larry. During PTA nights, all the celebrity parents would put on shows to raise money, and it was always great fun. So I was around the entertainment world while I was growing up. The thought of becoming a housewife — staying at home and raising children — didn't have any appeal for me, so I never married. Dad was always traveling for his work on films and TV and that's what I wanted. Like my dad, I moved to New York when I was 20 and started working in improv groups in The Village. Then I came back to L.A. around 1972 and joined the original Comedy Store Players when the Comedy Store first opened. I was doing improvs every night when Garry Marshall saw me and gave me TV work on *The Odd Couple* and that led to my wonderful gig as Big Rosie on *Laverne and Shirley*.

How did your dad handle the role of being a father?
He was a tender person and could get emotional about certain things, but as far as we kids were concerned, he always believed children should be "seen and not heard," which was fairly common in those days. He believed his family should act appropriately out in public because he was a professional, in the public eye, and we should behave accordingly. I remember one Sunday evening after we had eaten at Ah Fong's Chinese Restaurant in Beverly Hills, which was owned by actor Benson Fong, who played Charlie Chan's #1 son in the films with Sidney Toler. We left the restaurant and my sister and I got into the backseat of my dad's Cadillac convertible. We were at a red light

when dad saw his friend, Edd "Kookie" Byrnes, on the corner. He was the teen heartthrob star of the *77 Sunset Strip* TV show, which was hugely popular at the time. I had the biggest crush on him! There was also a popular song by Connie Stevens called "Kookie, Kookie, Lend Me Your Comb." Well, my dad pulled over to say hello to Edd, and introduced him to us. I don't know what came over me, but I stood up on the seat of the car and started to sing out, "Kookie, Kookie, Lend Me Your Comb." I was all of nine years old, but instead of finding it adorable, my father was mortified and he let me know in no uncertain terms that this sort of behavior from his daughter was completely unacceptable. I never did anything like that again.

Sounds like you were a pretty typical teenage kid from the '60s. What type of music did you like?

I was a Beatles nut as a kid and was one of those teenagers who had a whole bedroom wall covered with Beatles pictures and posters. I even got to meet them on my 16th birthday after their first Hollywood Bowl concert! Carl Reiner arranged for tickets to see the concert. The day after the show, August 24, 1964 — my birthday — Capitol Records had a charity event where you could pay $25 and stand in line to meet the Beatles. It was the thrill of my young life, and I have pictures of me talking with John Lennon and George Harrison. I was completely obsessed with them. I picked up their cigarette butts and cups that they drank from, and wiped the seats of their chairs with my gloves, and pasted them all in my Beatle scrapbook-typical Beatle-crazy teenager! I remember it was a very hot August day, and I invited them over to swim. Not that I expected them to come, but I figured I would give it a shot! Unfortunately, I didn't get their autographs. As my dad's daughter I was never permitted to ask celebrities for autographs. But getting to shake their hands and talking to them was enough. A little while back, my cousin in New York sent me a video clip taken by a film crew at the concert and there I am with my girlfriends. So that was fun to see after all these years.

How did your dad relax?

The truth is, my dad loved to work. He'd say he didn't need vacations and never wanted to retire — he loved to act. When I was very little, in the early '50s, I remember he used to "paint by numbers" which he found very relaxing. He and my mother were very social and held lots of parties and went to many. They would leave my sister and me at home with the maid and head off to some Hollywood party at Brando's house, or elsewhere. Tony Curtis and Janet Leigh were very dear friends, as were Gene Barry and his wife, and Red Buttons. Dad belonged to the Friars Club and you could often find him there having lunch with Milton Berle or George Burns. He loved being around entertainment people. I remember the parties my parents had at home and, at the end of the night, he and the others would be sitting around smoking and having cocktails and we would be sent out because he would be telling jokes that were sometimes "off-color." I would listen with my ear at the door and hear him telling stories, which he loved to do. He loved to make people laugh and actually did some stand-up during the years he worked for Maytag.

Your dad was always a supporting or character actor. Did he have any regrets that he wasn't the "Clark Gable" leading-man type?

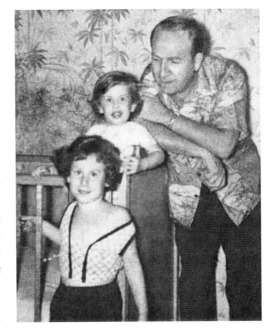

Carole Ita White, baby sister Janet, and their father Jesse White at their Beverly Hills home in 1954. (Photograph courtesy of Carole Ita White.)

No, he didn't mind. He still had plenty of women interested in him! That was just the nature of the business — young girls loved to hang around celebrities and he liked the attention. He made over 50 films with some big stars such as Greg Peck and Lauren Bacall in *Designing Woman* [1957], Esther Williams in *Million Dollar Mermaid* [1952], and Ron Reagan in *Bedtime for Bonzo* [1951]. He remained friends with Reagan, and a proud moment for him was when he attended a White House function with Reagan as president.

His last acting job was in a 1996 *Seinfeld* episode called "The Cadillac." Did he enjoy that?

My father suffered from Parkinson's during the last ten years of his life and it was not easy for him, but he did enjoy being back on a set. In the episode, Jerry buys a car for his father who lives in Florida, and my dad was one of the condo board members. Sandy Baron and Bill Macy (who played Walter in *Maude*) were in the episode. Bill was close to my dad for many years and helped him throughout the filming by bringing him lunch, helping him with his lines, and escorting him to the set. I drove my dad to the studio and everyone involved in the show was kind to him. My father was actually the first celebrity Jerry ever met when he was a kid! I think it was when my father was doing the *Harvey* revival on Broadway, and Jerry was walking down the street and saw my dad, and asked for an autograph. Dad only had a couple of lines in the *Seinfeld* episode, but he did have such fun doing it. But it was hard to see him getting frail in those last years.

What's one fact about your dad that most people probably don't know?

Did you know he had a glass eye? When he was 18, he was sitting in the backseat of his brother Al's convertible. Some kids were playing baseball nearby and the ball hit him in the eye. At first he didn't think the injury was too serious. They lived across the road from a hospital and eventually sought attention. But he eventually lost the eye. You really don't notice it in his films because he figured out how to work so it wouldn't be very noticeable. He was a little insecure about it all his life, but you'd never really know it. He came from "the streets" and wasn't going to let that get to him. Throughout his life he really was a "ladies man" and I think he always had to prove to himself that he was still desirable to women, despite having a glass eye.

He continued to act throughout the '70s and '80s, but got a lot of recognition as the Maytag repairman in TV ads. Was there a downside to being so well know for the commercials?

He loved the fact that people recognized him from the commercials wherever he went. However, he did miss out on some really good movie roles in that period because he was too recognizable as the repairman. He liked a lot of the roles that Jack Warden played and would loved to have had some of them. So that frustrated him somewhat. But he made a bundle of money from Maytag, working just a few days a month. Most actors are not that lucky!

Carole Ita White on Jesse White. Telephone interview on 3/8/11.

25

Noel Blanc on Mel Blanc

For most of his life, Mel Blanc (1908–1989) heard voices in his head. By collaborating with artists and animators, he was able to channel those voices through his incredible vocal chords and create some of the most iconic and beloved cartoon characters of all time. Blanc produced hundreds of voices, dialects, and sounds that echoed down the halls of Warner Bros. Studios and through the corridors of the Hanna-Barbera offices. From movies, such as Who Framed Roger Rabbit *(1988), to robots in TV's* Buck Rogers in the 25th Century, *Blanc was, quite simply, the most prolific voice actor — ever. What cartoon-loving kid of the '50s and '60s wouldn't have been envious of Noel Blanc, growing up with a father who infused life and personality into the likes of Bugs Bunny, Daffy Duck, Porky Pig, and Barney Rubble!*

When did your father begin doing voices?

He started as a kid in grammar school in the 1920s and could do many dialects and voices. He would shout up and down the school halls doing a loud laugh that later became the Woody Woodpecker laugh in the 1940s. He was also very musical. He played the bass fiddle and his parents encouraged him to entertain. When he wanted to join the band, he learned the tuba and, at the age of 22, became the conductor of the Oregon Orpheum Theatre orchestra and was the youngest orchestra leader in the country. He then worked in radio and met my mother, Estelle. They had an hour-long show every night in Portland called *Cobwebs and Nuts*. They played all the roles — my dad did all the male characters and my mother did all the female characters, so that's really where he got his start.

Did he do voices for you at home?

He started when I was a baby. When I was two or three years old, I would bring him the comic strips every day and he would read them and

Mel Blanc and his son, Noel, circa 1947. (Photograph courtesy of Noel Blanc.)

make up various voices for characters like Dick Tracy and Wonder Woman. I learned that he was the voice of Bugs Bunny and the others when I was very young because we had pictures of them all around the house.

How was he able to create such a variety of voices?

He had a pair of vocal chords that were simply amazing. In fact, he was rather upset with me when I once arranged for him to visit a specialist who wanted to photograph his vocal chords. But he became quite excited when the doctor told him they were the thickest vocal chords he had ever seen, even thicker than the vocal chords of Enrico Caruso, which the doctor had seen. I can copy about nine of his voices, but I don't do Yosemite Sam — it would wreck my vocal chords. People would often ask him if doing someone like Yosemite Sam would tear up his voice. While it was one of the most difficult, he never got a sore throat from that or anything else, and I never remember him ever becoming hoarse. Having those large vocal chords was like having large muscles in your biceps that enable you to do a lot more curls than most other guys could. Even when he had a cold, which was rare, he could still do the voices. He never did any voice exercises and only gargled with lemon juice in the mornings. Alan Reed, who did the voice of Fred Flintstone, had bad throat problems and used to drink lemon juice and honey to help his voice. But Dad felt that hot lemon juice in the morning helped by clearing the phlegm from the throat.

So this was a talent that he was just born with?

It was truly a God-given gift. But it was really just one of many — he had perfect pitch as a singer and sounded like Bing Crosby with his natural singing voice. He also had an eight-octave range and an ear that could reproduce any sound after hearing it once. He could do hundreds of dialects. His voice was actually insured with Lloyd's of London for a couple of millions dollars. His acting ability was also amazing.

When you say "his acting ability," was there more to his voices than just sounds?

He put personality into each voice and actually became the characters while he was doing them. He could switch from Bugs to Daffy and any of the others in a second. He really was an incredible actor and had such a rubber face — the man of a thousand faces as well as voices. When he was in the studio, you could turn the sound off and just watch him through the booth window. I could tell if he was doing Bugs or Daffy or Yosemite Sam just by the expressions on his face. I remember a photograph that Abbott and Costello signed for my dad after they worked together. They signed it, "To the greatest actor we know."

Were many of his voices based on real people?

Very few. Mostly, he would look at the artist's drawings and story boards, and develop the voices from those images. Possible the only one was the voice of Barney Rubble in *The Flintstones*. Fred's character was based on Jackie Gleason from *The Honeymooners*, and Barney was similar to Art Carney. They actually wanted him to copy Art Carney's voice, but he came up with his own version.

Was he popular with the neighborhood kids when you were growing up?

This is no exaggeration, but kids would come up to the door every day and ask him to do voices. Then they would tell their friends, who would come over, too, and they would tell their friends. This actually went on for several generations because he lived in the same house for 40 years and parents who had come over as children would have their kids come over! So every afternoon, after school, we'd get an enormous number of kids appearing at the door and he would really have to "audition" for them. But he loved doing it. He also loved doing dialects — he did something like 12 Yiddish, four Mexican, and three French dialects — he had so many, and the kids got a big kick out of them. He would also hand out signed animation cells to the kids. They really weren't worth anything at the time, but 25 years later, those same kids came back and said, "Thanks for putting me through college!" because the cells became worth thousands of dollars. These were the wonderful, hand-painted artwork that were photographed for cartoons, and 24 were used to make one second of film. So for just one seven-minute cartoon, thousands of these cells were used. The studios had so many, they didn't know what to do with them. Some could be washed and reused, but most were just thrown in the trash and the artists would often retrieve them. My dad took hundreds of them and turned them into Christmas cards. Over at Disney, there were millions of these cells from their features and they sold in the 1950s for about $5 at Disneyland. They just had so many, they were almost worthless at the time. Some of those now sell for $250,000. Halloween was an especially busy time at our house, too. Even more kids would show up — over 2,000 each Halloween — and my dad would give them candy and autographs. There were actually busloads of kids that would turn up at the house. It would start at two o'clock in the afternoon and my dad would sit in the doorway for about six hours and hand out candy with my mom, who would make up over 2,000 candy packages for them. When I moved to Beverly Hills in the '60s, I used to get about 1,500 kids at my door for Halloween, too.

Were there any characters that he did just for you, that no one else ever heard?

There was one character based on a tour guide he heard in Quebec. It was a Scottish/Irish/Canadian/French voice. He would also do an amazing face to go with the voice and it would break me up every time. The character had no name, all I had to do was say "Quebec," and he'd do it.

Did he ever get up to any mischief with his voices — play practical jokes?

I remember one story he told me. One day he called all the Chinese restaurants in San Francisco and told them that the water was going to be shut off to the area for two hours, so they had better start collecting and saving water which they needed for preparing the food. Later, he went down to Chinatown with his buddies and they watched as all the restaurant staff were running around with jugs and cans collecting water so they would have some when it was shut off! Another funny story I remember relates to the heyday of CB radio. It was in 1975 and I was driving along Wilshire Boulevard on a rainy night in my Jeep and had just left my folks' house. I was in a 35 miles-per-hour zone and going about 45. I was talking to my dad on the CB radio telling him about the bad weather and said, "Uh-oh, there's a flashing red light behind me; I think I'm being pulled over!" So a cop pulls me over and I left the CB mic on so my dad could hear what was going on. The officer told me I was going ten miles per hour over the speed limit and, just then, my dad broke in over the radio and says, "Eh ... What's up, Doc? Hi, officer, this is Bugs Bunny, please don't give my kid a ticket, would ya?" Well, the cop broke up and laughed like crazy. He gave me a warning, and I got away without a ticket!

You were 23 when your dad was in a coma after a bad car accident in January 1961. Is it really true that the doctor revived him with a little help from some animated friends?

Yes. On the day of the accident, he had returned from San Francisco where he had done a number of commercials that day. He came home for dinner and had a recording session to do at Glen Glenn Sound studios in Hollywood at eight o'clock in the evening. So he left home at about 6:45 P.M. so he could be at the studio at least a half-hour early. He was driving down Sunset Boulevard at a place called Dead Man's Curve — the same place named in the famous Jan and Dean song — which was right above the athletic field at UCLA. They figured Dad was only doing about 25 miles per hour when a kid in an big Oldsmobile jumped the double lines and hit him head-on. I think the kid only ended up with a cut on his knee. My dad was in an aluminum Aston Martin, which just folded right up on him, and it took about 30 minutes to cut him out of the car with a torch. Luckily, he was just a minute from the UCLA Medical Center, but he was in a coma for about 14 days. The physician, Dr. Conway, would leave the television on in my father's room so he could see the screen if he opened his eyes. Back then, the cartoons would come on at early every morning and one day, when a Bugs Bunny cartoon was on, my father opened his eyes. The doctor said to him, "Bugs, can you hear me?" And the first thing my father said was "What's up, Doc?" in Bugs's voice! Then the doctor asked, "Porky, can you hear me?" And Dad said, "I-I-I c-c-can hear you," in Porky's voice. The doctor then went through a whole repertoire of characters and got him out of his coma that way. I was there when Dr. Conway did it, and it was really weird. Years later, on an episode of *This Is Your Life* honoring my dad, the doctor came on the show and explained what happened. My father hadn't seen him in 25 years.

You also had an unusual accident, almost exactly 30 years after your dad's. What happened?

My father's accident was in 1961, and mine was in 1991. I was flying my helicopter with Kirk Douglas and we were up about 50 feet when a plane hit us from the rear. We fell to the ground and I broke just about the same number of bones in my body as my dad and was just as critical. I lost a lot of blood and the X-rays of our injuries were almost identical — at the same age! Two people in the plane were killed and Kirk suffered a back injury as a result. He and I have been friends for a long time. When he went to Australia in 1981 to finish filming *The Man From Snowy River*, he asked if I wanted to come along and I said, "I'd love to!" We even went down to Hobart, the capital of Tasmania, for the day. We walked through the town and it was so quaint. I can still remember a woman running out of a tea house and yelling, "Kirk Douglas!" Well, we must have had half the town following us around after that!

Did it bother your father that he didn't get screen credit in the early years, which was pretty common for early voice actors?

He was getting $45 a week in the early days which was barely enough to survive, so he had to live at my grandmother's house. He asked for a raise and was told he couldn't have any more money. So he asked for screen credit, and was the first of the voice actors to get screen credit. I would say he got it 20 years before the others got screen credit. Hanna-Barbera started flashing the credits all together on-screen very quickly in the early 1960s, so Dad wanted single-page credit from Warner Bros., which he eventually did get. So he got that instead of a raise, which turned out to be a much better deal because all the radio casting directors found out who had been doing all the voices. As a result of that, he ended up getting a lot more work and, at one time, was doing 18 radio shows a week.

Was it tough for him to be known only for his voice, rather than his image like most actors?

He didn't mind not being seen in films or television. He enjoyed working with Jack Benny on his TV show in the '60s, but didn't really like being in front of the camera because he had to memorize lines. When he did the American Express "Do You Know Me?" commercial in early 1970, his face became much more widely known. It received a tremendous amount of air time and it was the first in a series of "you may not know my face" type of ads. He also enjoyed public speaking, especially at college campuses. He was a guest lecturer at 189 colleges and literally holds the attendance record at all of them. I remember one time he went to speak at the University of Southern California and they were expecting a couple of hundred people because they were used to seeing the stars all the time. That day, over 3,000 turned up and speakers had to be placed in the quad behind the theater, which only held 1,700, so people could hear. The students had watched the cartoons growing up and wanted to see Mel Blanc in person. So he enjoyed the accolade that

Mel Blanc and friends, circa 1976. (Photograph courtesy of Noel Blanc.)

came with being seen in person, because he loved college students.

You'd think Disney would have signed Mel Blanc up to a long-term contract, but he only worked on one Disney film, didn't he?

He only worked on *Pinocchio* [1940] in which the director wanted him to do an inebriated cat. Dad did a great drunk, although he wasn't a drinker at all, so they hired him for eight weeks to do the voice of Gideon, the cat. But then Walt Disney came along and said they couldn't have a drunk in a kid's movie, so it ended up that the cat didn't talk. All they left in was one hiccup that my father did — they paid him $800 for one hiccup! But for most of his career he was contracted to Warner Bros., although he did do an early Woody Woodpecker for Walter Lantz. Disney would have paid him even less than the $45 a week he was initially getting from Warners. Disney used their local staff and even Disney himself did the voice of Mickey. My dad never lived to see the enormous salaries that voice actors now get. Big-name actors now get millions for doing animated films because lending their name to productions gives the project worldwide recognition, like Paul Newman in *Cars*

[2006]. The first big star I remember doing voice work was Dustin Hoffman in a television special in the '70s called *The Point!* about an Irish Setter, named Arrow, and a little boy. He was the first major star to get decent pay for voice work. But you really didn't see that in the movies until the '90s, after my father had passed away.

Aside from his radio, TV and film work, how else did he use his voices?
He did some voice recordings for answering machines, and I did some, too, after he passed away — a whole series with Daffy, Bugs, Porky, Tweety, and Sylvester. He also did the personalized birthday-grams in the mid–'80s. Machinery was used to insert a person's name using Mel's Bugs voice, so that instead of "What's up, Doc?" you could replace "Doc" with any of a thousand names. You could call a number a few days in advance of someone's birthday and this machinery, which was very archaic at that time in the mid '80s, would insert the person's name. So for a certain price, you could arrange to get the personalized birthday message by phone and a record of the message was also available. I redid them again in the early '90s with about 3,000 names and it was known as the Bugs Bunny birthday call. Later, in the mid–90s, I did some phone tapes for answering machines. By the way, my father didn't use an answering machine at home so he never did voices for a home answering machine.

Your wife, Kathleen, is also artistic and writes children's books. She wrote an interesting book in 2010.
She's done nine books and that one was *The Boy Who Conquered Everest* about Jordan Romero, the 13-year-old who climbed Mt. Everest. He lives at Big Bear Lake and we are up there eight months out of the year, so my wife talked with him and got his photographs and his thoughts of the climb. It was done as a picture book with hundreds of color photos. He's also climbed six of the other highest peaks in the world, including Kilimanjaro when he was ten and McKinley when he was 11.

You formed a company with your dad. Did you enjoy working with him?
I was in the Army for a time and after I left, we formed Blanc Communications. We made thousands of commercials, TV shows, and radio bits over the 30 years we worked together. I actually directed him for many years and he was fabulous to work with. There was nobody like him. All the actors we would hire were just in awe of him because he would do things that they couldn't. But to me, he was just a regular dad and he was never "on" like so many actors who always have to be doing their shtick. As I said, kids loved to come to our house because he was like a "pied piper" and loved to entertain

them. He was an extremely friendly person one-on-one with other people or in a small group, but he didn't like cocktail parties much. Johnny Carson was like that, too. If they were ever at the same place, they would just sit in the corner of the room and let people come over and say hello, rather than circulate through the room. There wasn't anything pretentious about Mel Blanc. You could have believed he was a shoe salesman from Kansas when you met him, rather than the most famous voice actor who ever lived.

Noel Blanc on Mel Blanc. Telephone interview on 12/1/10. Blanc's daughter-in-law's website is www.katherineblanc.net.

26

Mary and Harry Crosby on Bing Crosby

> *Was he a singer who could act, or an actor who could sing? Throughout his career, Bing Crosby (1903–1977) was both, and a lot more, including an early radio star and an Oscar winner — the original American entertainment icon. In 2009, hundreds of Bing Crosby items were rediscovered in the "Crosby Vault," including old radio programs, musical recordings, television programs, and a few surprises. The Bing Crosby estate began releasing material in 2010, and Bing fans can look forward to the release of new material from the veteran crooner for years to come. Crosby was a devoted husband to his second wife, Kathryn, and father to their three children, Harry, Mary and Nathaniel. Harry and Mary recount fond memories of growing up in a home where music and love were in plentiful supply.*

It sounds like it will take decades to release all the new Bing Crosby material that was recently unearthed. Is there really a "Crosby Vault"?

HARRY: It was the basement of the family home in the Hillsborough area of San Francisco, where I grew up. We moved to San Francisco when I was five and I stayed there until I was 17 when I moved away to college. My mother still lives in the same house. The kids are now spread around the country: I'm in New York, Mary is in Los Angeles, and Nathaniel lives in Florida. But I still consider that house to be my home and we get together there whenever we can. My father saved a huge amount of his old radio shows, songs, and television footage — some of which hasn't been seen or heard for decades. Robert Bader, from Bing Crosby Enterprises, has the daunting task of cataloging it all and transferring it to digital form for preservation. So we'll be releasing more material over time.

So your dad was a hoarder?

MARY: I wouldn't call him a hoarder. I would say he was smart enough to hang on to material he knew would be of interest one day. I think he made sure to save a master copy of everything he did. As a family, we're just happy to get this material out for people who are interested in it, and the quality is exceptional. Much of it has been moved out of the basement so it can de digitized, preserved, and eventually released. We realized we weren't doing anybody a service by leaving it in storage.

In the '60s and '70s, the family produced a Christmas TV special each year. Was that fun for you or did your parents drag you into it?

MARY: Harry and I were hitting each other over the head to get in front of the camera — we were hopeless extroverts! I always felt we were so lucky because everyone else in the world got to celebrate one Christmas, but we really had two: first in November, when we would record the Christmas special, then in December. So the shows were great fun for me.

HARRY: I loved it. Every September we would get out of school for several weeks to do the show and even traveled to England to record some of them. But, apart from that, we really had more of a normal childhood than you would think. I took the bus to school, had my own friends, and we tried to be like the other kids. Of course, I realized my father was a popular entertainer, but I really just thought of him as my dad, friend, and companion.

What was Christmas like in the Crosby household?

HARRY: You'd be surprised. He would actually startle our neighbors by taking the family out caroling. People would open their front doors and there would be Bing Crosby and family serenading them with Christmas carols! Many were friends, but he would also wander down the road, pick out a house and say, "Let's bang on that door." What a Christmas surprise it was for some families. But apart from that, we had a very traditional Christmas. We went to church in the morning, came back for lunch, opened gifts, and leading up to it there was a lot of singing. My mother made sure that we also wrote thank-you notes to the people who sent us gifts.

MARY: We didn't have a lot of other people over at Christmas, just the family. We had a big tree, and I remember Mom would cook pan-fried quail in the morning. When Dad died, it was very hard at Christmas time because he was the heart of the family. It was rough for a few years, especially when we would hear his music or see him on TV all through the season. But after a few years it became sweet again, and now I love to hear his voice at Christmas and sharing him with my two kids.

A DVD collection was released for Christmas 2010, that featured Bing's final TV appearance in the 1977 *Bing Crosby's Merrie Olde Christmas*

This image was used by the Crosby family — Kathryn and Bing with children (left to right) Harry, Mary and Nathaniel — for their 1970 Christmas card. (Photograph courtesy of Robert Bader and the Crosby family.)

where he sings "The Little Drummer Boy/Peace on Earth" duo with David Bowie. Do you remember that show?

MARY: I remember the buzz going 'round about David Bowie appearing on the show. He was hugely popular in the '70s. David was going through his "androgynous period" at the time, and we were all sitting around on the set when he walked in wearing a full-length mink coat. His wife had one on, too, and they both had their hair cut very short and the same color. I remember looking at them and gasping, and thinking, "Oh gosh, how is this going to work with Dad?" It was fabulous once David sat down at the piano with Dad. David said he had to sing in a particular key, and Dad said something like, "Don't worry, I'll just squeeze it in there somehow." Both recognized the other was a talented musician and the moment they started singing, you could see them saying to themselves, This is going to be just fine! I think they made some magic that day.

HARRY: I remember it like it was yesterday. The most creative aspect of that show was to mix David Bowie's modern style with my father's traditional music. Despite their age difference, Dad and David hit it off immediately. "Little Drummer Boy" is a timeless Christmas ballad, and for two singers with such different musical styles to blend so well — so simply and purely — was a testament to both their talents. They rehearsed the number once and recorded it. The arrangement was terrific and it has been a popular YouTube clip for ages. David was a wonderful guy. Dad wasn't intimately familiar with his music, but he followed all styles of music and had enormous respect for David. It was a shock to all of us when Dad died suddenly, just a few weeks after recording that Christmas show.

Was there any sign that he was ill?

HARRY: No, he seemed in good health and no one could have anticipated it. I was 19 when he died, and it was totally unexpected. We were at the Palladium and he decided to cut short the tour. I had dinner with him one night, then he went off to Spain. I had taken a year off from college in order to do the year's tour with him, along with Rosemary Clooney and a host of other performers.

Did your dad spend much time with you as kids?

MARY: Dad was somewhat retired when we came along, so the family was lucky and we got to spend an incredible amount of time with him. We did all the good things a family does, and he treated me just like one of the boys by teaching me how to hunt and fish — no dolls for me, which was the way I wanted it. And there was always music in the house. He didn't necessarily sing all the time, but he would be humming, and he was an incredible whistler.

A family portrait of the Crosbys, taken at their home in Hillsborough, California, in 1968. Left to right: Kathryn, Mary, Bing, Harry and Nathaniel. (Photograph courtesy of Robert Bader and the Crosby family.)

So I was hopelessly spoiled in that regard — not too many kids grew up with Bing Crosby humming and whistling around the home every day!

    HARRY: He spent a lot of time at home with us. He was on the road less in the '60s, when I grew up, than he had been in previous decades. A lot of times after dinner, I would play the piano and he'd sit and listen and we'd work on different songs, and sing. He loved golf, so we spent a lot of time at the local golf clubs. I was a big Giants fan, and dad was part-owner of the Pittsburgh Pirates, so we were always at games together. When the Pirates were playing, someone would come over to me and give me a mitt and ball, which was cool, but I was more impressed watching the local Giants and two Willies — McCovey and Mays!

Speaking of baseball, what was the surprising sports discovery in the Crosby Vault?

HARRY: As an owner of the Pirates, Dad was really nervous about being around the team when they reached the World Series in 1960 and were playing in the deciding seventh game. So he went to France and stayed with a friend and listened on the radio. But before he left, he arranged to have the game filmed by kinescope, which predated videotape and was the early way to film live television. He was able to watch the game when he returned. The networks apparently lost or destroyed their copy of the game and for years only a short clip was known to exist. So when the 16mm films of the game were discovered in the basement, and in excellent condition, it was a big find.

Your dad was in his fifties when you were born. Was it difficult having an older father?

MARY: He didn't feel old to us. He was very active and strong. We played tennis and went hunting and fishing so it didn't feel like we were living with a much older father. In typical Crosby style he died with impeccable timing: he had been healthy, had complete possession of his faculties, and died on the golf course — he even shot 80 that day! He died when I was 18, so we only had a short time together, but it was high-quality time and I'm so grateful for that.

Mary, you inherited some Crosby acting genes. How did your dad help your career?

I grew up doing the TV shows with the family and some commercials, and I really liked it — the business can be a very "heady wine" — so I was hopelessly in love with that world. But my dad was very clear that he didn't want me to be a serious child actor. After we did the Christmas shows, offers came in, but he wanted me to wait until I was older — to my fury, I might add! So I studied acting and trained to be an actress. I did a few TV movies of the week and some summer theater, with my mom who was in a lot of films in the '50s, but that was pretty much it. Then in the '80s and '90s, I became more involved in movie and television work. I moved to L.A. after Dad died. When I got the role of Kristin Shepard in *Dallas* — yes, I'm the one who shot

JR!— the producers were worried because they were concerned that the public wouldn't accept Bing Crosby's daughter doing all those nasty things to JR. But they took a chance, and it worked out well for me and the show.

Harry, much of your career has been in investment banking and finance, but you did some acting and singing, too. Did you have any serious thoughts about an entertainment career?

Dad was on the *Hollywood Palace* in the '60s and I went to watch him when I was six or seven. One of the producers came up to me and asked if I also sang and if there was a song I knew. I said I knew a Christmas carol, so I sang my first song on the Christmas show. The next year, the whole family was invited to come and that's what led to the Crosby Christmas shows.

Aside from the TV shows, part of my interest in entertainment came from touring with Dad. In terms of performing, I never tried to do my father's style. I loved to accompany him and I loved performing, but I wasn't trying to be a Frank Sinatra, Jr., because that wasn't really me. I had my own look and different interests in all kinds of music — Latin, pop, rock, R&B, and I played guitar that was more of a classical technique. I thought about following him because music has always been a part of my life, but it was not my vocation.

Aside from all of his entertainment achievements, Bing introduced some important technological ideas. What were they?

MARY: Dad was one of the original investors of Ampex, a company that produced sound recordings. He used the technology to record his radio shows, which were all done live at the time. Of course, the reason he originally did that was because the live radio shows were cutting into his fishing and golf! He even recorded some of the radio shows in the hospital when he had an operation for kidney stones. He was also an early investor in the frozen food business, for products like Minute Maid, and the family did those commercials. I wouldn't necessarily say he was a brilliant businessman, but he was a brilliant innovator.

The great comedy duo of Bob and Bing — were they friends off screen?

MARY: Dad had his hunting buddies and his working buddies and stayed connected with the people he cared for, and Bob Hope was definitely one of them. Bob wasn't a regular visitor to the house — he lived in L.A. and we were in San Francisco. But when he was in the neighborhood, which wasn't often, they would meet for dinner or go golfing. On the Road pictures, when they were together a lot, they would go golfing at the Lakeside Country Club on their lunch breaks and the assistant director would have to chase them down to get them back to work on the picture.

Growing up, did you think your dad was cool or old-fashioned?

HARRY: I thought he was very cool from a musical standpoint and not just because he was my dad. Musically, he was always curious, right up until the end. I performed with him at his last performance in Brighton at the Palladium, just before he went off to Spain. He had an enormously unique talent of being able to tell a story in a musical way. He could get the words across better than most. He covered an enormous breadth of styles and influences, too — Irish music, Hawaiian sounds, jazz, blues, and ballads.

Is Bing Crosby's music still relevant today?

HARRY: Absolutely! Just look at all the movie soundtracks that continue to use his music. And what would Christmas be like without Bing Crosby? You hear him on TV shows, in commercials, and in department stores. I'm amazed how many young people recognize his music.

MARY: One of the things that makes my dad extraordinary is that his music was pertinent to any time. It's not just my mother's generation that loves him. I see people who hear his music for the first time say, "Oh, my God, this guy's incredible!" So his music continues to reach all kinds of people across the generations. Whether he was singing or acting, Dad had such a natural, easy-going style. I think that was really who he was and it's what people recognized in him and loved him for. He really did seem like the guy next door, who just happened to have an amazing voice. People identify with that type of character as much today as they did back in 1940 because it's absolutely authentic, and that's why he can still be appreciated today.

Harry and Mary Crosby on Bing Crosby. HARRY: Telephone interview on 11/29/10; MARY: Telephone interview on 11/29/10. The official Bing Crosby site is www.bing crosby.com.

Index

Entries in **_bold italics_** refer to photographs